T0353983

Watch what you DO!
Watch who you do it TO!
They might tell the world on YOU!

Dr. Frankie J. Monroe-Moore

authorHOUSE®

AuthorHouse™
1663 Liberty Drive
Bloomington, IN 47403
www.authorhouse.com
Phone: 1-800-839-8640

© 2011 Dr. Frankie J. Monroe-Moore. All rights reserved.

No part of this book may be reproduced, stored in a retrieval system, or transmitted by any means without the written permission of the author.

First published by AuthorHouse 3/18/2011

ISBN: 978-1-4567-5664-2 (sc)
ISBN: 978-1-4567-5663-5 (e)

Library of Congress Control Number: 2011904646

Printed in the United States of America

Any people depicted in stock imagery provided by Thinkstock are models, and such images are being used for illustrative purposes only. Certain stock imagery © Thinkstock.

This book is printed on acid-free paper.

Because of the dynamic nature of the Internet, any web addresses or links contained in this book may have changed since publication and may no longer be valid. The views expressed in this work are solely those of the author and do not necessarily reflect the views of the publisher, and the publisher hereby disclaims any responsibility for them.

Watch what you DO! Watch who you do it TO! They might tell the world on YOU!

Contents

A favorite quote of my grandmother (Mary Torry-Patton), "Your darkest hour is just before the break of dawn. If you can hold on until daylight everything will be alright."

A favorite quote of my mother (Addie L. Standifer), "You are a light in a dark place you are Gods agent let them know you serve a God of Love, Life, and Living.

I think I see daylight breaking through the darkness. I can finally move past my own hurts and be a light to others.

Forget the past and look forward to what lies ahead

Philippians 3:13

Prologue

Listen, I have to tell you something before it's too late. I have this overwhelming feeling that someone is going to try and stop me because if this gets out it could have dire consequences for them.

This might serve as a wake-up call to all those out there that feel they can get away with treating people anyway they choose. It doesn't matter if they are employers, government agencies, or medical facilities. There is always the possibility someone like me is waiting patiently for the right moment to expose them.

In my last book "Dead Woman Talking but God's Got This!", I shared with you that I've tried not to cling to past hurts, move on into the present, and be a positive influence on the future, but of late old hurts from my past keep resurfacing. I went on to say; I have loved Corpus Christi, Texas but it hasn't loved me back. It's important for me not to paint the entire city with a broad brush and say everyone that lived here treated me bad. There have been some who have shown me extraordinary love and compassion on a personal level especially my close friends, students, parents, and some co-workers, but for the most part I was treated badly when it came to advancing in my career. In the first book I promised I would tell you what evoked those emotions of deepest, darkest, despair when I published the next book entitled "Watch what you **DO**! Watch who you do it **TO**! They might tell the world on **YOU**!" The time has finally come and I need your help to bring about change.

As I did in my first book I want to give my soon to be released trademark disclaimer.

"Before I begin my story please don't think too harshly of me when you come across grammatical or typographical errors. I just don't have time for anyone to proofread this. It's as if God is telling me to hurry. This isn't the first time something prophetic has occurred immediately following this feeling of urgency I am experiencing right now. So I beg of you to just get the message not the mistakes."

Unknown Artist

Chapter I

Signs

The First Sign

I had been threatening to expose everyone I felt treated me unfairly and gotten away with it, on the job or in the courts for a few years but procrastinated. The first sign that stirred me to action happened while I was listening to a conversation Judge Jeanine Pirro, a television judge, had with Rodney King. I don't know if you know who Rodney King is. He was the Black gentlemen that had been severely beaten by the Los Angeles police in 1991. He won millions in his civil lawsuit against the police department for police brutality. Judge Pirro expressed how she felt Rodney had the potential to change so much in this system. He could be a bellwether. She suggested that Mr. King go around the country and talk about what it's like to be in the minority community and be the one that has been targeted. Perhaps this would promote change in a flawed system.

When I first heard the term bellwether I had no idea what it was so I looked it up in the dictionary. It said a bellwether is any entity in a given arena that serves to create or influence trends or to presage future happenings. It can promote a power within you to change a system and serve as a wake up call. The alarm had finally gone off in my life and I wanted to be a bellwether. I was wide awake, fired up and raring to go but the phone rang and that fire dwindled.

The Second Sign

It was a Friday morning around 3:30 a.m. I'm not sure what woke me up but the television was on and I vaguely remembered hearing the newscaster say a professor in a Huntsville, Alabama university had killed three of her colleagues and injured three. They went on to say she did this because she had been denied tenure. I didn't learn anymore about her until later that day. Her name was Amy Bishop, apparently she was disturbed because she had tried to get tenure at the university but was voted down by some of the people she shot. No one knows exactly how she found out who voted against her but it had deadly consequences.

As the days progressed more and more information was released about this professor. She was married and had four children. She had accidently killed her brother when she was 18. She had been questioned in a pipe bombing case but it was never proven she was the one that did it. She had also been charged with assault in an IHOP restaurant incident for striking another woman. It stood to reason Amy had been emotionally impacted by the death of her brother which probably influenced some of the erratic behaviors she displayed over the years. Apparently she had become disenfranchised and didn't feel she had anything to live for and wanted to take down all of those she felt were responsible for her downfall.

The one thing that struck home for me was the career path both Amy and I had taken. We were both in education. We were both driven and dedicated to our jobs. We both poured everything we had into our work and sought to progress to the next level in our careers only to be rejected time-after-time. When I heard Amy had filed a lawsuit against the university on the basis of gender discrimination and the university denied it saying she acted as if she were entitled. I felt I had been eviscerated. This is exactly what was told to me when I filed charges of discrimination against Corpus Christi Independent school district (CCISD) based on race, age, and retaliation in 2005. The school district's attorney told me in a mediation meeting, which was ordered by the judge, I acted like I was entitled but added that it didn't matter how many certifications and degrees I earned the school district had the right to hire whomever they wanted. In that same meeting I responded by saying, I wasn't acting like I was entitled I had earned the right to expect to advance in my career if I worked diligently to improve myself. Even though Amy and I both experienced similar situations in our careers; I never had a run in with the law or contemplated striking out physically to hurt those I believed had wronged me. This story was slowly replaced by some other tragedy in the news and I soon forgot it.

The Third Sign

The third sign that provoked me to share what happened to me occurred on February 9, 2010. I received a letter from Mr. Scott Elliff, the Superintendent of Corpus Christi ISD. In the letter it stated my resignation letter had been received and presented to the school board. They had accepted it and I wouldn't be allowed to withdraw the resignation. The letter went on to say if I wanted to get any of my records I was free to do so. Needless to say I was floored. I couldn't believe this. After 20+ years of dedicated service I was kicked to the curb, as my students would say.

I shouldn't have been surprised at these actions; after all I did something that was considered career suicide. I had the audacity to challenge certain policies and procedures the school district had in place by filing charges of discrimination with EEOC and eventually a lawsuit through the courts. Several school board members and top administrators hoped I would have left the district after the lawsuit I filed against them was thrown out by the judge, six days before my case was to go to trial but I stayed.

The judge actually ordered both camps into mediation during the pre-trial hearings and was well aware of the breach of contract on the part of the school district. They had signed a $25,000.00 settlement agreement with me and rushed to court to have my entire case thrown out. It was stated the reason the school board was not going to honor the agreement was because they had decided to be good stewards of the taxpayers finances; which had been entrusted to them. They had unanimously decided they would no longer settle any agreements involving charges of discrimination but would instead fight to the fullest extent of the law through the courts. My question was if you knew you weren't going to honor the agreement why sign it in the first place. In the end they paid a law firm over a $100,000 to uphold this decision when they could have easily shut me down for just $25,000. How fiscally sound was that move? I can't lie I was quite pleased about their decision to breach the agreement because I didn't want to settle anyway. I wanted to tell the world what was going on. I settled only because my attorney and the court appointed mediator convinced me it was the best thing to do. Once the school district didn't act in good faith and honor their portion of the settlement agreement I felt the entire agreement was null and void. Therefore; this breach enabled me to freely discuss any parts of the agreement with whoever I chose without any fear of repercussions. Despite this treatment I remained silent because I didn't want to loose my job.

The Fourth Sign

It wasn't until my death experience that I developed the ability to look at things with fresh eyes. Situations which normally rattled me in the past didn't affect me in the same way anymore. I didn't obsess over bad situation the way I had. I simply stilled myself and listened for God to guide me. I can't explain it but I felt this urgency to go home to Gary, Indiana. I hadn't been home in five years. I don't know; it just didn't feel right going home after Madea died and frankly I didn't have the finances to go since my injuries and subsequent illness caused me not to be able to work as an adaptive education teacher. I'll discuss my injuries in greater detail later.

I was getting a small disability check from a disability insurance policy I had taken out while working for Corpus Christi ISD, but nothing more. I was barely getting enough to cover the monthly expenses we had. At the urging of my brother, Martin, who financed the trip, my husband, Ed and I agreed to come. The visit was twofold; first I wanted to visit a critically ill cousin who had been asking for me. Secondly, I wanted to promote my first book "Dead Woman Talking But God's Got This."

Martin had been selling a few copies of my book to some of his church members at New Hope Missionary Baptist Church, in Hammond, Indiana. Several of the members agreed to purchase the book if they knew for sure I would come and sign their copy. I was quite thrilled to know they thought enough of me to want an autographed copy. Martin had gone to his pastor, Reverend Herman A. Polk, and asked would he be willing to allow me to come and launch my very first book signing campaign at their church. After much deliberation Rev. Polk, who didn't feel it was appropriate to promote the selling of any products in his church agreed; especially after reading how God had performed a miracle in my life.

In late June I received a call from someone named Jonathan, from Riverside Mediation. He left a message on my cell phone requesting that I return his call. I returned the call and apparently Corpus Christi ISD had agreed to a mediation meeting with me through EEOC. This was a curious state of affairs. In 2004 when I first filed charges of discrimination with EEOC against Corpus Christi ISD they refused mediation. It was their policy according to their in-house attorney, Mrs. Imelda Martinez, not to mediate.

Jonathan asked if I would be available to attend a mediation meeting about two days in July. I explained to him I was planning to leave in early July because my cousin had suffered a catastrophic illness and was asking for me, but I would be available the last week in July. He asked if I could make it around the 19th or 20th of the month. I agreed to those dates and he promised to call me back to let me know which day would be best for Corpus Christi ISD. Well a week or so passed and I hadn't heard anything. I figured he would call me back on my cell phone, which was his initial mode of contact, once a decision was made, but I didn't hear any thing from him. My husband and I continued making preparations to leave.

It was no easy task preparing to go on this trip especially since Ed, was battling kidney failure and was on dialysis. We had to prepare almost a month in advance. He had to get a complete physical examination including x-rays to be allowed to travel. He was normally required to take three dialysis treatments a week for five hours each visit. These treatments had to be setup in two states, Mississippi and Indiana. I also had to get permission from my doctor to travel especially since I had been critically ill and was still recovering physically.

Martin didn't have enough money to get plane tickets for both of us and Ed didn't feel comfortable letting me travel alone because I hadn't been feeling well; so we decided to drive. I hadn't been to my sister, Debra's house in Summit, Mississippi in five years and her house was the midway point between Texas and Indiana for us.

When the day finally arrived, Ed loaded up the car, I stretched out on the back seat, and we were off on our adventure. We figured, given that it was a Sunday and the 4th of July weekend, we wouldn't run into too much traffic. We left around 5:00 a.m. so we could drive during daylight hours. We planned the trip this way because Ed had some difficulty driving at night after getting laser treatments to stop some bleeding in his eyes brought on by diabetes. When he drove at night he would catch glares from the headlights of cars which made him uncomfortable driving during that time; especially on unfamiliar roads.

It took about 11 hours to get to Debra's house. We spent (5) days there. This allowed Ed time to rest and get his dialysis treatments since he did all of the driving. After a few days of resting up I was ready to visit Algeria, the area in McComb, Mississippi, I wrote about in my first book. The old shot gun house we lived in had been demolished and nature had reclaimed the spot it once stood on. Child's house was still standing but barely. Part of the roof had caved in and some of the windows were busted out. When I looked across the narrow paved road to where Fat's house once stood was a neatly manicured lot. As I stood gazing at these little pieces of my history, I
was able to reach into my memory and envision what it once looked like. It brought back so many good and bad memories that had such an impact on my life.

We left Mississippi and headed for Indiana early Friday morning. This portion of the trip took about 12-13 hours. It was late when we arrived at mom's old house which Martin (aka Marty) now owned. As we approached the house a brief moment of melancholy seeped into my spirit because I knew Momo and Madea wouldn't be there to greet us, but that feeling quickly passed. Marty had really fixed up the old place. I have no doubt if mom had lived to see it she would have been so proud. Marty advised that we not park in the front of the house but go around and park in the back. He had been having some problems with new neighbors from Chicago and didn't want anything to happen to our vehicle.

He shared with us something he had been told. Mind you this is merely hearsay and don't quote it as gospel, but apparently Chicago had been busy tearing down one of the biggest housing projects in Chicago. I believe it was called Cabrini Greene. It was told to Marty an offer was made to the displaced residents they couldn't refuse. The residents were offered vouchers of some sort to get reestablished but there was one stipulation; they had to leave Chicago. Many of these people took them up on their offer and poured into different areas of Indiana such as Hammond and Gary. They wouldn't be in Chicago but they could still visit since these areas were only about 30 minutes away. This is what school administrators called passing the trash.

Marty said he really had a problem with this. Evidently Gary had no ordinances in place to discourage this kind of dumping behavior from other cities. It was bad enough the city was already an economically depressed area and plagued with its own criminal elements but to burden it with additional problems caused an even harder drain on the fragile local economy. The new residents started going to community assistance programs offered in the city asking for help. There was already limited assistance for the long time residents who had difficulty paying huge utility bills, and keeping food in the house until the end of the month. With additional people needing help the limited funding would run out sooner.

When the new neighbors first arrived in the neighborhood Marty said he went over and introduced himself and offered to cut their yard since the grass had grown quite tall since they had moved in. Marty is like the neighborhood watch person and takes a great deal of pride in the neighborhood. He actually purchased a riding lawnmower to cut the lawns of several empty lots and abandoned houses on the street just to keep it looking nice. To instill this same pride in the neighborhood Marty paid young people, out of his own pocket, to help him clean up the vacant lots, by picking up trash and bagging it for the trash man. He was never compensated for doing this nor given a thank you from anyone. Just seeing the end result was enough for him. He told me if people would just take pride in the place they lived regardless to whether they owned or rented it the city would be revitalized.

As time went on Marty began to notice trash being thrown on the ground in front of the new neighbor's house which eventually found its way into his and several other neighbor's yards. He knew of a trash can behind him that wasn't being used because the house it belonged to burnt down. He went and retrieved the garbage can, took the trash in it to the garbage dump and offered it to the new neighbors. They took the garbage can and put some of the trash in it but didn't close the lid. Every time a gust of wind blew through or the dogs and cats got into the trash cans there went the trash all over the place.

I explained to Marty that apparently the new neighbors weren't use to anything nice. After all, from what he told me, they had come from a bad environment. In their previous residency they were surrounded by trash, graffiti, urine smells in the halls, drugs and gang activity. It would take time for them to adjust to something nice. In many instances you do better when you know better. They just needed to be shown the way.

Marty didn't really want to hear what I had to say because he was a peace loving soul and the new neighbors had rocked his world. Most of the neighbors had lived on this street for 40 years or more. Their children had grown up and moved away. Marty was the youngest homeowner on the street. Everyone knew each other and pretty much took care of each other.

Marty proceeded to tell me what occurred that upset him so. With a disturbed look on his face he started to talk, "Look Frankie, I know what you're saying but this just isn't right. I use to sit on the porch, early in the morning, enjoying the cool breeze and quietness of our neighborhood, just as winter gave way to spring. I knew of other areas of town that weren't so peaceful but that didn't apply to Hanley Street. Then one day everything changed. The old neighbors across the street moved away and their house was purchased. The new owners fixed up the house and rented it out to people on section eight. This is a government subsided home. The tenants only have to pay a small portion of rent and the rest is paid by the government." I told Marty I was familiar with the program.

In an agitated voice Marty continued talking, "It seems to me when people don't own or have to pay for things they take less pride in it. It was bad enough the trash was being strolled all over the place, to add insult to injury strange cars began pouring into the neighborhood at all hours of the day and night. They had their speakers cranked up so loud it rattled the windows at my house. Do you know one night I had to get up out of my bed, go over to their house around 1:00 a.m. and ask if they could tone it down because I had to go to work later that day and needed to rest? They did cut it down but the very next night the same thing happened. I went back over and they once again lowered it for a little while then cranked it up again. Then gunshots rang out and I couldn't take it anymore I had to call the police."

I told Marty he did what he had to do to protect Angel, his daughter and himself. Then He continued, "I can't believe the quiet neighborhood I have lived in for over 35 years has been transformed into this loud, dangerous neighborhood. Their children are running wild in the streets, and the cussing, drinking and partying all night long, has become the norm."

The older people in the neighborhood were afraid to call the police and just hoped it would all go away. Marty was the youngest homeowner in the neighborhood and took it upon himself to call 911 and complained more than once. He never saw any patrol cars answer his call. Because the behavior continued after the police were called he decided to visit the police department to get a report and found they didn't even have a copy of his 911 complaint on record. Marty had never been involved politically in the city but because he was being sucked into this conflict he decided to take his complaint to the mayor's office. He was sent to several public officials and was eventually directed to the assistant mayor's office. When this excursion was finally over Marty came to the conclusion that Gary's political system was like a Lion with no teeth. They were simply powerless to truly protect its citizens. He said this was the first time in his life he ever considered selling the house and moving out of town.

As I listened to Marty vent about his concerns I was quite moved and felt I had let him and Gary down. I moved away like so many others did when things got bad in Gary. There was a great exodus away from the city in the late 70s and early 80s when the steel mills started outsourcing jobs overseas which caused massive lay offs in Gary and surrounding area. As people found it harder and harder to find employment they started uprooting and moving to other cities that offered a better living, which was understandable. Those that could get out left and those that had nowhere else to go stayed. Then drugs and gang activity took over.

For a while it was like the "Wild, Wild, West" actually earning Gary, Indiana the dubious title of *Murder Capital of the United States* at one time. The last time I went home before mom died, I witnessed a shootout while at a gas station. This car sped by with people shooting back at a police car that was chasing them. I ducked down behind my car to protect myself. I knew bullets didn't have any names on them. Then I looked up in this tree and saw a guy shooting down at the police car as well. I couldn't believe this. I made my way back to Madea's house and begged her to leave Gary and come live with me in Texas. She said Gary was her home and God would protect her. She was right. The entire time she was there nothing ever happened to her. She never put bars on her windows, like so many others did, and she was never personally hurt or robbed.

I'm sure some of you reading this would say this is no different than any other economically depressed area, but I have a personal connection to this particular city and I have to work from my own of frame of reference.

The next day, which was Sunday, we prepared to go to the 11:00 service at New Hope Missionary Baptist Church. Weeks earlier Marty had asked if I would send the secretary of their church a brief bio about me along with a picture. When we arrived at the church Marty dropped us off in front and he went to park the car. Just inside the church doors, posted on their church bulletin board, was a picture of me and the brief bio I sent. There was also an announcement of my book signing which was to take place immediately after church service in the lobby. As other members of the church gathered to wait for Sunday school services to end they started reading the bulletin and then gave double takes at me. I smiled politely as Marty introduced me. I had visited this church on other occasions when I came home and every time I attended, it felt like I belonged. This time was no different.

My cousin, Pastor Vera Johnson, who is the pastor of Fifth Avenue United Methodist Church, finished services early at her church and came over just in time to get her copy of my book signed. I finished signing books for everyone that had purchased them and then took pictures with Rev. Polk.

Vera offered to take us all out to dinner. She took us to this rather new buffet styled soul food restaurant in town. I think she said it had been called Dusty's at one time. I hadn't been to a soul food restaurant in years. In my neck of the woods there were mostly Spanish restaurants. This restaurant wasn't to far from the new baseball stadium they had built. The food was "Slammin" as my daughter-in-law, Bridget would say. They had collard greens, cornbread, ribs, fried chicken, fried green tomatoes, mash potatoes, sweet potato pie and sweet tea so sweet it could cause instant cavities. I went back a few times for the fried green tomatoes.

I ran into one of my old high school classmates while we were at the restaurant. I hadn't seen her in years and was surprised I remembered her name. In high school she was Delores Miles. I don't know what her married name was. She told me about Emerson High Schools 40th class reunion which would be held in mid-August. I told her I wouldn't be able to make it because I had a prior commitment. She kept saying I didn't look like she remembered me. I told her maybe because I was older and heavier. She said, "No I remember you darker." As I finished eating, I couldn't forget what Delores said about remembering me being darker. Then I remembered something. She was probably talking about Jessie Elliott. When we were in high school they use to call me Jessie and Jessie, Frankie. We looked quite a bit alike; in fact we could have been twins. We were the same height and weight, our hair length was down our backs and we both wore ponytails the majority of the time. The only difference was I was slightly lighter than Jessie. No matter how often we corrected people they kept getting us mixed up; so we just stopped trying to explain and answered to each others name. When we talked to each other we simply shared what was said.

As we finished our meal and prepared to leave Vera invited me to go to a prayer breakfast the next day and I agreed. I didn't realize I would have to get up at 4:00 a.m. just so I could get showered and dressed, because the prayer breakfast started at 6:00 a.m. It lasted until 8:00 a.m. There were about 10 people in attendance. Vera said many of the members had attended these meetings for over 30 years. As we prayed and discussed the bible I discovered that every one of them had experienced miraculous healings of their own. They truly blessed my soul. Vera had to be at work by 8:30 and dropped me back off at Marty's by 8:15.

I had promised to call Aunt Bernice and make plans to meet with her, so as soon as I got in I called her. Aunt Bernice had been one of Madea's best friends growing up. They actually married two brothers. We made plans for her to pick me up around 12:00 noon so she could take me to see my cousin Sheryl. She was one of Aunt Bernice's four children. Sheryl had already been diagnosed with MS years earlier but was still able to somewhat take care of her self.

Aunt Bernice was 75 years old, but to look at her and watch her move around you would have thought she was in her 40s or 50s. She had more energy than anyone I knew. Given she had two mentally challenged sons and a physically handicapped daughter that she was responsible for; I guess that kept her young.

As Sheryl's MS became more debilitating she had to have more help. Aunt Bernice, Yvonne, Sheryl's sister, and Sheryl's daughter, would take turns going to her apartment to help her take a bath and cook for her. One day Sheryl went to get her teeth pulled and ended up with this massive infection throughout her body. If I'm not mistaken I think she had several strokes. She was in critical condition and they didn't think she would make it. In the end she pulled through but she was now a complete invalid. The family couldn't continue to care for her at home and Sheryl was moved to a rehabilitation hospital.

As I entered the hospital it reminded me of my own near death experiences and the plans that were being made to put me in a facility much like this one. Through lots of prayer and faith in God I pulled through. My whole purpose for the visit was to share what happened to me and encourage Sheryl to trust in God and know that all things were possible through Him that strengthens us. After visiting with her for about an hour Aunt Bernice had to go because she had to pick up her son, Roland, from work. Even though he was mentally challenged he was high functioning and could hold a job. I kissed Sheryl good-bye and we left. Aunt Bernice

dropped me back off at home. Whew! This had already been a world wind visit. On Tuesday Ed had to go for a dialysis treatment. It was going to last for about five hours. The entire time he was gone I slept. About five minutes before he was due to return I woke up and ate something. Then I went straight back to sleep.

After catching up on some much needed rest, the next day Marty took us on a tour around Gary. Even though there were a lot of abandoned buildings and over grown lots I saw quite a few signs of new life in the city since the last time I had visited. I wanted to take a nostalgic trip down memory lane. Our first stop was the old projects were we grew up. My cousin Vera told me I couldn't use the term projects anymore it was now called St. Johns Housing Development. As I rode through the old neighborhood it had become a gated community. Where there had been two ways leading into and out of the housing development the entrance near the railroad tracks had been closed off. I saw tremendous improvements since we lived there 40 years earlier. The big, dusty, open field in front of our apartment at 2277 Carolina Street, now had a beautiful grass covered lawn and a playground smack dab in the middle of it for the kids to play. It would have been nice to have had this when we were growing up. All of the apartments had been remodeled. The Good Corner, directly across from where we lived, which consisted of a laundry mat, shoe store, liquor store, restaurant and a Kroger grocery store were gone. This is where I first saw the Jackson Five perform before they became famous. The factory directly behind it was being demolished.

I couldn't resist, I wanted to get out and walk down the sidewalk I had walked down as a kid and head for the apartment we shared with Madea, Momo, and Pawpaw who had long since past. Ed and Marty didn't feel comfortable doing this but Vera was game. I walked up to the apartment door at 2277 Carolina Street and knocked on it. I didn't want the new occupants to think I was investigating them or something. This gentleman that apparently lived there opened the door and I explained what I wanted to do. "Hello sir, my name is Dr. Frankie J. Monroe-Moore, I lived here about 40 years ago and I just want to make a video of the front view of the apartment and take a few pictures. Is that alright with you?" He smiled and told me it wouldn't be a problem and then shut the door gently.

After that I wanted to go visit a couple of the old schools I had attended as a child. First I visited Pulaski Jr. High and then Emerson High School. I was a bit distraught because they had fallen into such disrepair plans were in the works to demolish them. We visited a few other sites and then Marty decided to take us out to Crown Point, Indiana to eat dinner at Ponderosa. Vera couldn't go with us because she had some prior commitments so Marty, Ed and I struck out on our own. I remembered there being a Ponderosa restaurant closer to Gary but Marty said it had shut down.

The drive took us straight out Broadway about 5 or 10 minutes away from Gary. As we traveled down Broadway I reminisced about walking these streets as a kid. We never owned a car so the only way we got around was either by bus or walked. Back then Broadway was the hub of the city of Gary. This is where you came to buy clothes, go to the doctor, get your prescriptions filled, go to the movies, and get something to eat. The city was simply alive with activity back then. But now, it was a mere shell of its former self.

Something else I thought was unique about Gary when I was a kid, if you got lost and couldn't find your way home all you had to do was find your way to Broadway. Broadway was the dividing line between the Eastside and Westside of town. The Eastside of town consisted mainly of streets with state names such as Carolina, Virginia, and Connecticut. The Westside of town consisted mainly of streets with names of presidents such as, Adam, Washington, and Taft. Broadway wasn't just a part of the city of Gary it was part of several cities. I guess you could say it was like a highway taking you from one area to the next.

Marty said something that caused me to refocus. He said, "When we come back I'm going to point something out to you." I was curious about what he wanted to point out and kept asking him "What is it?" He told me, "You'll see just wait." We reached the restaurant and went inside. It reminded me of Golden Corral back home. I ordered a medium rare sirloin steak dinner with baked potatoes and green beans. Ed and Marty ordered the buffet. This was another delicious meal.

When we finished eating and headed back to Gary, Marty told us to pay close attention to Broadway Street. I had already notice how much more life and vitality was in this particular area than in Gary. Then I paid more attention to the street itself. When we left the restaurant and headed back down Broadway, towards Gary, I noticed the street was beautifully paved, but the closer we got to that section of Broadway that belonged to Gary the street became drastically different. First you began to see more and more potholes.

I know potholes are nothing new in any community throughout the United States that has harsh weather. They're especially bad where it snows excessively and freezes causing ice on the roads. Many states use salt to help melt the ice. Once winter is over and all the snow melts, the residue left behind from the salt, reeks havoc on the roads.

As we proceeded down Broadway we observed more and more potholes. Some potholes were small but others were so big if you weren't careful you could cause damage to your car. By the time we reached the part of Broadway that belonged to Gary, Ed said, "This part of Broadway is almost gravel." Ed knew what he was talking about because he had been a heavy equipment operator for the street department in Corpus Christi, Texas for nearly 19 years before getting hurt. You could see patches of grass actually growing up through the cracks in some parts of the pavement on the street. I just couldn't phantom why Broadway at least wasn't treated the same in all areas given that it was still part of Indiana. It wasn't like traveling from one state to the next as we had done and noticed differences in the roads.

It really was a shame how Gary was being neglected. I've overheard other groups of people say, "That's all Blacks want to do is blame others for their problems." In this instance I do feel the treatment the citizens of Gary were receiving was mainly due to the fact that the majority of the general population is Black. The city has been tarnished with the reputation of being considered the scourge of the State of Indiana. Many people in the surrounding areas have nothing but bad things to say about Gary. The sad thing is the people in Gary themselves speak badly about the city. I guess it's like a child that's been verbally and mentally abused. If you say their not good long enough, they start to believe it themselves.

Marty shared several other disturbing things he had overheard. He told me how different groups of people had come to Gary pretending to have its best interest at heart. But in fact practically all of them had ulterior motives. They merely wanted to swoop in like *"Vultures"* and ravage Gary with empty promises and pluck its carcass clean, all in an effort to line their own pockets. No wonder the people were so pessimistic and leery about anyone coming in with grand plans to help the city. Just like a protective mother defending her young even though she knows her child has problems, I

felt defensive. It has always been my

nature to choose the side of the underdog in any situation. I stayed true to form and started voicing some concerns of my own. I can only say to those abusers out there, "There but by the grace of God go you."

On the way back I told Marty before we went home I wanted to see the childhood home of Michael Jackson and the Jackson Five. After all these years, I never visited their home even once. I know, I know, it's shameful, but it is what it is. I had heard before I left Corpus that they had dedicated a Jackson monument made of granite, at the Jackson families original family home; commemorating the life and death of Michael. When we arrived there were several people there taking pictures and talking. I whipped out my camera and started taking pictures as well. I overheard a lady say she was glad she came and took pictures before the wrought iron fence had been put up. She was able to get much better pictures without this obstruction. I

finished taking pictures and then we headed for the house.

You would have thought one visit would have been enough but for some reason I felt compelled to go back to this site two more times. My cousin Vera took me on one of these trips. I can't explain it but I sensed Michael's presence there and when I returned to the site I decided to create a video and discuss my book in front of the Monument. After all Michael had been included in my first book. In the Prologue I discussed Michael Jackson, Farrah Fawcett, Karl Malden, Patrick Swayze, Senator Ted Kennedy and Willie Maxine Perry, Tyler Perry's mother and how we had several things in common. There was one unique thing we shared and that was we all died in 2009 but I survived death.

After visiting the Jackson Monument; Vera suggested we go to the Gary Public Library. She knew of a plaque which had been dedicated to Karl Malden, a famous actor that stared in the Streets of San Francisco. He also graduated from Emerson High School, the same high school I graduated from. We arrived at the library just before it was time to close. We rushed to the door and explained to the security guard what we wanted to do and he allowed us in. We

videoed and took pictures of the plaque as well as a picture of Karl Malden. How neat was that?

On the last day of our visit before heading back to Corpus, my cousin Shirley Stamps called and told me she planned to visit but I guess something came up because she didn't make it. I only had one other brother in town, Melvin. He, his wife

Jean, son Aaron, and daughter Chandra visited us the first few days we were in town. All the other relatives, besides Aunt Bernice, that lived in Gary were cousins. I don't know if the other cousins were aware that I was even in town but I do plan to catch them on the next trip.

Even though I didn't get to see many of my cousins Vera, Rosemary, and Gloria did make it over to see us the last night we were there. Vera and Rosemary arrived a little before Gloria did. After all the hugs and kisses we all took a seat in the heart of the house, the kitchen. Here sat three sister's daughters. Pastor, Vera Johnson, and Rosemary Williams were the daughter's of my late Aunt Rose. Pastor, Gloria Dawson was the daughter of my late Aunt Sweet, and then there was me, Dr. Frankie J. Monroe- Moore, the daughter of the late Addie L. Standifer, aka (Madea).

As we talked and shared different things going on in each others lives Vera said something that stuck with me. She said, "Why are we so *UNLOVABLE*?"
Since I had been focusing on all the negative things going on in Gary I chimed in saying, "I just don't know why the world seems to target Blacks." She stopped me saying, "No I don't mean just Blacks, I mean us sitting at this table." She continued talking, "I know several people that find favor from others, that are Black, but for us everything seems to be a struggle. In anything we try to do, that we consider right, we have to face tremendous obstacles that push us to have to fight for justice." I thought about what Judge Jeanine Pirro said about the bellwether and then said "Even though we all have had to endure so many struggles in our lives we overcame a great many of them.

I also remembered what happened to me while I was hovering between life and death in the hospital. I heard these drums and tribal chants similar to those made by Indians and Africans. Even though these chants were separate I heard them intermingled. I kept asking the nurses did they hear them. But no one did. Then I felt I knew the true answer to Vera's question and I said, "We come from strong stock. Our heritage, which includes African, Indian and White blood, has infused in us this warrior spirit. We are not fighting on an earthly plane. We are in constant spiritual warfare. In Ephesians it speaks of this.

Ephesians 6:12, "For we wrestle not against flesh and blood, but against principalities, against powers, against the rulers of the darkness of this world, against spiritual wickedness in high places"

When I said this we all remember who we were and who we belonged to. **GOD**! As we sat talking I felt this cool breeze sweep over me and I sensed Madea's presence in the room. I knew she was pleased.

Since my death experience, I've become keenly aware of things spiritually. When everyone left I shared something I saw in a vision with Ed and Marty. I said to them, "I feel the winds of change coming to Gary. I feel this change will be like the Phoenix, a mythical sacred firebird. The story goes like this. " Near the end of its 500 to 1000 year old life cycle, this sacred bird returns to its place of birth and builds itself a nest made of its own feathers, twigs and leaves and creates an egg filled with this flammable substance that is ignited by the sun. Both the nest and egg burn fiercely and is reduced to ashes. From the ashes a new Phoenix is reborn to live again." This is what I see for Gary. I see it becoming the head and not the tail of the State of Indiana. I see its roads being fixed like the county roads I saw in Crown Point, Indiana. I see old buildings being demolished and new business establishments springing up. I see better schools being built to accommodate the new families that will be moving into Gary. I see newly hired police officers protecting its citizens and I see its citizens lifting their heads up with pride when Gary, Indiana is mentioned in the media instead of shame. The city can finally reap the benefits from its hometown heroes, the Jacksons, just like Nashville benefited from and is still benefiting from Elvis. After all Michael was born in Gary, Indiana and was called the King of Pop despite what others wish. His birth place is and always will be (**Gary, Indiana! Gary, Indiana! Gary, Indiana!**)."

Please keep in mind I am in my healing process and the only way I can completely heal is let go of everything that is burdening me down. Racial prejudice is a burden I have carried for more years than I want to talk about. I promise to promote Gary in a positive light whenever I speak about it. It's like the self-fulfilling prophecy. If you hear it enough times you eventually believe it and act accordingly. Perhaps Gary will have another hometown hero (Me!). I wish nothing but blessings on this city. I tell you; it has been a long time since I visited Gary and left feeling this good about the visit. I truly enjoyed it.

The Fifth Sign

When we returned home I discovered the phone had been turned off accidently. Before we left we turned off switches and unplugged all the computers and televisions. I forgot we had changed services from AT&T to Time Warner Cable to save money. When the power was cut off it also disconnected the phone.

I hadn't received a call from Jonathan the gentleman I told to you about earlier, from Riverside Mediation for EEOC on my cell phone and decided to give him a call. After all we had discussed a meeting that was to take place but I hadn't received any information in the mail and had no way to leave a message on the home phone given that it had been disconnected by accident. I told Ed I didn't want to take any chances this time by not documenting the contacts I had involving EEOC or Corpus Christi ISD and decided to record the conversation. Before I called I turned on my tape recorder.

Jonathan answered the phone and I told him who I was……. "Hello, Jonathan this is Dr. Frankie Monroe-Moore. I'm contacting you now because I need to know if the meeting is still going to take place on the 20th of July. If it is I need to know where and when."

Jonathan replied, "Corpus Christi ISD's representatives couldn't attend the meeting on the 20th but would have been available on the 23rd." I told him, "That works for me."……

Before I could finish he interrupted me and said, "Because I hadn't been able to contact you to confirm that date we had to change it to the middle of August."

I asked him, "How did you try to contact me?" He stated, "I left several messages on your home phone as well as your cell phone."

I immediately knew he was lying and all kinds of red flags went up. "Here we go again!" I thought to myself. I told him I hadn't received any messages but in the future I needed him to leave messages on both my cell phone and home phone to make sure he reached me even if I didn't answer.

This was the third time I had tried to give EEOC the benefit of the doubt and they appeared to be up to their old tricks again. I'm glad I was going through this process for documentation sake and not because I was really depending on them to represent me. I will go into greater details about my trials and tribulations over the years with EEOC and Corpus Christi ISD in later chapters.

The Sixth Sign

Mary Russell called me a few days after we got back from Gary. She was very excited as she began to explain a phone call she had received from one of her friends. A story had been published in ***We The People***, a national newspaper that's distributed locally and free to the public. It was my understanding that this newspaper was started because a lot of the stories of injustices would not be published by the larger newspapers in different cities, in our case it would be the "Corpus Christi Caller Time." The larger newspapers claimed they had to report responsible journalism. I felt what they were really saying was; they had to protect their bottom line, especially if the story impacted large corporations in a negative way. These corporations supported the newspapers and invested heavily in advertisements with them. This particular story concerned a teacher that worked for Corpus Christi ISD. She filed charges of discrimination with EEOC and the school district terminated her.

The article was written by John Kelly on 5/26/2010 and titled, "*CCISD Retaliates Against Teacher for Filing EEOC*". According to the article a teacher was reported to Child Protective Services by her campus principal for abusing a child. An extensive investigation was conducted which included the support of the child's parents, it was ruled that the teacher was not guilty as charged.

Despite these findings the teacher continued to be barred from the campus. She went before a Hearing Officer to plead her case and won. Corpus Christi ISD was ordered to reinstate her. The school board refused but offered to give her a settlement of a year's salary provided she didn't file charges with EEOC. The teacher refused their offer and launched a complaint with the Commissioner of Education. He did his own investigation and ruled in the teachers favor. The commissioner ordered the school board to rescind their decision not to allow the teacher to return to work but they refused. She then filed charges of discrimination based on retaliation with EEOC. She was later contacted by her EEOC investigating officer and told the school district had officially terminated her.

This clearly gives you an understanding of just how haughty this school board appears to be. They were ordered by the Commissioner of Education, who is a governing official over all the school districts in the state of Texas, to reinstate this teacher because their charges were unfounded and they refused.

As I finished reading the article it brought back so many painful memories. It was just like De Ja Vue. It reminded me of my own challenges with Corpus Christi ISD. According to this article apparently something had changed though in the way the school board operated. If you remember earlier I shared with you the school boards explanation for not honoring their part of the signed settlement agreement with me. They proclaimed they were going to be fiscally responsible with the taxpayer's finances and let the courts settle the dispute. Well apparently all that changed when this teacher filed charges. They offered her an entire year's salary to settle as long as she agreed to their terms. How about that? I'm sure she earned at least $50,000 a year with 22 years of experience. The most I was told I could expect was $25,000. Was it because I was valued less due to my race (Black)? It's not fair for anyone to experience discrimination of any kind but this makes you want to go (Hummm).

About a week later I got another excited call from Mary, she said, "Frankie you're not going to believe this! I was out shopping and ran into my friend Beatrice. She had this other lady with her and then she introduced her to me. You know the lady I told you about that filed retaliation charges against Corpus Christi ISD with EEOC, well she was with her. Her name is Rene Garcia, I told her about what had happened to you and she really wants to talk with you. I wouldn't give her your phone number because I wasn't sure it would be alright but I did take hers and she wants you to give her a call." I assured Mary I would.

I told Ed about the conversation Mary and I had and he said, "You know babe, you have to be careful. We just don't know who to trust. You remember all the dirty tricks Corpus Christi ISD pulled before. It could happen again. People already know you're writing a tell-all book about the district and they might be setting you up." I agreed with him and decided not to call.

On Sunday, August 8, 2010, Mary called again with a message from Mrs. Garcia. She said, "Frankie I just got another call from Rene Garcia. She asked would you please call her. She needed to talk to you before she went out of town."

Something moved in me and I decided to relax my suspicions and told Mary as soon as I hung up with her I would call. Ed warned just before I called, "Frankie, don't give too much information away." I promised I wouldn't then I picked up the phone and dialed the number. The phone rang, Rene answered and I introduced myself, "Hello, Mrs. Garcia, this is Frankie Monroe, Mary Russell's Friend. She told me you were really anxious to speak with me."

I could hear the hesitancy in her voice as she spoke. We both had been through so much and wasn't sure who to trust. She said, "Yes, Mary shared with me that Corpus Christi ISD had agreed to a mediation meeting with you through EEOC some time this month. How were you able to get them to agree to a mediation meeting? I've tried for almost two years but they absolutely refuse."

I told her, "They originally refused me as well when I initially filed discrimination charges of race, age, and retaliation against them through EEOC. It wasn't until I was able to secure a lawyer and the judge court ordered them to hold a mediation meeting that I met with them."

I told her, "Well, I'm not holding my breath this time either because a meeting was suppose to have taken place on July 20th but the mediation person from EEOC never called to confirm it or give me a place and time. After, I made contact with him; he did the usual song and dance routine that I've grown accustom to with EEOC. He did call back though and gave me three other dates that would be available to meet. I agreed to August 26 2010, but I still haven't been contacted to see if that's a confirmed date or not."

We both relaxed and started sharing information. She said, "The reason I was so desperate to talk to you was because I'm going to a hearing in Austin to meet with the Texas Education Agency (TEA) tomorrow concerning my treatment from Corpus Christi ISD. I wasn't sure when you were scheduled to meet with them and wanted to tell you not to trust them and definitely don't meet with them without an attorney present. You have no idea what I've gone through"

I assured her I knew just what she had gone through. I'd been there myself many times. I told her, "I don't really care about this meeting; I just want to document it. These two groups have never treated me fairly and I don't expect them to change now. They're only going through this just to see what I have but their going to be in for a rude awakening this time."

Then we started comparing the similarities in our cases. We were both in our fifties, I was 58 she was 56. We both taught special education. We both held superintendent certifications, we both had been passed over in our quest to advance in our careers for younger females, with much less experience. We both had been pretty much shut out of jobs because we had exposed Corpus Christ ISD and their discriminatory practices. As far as I was concerned this validated what I claimed in my initial discrimination charges of age and retaliation in 2004.

I told Rene, "You know, I was told by Corpus Christi ISD's in-house attorney when I first met with her, as well as several other people, the reason I was probably not being allowed to advance was because I taught special education students, unlike the teachers that teach general education students in subjects like math and history. My response to them was I know people that have taught homemaking and moved into administrative positions. That is just not an acceptable answer."

We continued talking and then I said, "You know, what I truly believe people think is, just because we work with a special student population, we ourselves are mentally challenged and that is the farthest thing from the truth. We, as special education teachers have to actually get more training than the general education teacher. As far as advancing into an assistant principal position, who better to know how to handle discipline problems than a special education teacher who has been trained to control behavior?

In an inquisitive voice Rene said, "Mary told me you had written a book about your illness and then shared that you were now writing one on the treatment you received from Corpus Christi ISD."

22

I confirmed that and shared with her that I was including her article in it. She asked, "What's the title of your book?" And I proudly told her, "Watch what you **DO**! Watch who you do it **TO**! They might tell the World on **YOU**!" I could actually hear a twinge of glee in her voice as she said, "*I LIKE IT*!" and can't wait to read it."

We talked a little while longer and she asked me to pray for her because she was leaving the next day and didn't know what was going to happen but she wasn't giving up. I assured her I would and we hung up the phone.

After that conversation I reflected on the treatment I received from Corpus Christi ISD as well as the courts and felt the sting of that betrayal. Despite that treatment I refused to quit working for the school district. I worked hard not to provide them any ammunition that could be used against me as far as the quality of my work was concerned. I knew they were looking for anything to terminate me. But as fate would have it the wheels of termination were set in motion the minute I fell at school injuring myself on November 12, 2008.

I remember that day just as clear as if it were yesterday. While rushing to the aid of one of my students who had a life threatening seizure, I tripped over the chair he was sitting in and went airborne, landing head first on the right side of my face, right wrist, left knee and foot, injuring myself. My right cheek and left knee immediately began to swell. Mary Russell brought the necessary forms for me to fill out so I could go and get treatment. I went to the principal's office to complete the forms and got it signed by one of the assistant principal, Mr. Chavez. I called my family doctor only to discover he couldn't handle workman compensation cases.

The school secretary provided me a list of facilities and doctors that worked with Corpus Christi ISD and I opted to go to the Doctor's Center located on Saratoga. After being examined, given a knee brace, that was too small might I add, a Celebrex prescription and an appointment to return to the office for a follow up visit on November 21, 2008, I was sent home. I took the Celebrex but it didn't help with the pain. By the next day I was in excruciating pain from my hip to the bottom of my left foot and remained in bed until Monday, November 17, 2008. I couldn't wait until Friday, November 21, 2008 I needed some relief from the pain and returned to the Doctor's Center on the 17th.

I was seen by a male I assumed was a doctor. The reason I assumed he was a doctor was because at the very top of every form I was given at the end of each visit was written physician.

The DOCTORS' Center   Follow up
A Service of One Med Corporation
Northwest · SPID · South

CHECK IN 1040A
CHECK OUT 1131

History/Physical/Treatment
INJURY

Patient Name Monroe, Frankie Date 11708 MR# _____ DOB 32952
Nurse BC _____ Room # _____ Physician Burkerbine

Complaint: Pt F/u on (R)side face, (R)wrist + (L)knee, face + wrist OK
(L) knee hurts
DOI 11-12-08 Work Related? (Y)/ N

Later I found out he was a Physicians' Assistant (PA). I explained to him how bad my
entire upper left hip, left leg and foot were hurting as well as this massive headache I was
experiencing. He stated that my blood pressure was up. I had already taken my blood
pressure medication for the day and asked could my blood pressure be up because of the
pain I was experiencing. He didn't respond to that question but said what I was
describing, as far as my leg was concerned, sounded like a Taylor's nerve pinch. I had
never heard that term before. He said, "It happens when a nerve is injured." He then told
me he was sending me to get an MRI on November 19, 2008 and I was to return to him
on November 21, 2008. I did as I was instructed but I still hadn't gotten any relief from
the pain by the next visit. The male PA told me after examining the MRI it appeared I
had slightly torn a ligament in my knee and had some minor arthritis. He was sending me
to an orthopedic surgeon to see if I needed surgery. This visit was scheduled for
December 1, 2008. I continued to take the Celebrex but I still hadn't gotten any relief and
now I was developing stomach problems.

On December 1, 2008 I went to the orthopedic surgeon's office. As I was lead into the
examination room the admitting nurse asked what happened. I told her about the fall at
school and how I was experiencing this horrific pain. The best way I could describe it
was like a knife cutting me from the inside, running from the top of my left hip, around to
the groin area, down to the inner part of my thigh, around the knee, down the back of the
calf of my left leg, to the heel of my foot and arch. She said it sounded like sciatic nerve
damage. I told her I had forgotten about the x-rays I was instructed to bring to them from
the Doctor's Center. She told me it was okay they could take additional x-rays if needed.

There was no mistake about the credentials of the Physician's Assistant at the orthopedic
surgeon's office because his name was stenciled in on the receptionist's window with PA
next to it. When he came in to talk to me I told him the same thing I told the nurse. He
proceeded to tell me he could only address what was on the workman compensation
report and in this case, that was the knee. He said the ligament wasn't torn enough to
warrant any surgery at the time but perhaps with some physical therapy it would improve.

24

I asked was there something he could give me for the pain. For the past two weeks I had asked for something to alleviate the pain but was never given anything from the Doctor's Center. In a sarcastic tone I said, "Even dog's are put out of there misery sooner than this." He told me the best he could do was give me a cortisone injection to relieve some of the pain for a while and provide me with a prescription for the pain. I was prescribed Ultracet.

After taking the Celebrex I had been prescribed to relieve the swelling in my hip, leg and foot, an additional problem was set off. For years I had suffered from acid reflux but it had been under control. Not only was I suffering from pain in all these different areas of my body, now my stomach was on fire. I called my family doctor immediately after leaving the orthopedic surgeon's office and asked if I could come in to discuss my stomach problems. When my doctor entered the examination room I began unloading all the problems I was experiencing on him even though I knew he couldn't do anything about the problems involving my leg and foot, because it was a workman compensation case. He reiterated that he couldn't do anything involving workman compensation but he could help with my stomach problem. He suggested I discontinue taking Celebrex because it was probably setting off the acid reflux and told me to start taking Zantac again. I left his office with a very pronounced limp now and went to pick up the pain pill prescription the orthopedic surgeon had given me. I already had over-the-counter Zantac at home so I started taking that as soon as I got home.

Over the next few days I took the pain pill (Ultracet) as directed but was still not getting very much relief in my left hip, leg and especially in my foot because nothing had been done to address that issue. I decided to call the workman compensation representative, Samuel Cardona, at Corpus Christi, ISD and asked could he please set it up so I could have my workman compensation information amended to include care for my left hip and foot. He told me he was only responsible for reporting the injury to the workman compensation department. The school district had another agency, Cambridge Integrated Services Group, that handled the actual care and provided me the number I needed to call.

I called and was told who my caseworker was. It was a Mrs. Iris Budjick. I asked to be connected to her office. When I finished talking to her I asked if I could have her e-mail address so I could send her a follow up letter to discuss what was discussed during our conversation and what I needed for her to do. I don't know why it was this way; but for some reason everyone involved in my case wanted to only concentrate on my left knee. No one wanted to address the additional problems I was having which resulted from the fall.

Below is a copy of the letter I sent Mrs. Budjick describing what had taken place. I also submitted this to the Texas Medical Board because I felt I had been medically neglected by Dr. James K. Rose and Mr. Robert Burkenbine, PA. In other communication from Cambridge Integrated Services Group as well as the Texas Medical Board, it was implied that Dr. James K. Rose had been involved in my medical care. I told The Texas Medical Board, in the complaint I filed with them, Dr. James K. Rose wouldn't have been able to pick me out in a police line-up if his life depended on it because he had never seen me. Each time after my initial visit on November 12, 2008 I was only seen by Mr. Burkenbine, PA, whom I was lead to believe was the doctor but later discovered he was the physician's assistant.

December 16, 2008

Mrs. Iris Budjick,

I contacted you during the week of December 8, 2008. At that time I described the problems that I was experiencing. I told you that I was having pains running through the upper left hip area, around to the groin area, down the inside of my thigh, around the knee, down the back of the leg to the heel of my foot and all the way to the toes. I told you that the best way that I could describe the intensity of the pain was to imagine a knife cutting you from the inside. You stated that this sounded like the sciatic nerve which was initially suggested by Mr. Robert Burkenbine, PA which he called a Taylor's nerve pinch on November 17, 2008 as well as an x-ray technician on December 5, 2008 from the Doctor's Center at 5440 Everhart Suite 1. It was also stated by a nurse at Dr. Robert Williams' office at 5920 Saratoga Blvd on December 1, 2008. Up until this point I was only given Celebrex and did not receive any relief for my pain until I visited Dr. Williams' office on December 1, 2008.

I explained to you that each time I complained about this during any of my office visits after my initial visit on November 12, 2008 the day of my injury, I was told that the only thing they were allowed to address was the knee injury because it did not appear that I was having problems with the head or wrist injury. I contacted Mr. Samuel Cardona, who reported my injury to workmen compensation. He suggested that I contact you to see if I could get the workmen compensation report amended to include the additional problems I was experiencing.

On December 3, 2008 I received a call from Mrs. Sheryl Lawson, who introduced herself as a CCISD nurse case manager. I explained to her the problems I was having getting anyone to address the pain I described to you. She asked when my next office visit was scheduled at the Doctors Center. I told her that Friday December 5, 2008 was my next appointment. She said she would meet me there to see if she could get this cleared up. She did meet me there on December 5, 2008. She went with me to the patient room at which time I explained to Mr. Robert Burkenbine, PA that she was there to okay examination of the additional problems I had described to her.

He made the comment that he saw this all the time. People got hurt on the job and kept adding on and adding on some times up to one year later because they had workmen compensation. I stopped him and told him that this was not an add-on. I had been scheduled for my follow-up visit on November 21 but was in so much pain I had come in on November 17, 2008 four days after my initial visit and was complaining about the pain previously described. I also informed him that if he was insinuating that I was profiting from being hurt he was mistaken because I was receiving only a little more than half of my salary from workmen compensation. He also made the comment that all that was needed was someone to say that there was a problem and people start imagining that they had it.

I asked was he implying that I was psychosomatic and the pain that I was describing was all in my head. He didn't respond but proceeded to set me up to be examined. He did some sort of scale test to determine the intensity of the pain. When he finished I was sweating and moaning because I was in so much pain. My foot began to throb. He ordered me to get dressed and left the room.

Mrs. Lawson asked was that the first time anyone had examined me for the level of pain I was experiencing. I told her yes. She said that was strange. After that examination I was taken to get additional x-rays of my left knee, thigh and hip. When I asked if I could be given an x-ray of my foot, which I had continuously reported as well, I was told no. Once the X-rays had been taken I joined Mr. Robert Burkenbine and Mrs. Lawson out in the hall. They were examining my x-rays. They told me I had a great deal of osteoarthritis and said my problem was the arthritis. I acknowledged that at my age it would be expected for me to have some arthritis but this had not been debilitating for me until I had fallen and tore ligaments in my knee as well as other injuries. A prescription was written for physical therapy treatments, by Mr. Burkenbine and given to Mrs. Lawson who volunteered to hand deliver it to Shea Physical Therapy. I asked her would they be providing therapy for all the other things I had been describing she said they would.

I received a call from Shea Physical Therapy on December 8, 2008, in which they stated they had received orders to provide physical therapy for my knee. I asked had they also received orders to include therapy for my hip, thigh, leg and foot area as well. She said no only the knee. I hung up and called Mrs. Lawson. I informed her of the call I had received from Shea and asked was I going to be getting more therapy than the knee. She said she would try to talk to Dr. Rose to see if he would order additional therapy for my hip. I asked her would this help with the additional problems I was having she told me she didn't know I should just tell Shea Physical Therapy what was happening with me.
I went to physical therapy on 12/9/08. At that time I was told they were pretty much obligated to follow what was provided by workmen compensation and could only really address the knee injury. They stated they had received a call from Mrs. Lawson and she was trying to get Dr. Rose to give additional orders to address the hip but knew nothing about the other things I was describing.

This has been going on for over a month now I have been in continuous pain. I don't feel my health issues are being addressed adequately and I asked you could I seek someone else for care. You told me that I had 30-60 days to seek other medical assistance. I did get a doctor to agree to assist me on 12/10/08. He should be contacting you soon to inform you that he is now taking over my medical care.

If this will be a problem please feel free to contact me.

Your cooperation will be greatly appreciated.

Respectfully submitted

Frankie J. Monroe

This letter was written a few days after being rushed to the hospital on December 11, 2008. I hadn't been feeling well for several days before going to the hospital. On that day pain was racing through my left hip, leg and foot. I hadn't taken any pain medication (Ultracet) that day so I decided to take it and fell asleep. When I woke up I was still experiencing severe pain in my left hip, leg and foot but I was also experiencing a severe headache, numbness on the left side of my face, lip, chest pain as well as numbness in my arms and hands. Mary called to check on me and I described what I was experiencing. She suggested I go to the emergency room because that didn't sound good. Ed overheard the conversation and immediately started getting dressed to take me.

When I arrived at Doctor's Regional Hospital I was immediately taken into the admitting room. I explained to the admitting nurse, who was taking my vitals, about the pain I was experiencing as well as the other things going on. I told her I didn't know if I should be admitted under workman compensation or my own personal hospital insurance coverage (Blue Cross Blue Shield). She said she was going to enter everything I told her into the records about the hip, leg, foot, wrist and head injury as well as all my other issues. They would make a decision about payment later. The emergency room doctor came in and asked questions. Several tests were run, including a CT scan. They noticed I had a magnesium deficiency and gave me medication for that but couldn't see anything else wrong. I had a follow up visit scheduled for the next day with my family doctor, Dr. Breeling. He ordered a MRI because he was concerned about me having mini-strokes, which was causing bleeding on the brain.

Over the next few weeks I got progressively worse. I was really dragging my leg around and eventually couldn't get out of bed. On January 5, 2009 I was so sick I went to my family doctor because I thought I was coming down with the flu. After the doctor's visit I was too ill to handle the trip to the pharmacist to get the prescription filled. I told Ed to wait and pick up the medication later and just take me home. By that evening I had come down with a fever of about 103. I knew it was too high and decided to take a cool shower. As I sat in the shower and let the cool water wash over me I felt this massive explosion erupt in my head. I remember grabbing my head with both hands and stumbling out of the shower. I let go of my head just long enough to slip my nightgown on over my wet body and fell across the bed. If you read my book "Dead Woman Talking But God's Got This" you will find out more details. I entered the hospital clinically dead. After spending 25 days in the hospital; 17 of which were spent in two intensive care units, I was released from the hospital on January 30, 2009.

I had to learn how to walk all over again. The physical therapist came to my house three times a week to assist me as well as a home health nurse. As I struggled to regain my strength the school district's insurance carrier was busy trying to get my workman compensation payment terminated. In February of 2009 I was sent to what the school districts workman compensation carrier, Cambridge, claimed was a neutral physician. He examined me and stated that what happened to me had nothing to do with the fall I sustained in November of 2008. Based on this decision they rushed to stop my workman compensation payments.

The Seventh Sign

I was too weak to fight workman compensation's decision to discontinue helping me at that time, but something happened in late June 2010 to change that. I knew I had additional disability coverage but I couldn't remember what or where it was. One day I noticed an automatic deduction had come out of my checking account which I couldn't account for. I went to the bank and found out it was Hartford Life Insurance Company that had withdrawn the money. The Teachers Credit Union offered all of its customers a $2000.00 life insurance policy free of charge annually all you had to do was sign off on a form they sent you. If we wanted additional accidental coverage we could select to pay for it. Apparently I had selected to pay more for the additional coverage which not only included life insurance coverage but accident and disability coverage as well . Go figure. I discovered they had been deducting this coverage from my checking account since 2007, but I hadn't noticed because it wasn't taken out monthly but quarterly. That'll teach me to check my bank statements more closely.

I requested a claims form be sent to me from the insurance company. A few days later I received the form in the mail and begin to read through it. It instructed me to send all the hospital records I had to see if I qualified for the insurance benefits. While searching through medical papers I discovered what I truly consider a blessing from God.

I had repeatedly asked over the past 16 months, "What happened to me?" No one could give me a clear answer but here in black and white was a diagnosis. The emergency room report diagnosed me as having Septic Shock. I remembered hearing this term before but wasn't quite sure what it was so I Googled it. This is what they said.

> Septic Shock can occur when bacteria enters the bloodstream. This may be caused by an injury, wound or infection which enters the bloodstream causing fever and potentially life-threatening conditions. In my case I was told I entered the hospital clinically dead due to acute respiratory and acute kidney failure.

I don't think you understand just how happy this made me feel! I was shouting for Ed to come and see what I had discovered. Even if the insurance company didn't honor the claim, but I hoped it would, at least I now knew what happened to me.

I discussed this with my daughter-in-law, Bridget, and she said based on what I had told her; what happened to me was called a **Sentinel Event** which results in serious injury, illness or death brought on because of missed diagnosis. In this case I blamed the Doctor's Center because I had gone to them over the course of nearly a month and asked repeatedly for help because I wasn't getting any better. Instead of a medically certified physician coming to examine me, especially after coming in with the same complaints repeatedly, I was never seen by the doctor that signed off on my workman compensation documents, and as a result suffered this life threatening event. I had also been denied financial support from workman compensation because they claimed what happened to me had nothing to do with the injury I sustained when in fact I felt it had everything to do with it.

The Eight Sign

It had been a very trying time for me during my illness. Not only had I been tested physically, and financially but emotionally as well. What I'm going to share might be considered petty and minor to some of you, but at the time it was huge to me. When I first became ill some of my close colleagues took up a small collection and purchased two $25.00 gift cards so my husband could eat a couple of decent meals while I was in the hospital. I also received several get well cards and a beautiful plant which was very much appreciated. Not only did my good friend, Mary Russell, come by the hospital almost daily to monitor my progress, she posted that progress on GroupWise, so the staff would know how I was doing. When I got strong enough to communicate my appreciation to everyone that prayed for me I did so by e-mail.

What hurt me most of all; while I was recovering from my illness was the principal of my campus never once called to see how I was doing even though she was well aware of the injuries I sustained at school and subsequent illness that followed. The only administrator that checked on me was the assistant principal assigned to the Special Education Department.

Now, I realize the principal of a large high school like Ray has a lot on their plate to contend with and may not have time to address every staff member's medical issues. But I felt given the severity of my illness she would have taken the time to personally check on me. I think what hurt me most was something the principal did for another co-worker a few months after my major illness. As I struggled to regain my strength another co-worker of mine had a medical emergency with a family member. I immediately sent an e-mail out offering prayers for a swift recovery. A few days later an e-mail was sent out to the staff from the principal, requesting a collection be taken up to help out with expenses for that family. It was later announced that about $3000.00 was raised. I even read where the principal sponsored a fundraiser where she was going to participate in the dunking booth and invited staff to participate to raise additional money for the family as well. Perhaps, I'm being petty, or having a pity party but it hurt. I felt no one knew or cared about how my husband and I were struggling financially, to stay above water. I know if it hadn't been for my faith in God and the support of my family and close friends I wouldn't have been able to make it this far.

The Ninth Sign

After getting out of the hospital in January, 2009; I worked hard to regain some of my strength back. My physical therapist was like a drill sergeant and going through his routine was no easy feat. In July 2009, I applied for the position "Special Education Behavior Intervention Specialist" posted on the Corpus Christi ISD website. I knew I was qualified for this position because this is what I did for over 20 years. I wasn't quite strong enough but I thought perhaps I would gain enough strength by the time school started to handle this position. I felt it would be less strenuous than the position I held before. This particular position didn't require me to lift students weighing up to 100 + pounds. I also felt my doctor would agree to let me work in this position. He had been unyielding in his decision not to allow me to return to work in the previous position I held as an adaptive education teacher. He wouldn't take the chance of releasing me back to work without restrictions, knowing full well I wasn't physically able to do that job. Not only would he be putting my health at risk he would be jeopardizing his own medical license.

I was getting quite panicked by August of 2009 because all the extended sick leave income I had been receiving from the school district had been exhausted. I didn't know if the disability insurance payments I was receiving would continue. To make matters worse I was now being told I had to pay all my own health insurance coverage. The school district wouldn't continue to pay its portion and I still needed medical care. I hoped and prayed Corpus Christi ISD would see fit to allow me to interview for this position but of course I was denied an interview because my application was never submitted by the intake person. This had happened repeatedly over the years and it was no different this time.

Just before the 2009-2010 school year began, I contacted Risk Management to see if I could return to work with restrictions. I was told they had to discuss this with the principal of my campus. Before a decision was made and I thought I might be allowed to return to school with restrictions, I prepared and submitted lesson plans on the districts website. All teachers were required to upload their lesson plans about three weeks in advance.

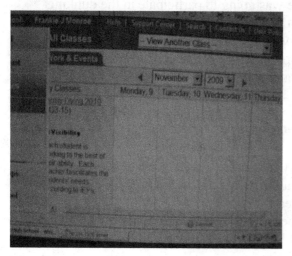

I didn't want to be behind if and when I returned to work this is why I did it as well. I also submitted these same lesson plans along with my paraprofessional assistant's duties to the special education department chairperson, and the assistant principal who had been assigned as the special education contact administrator.

After not hearing from Risk Management for a few weeks I contacted them and was told a decision had been made concerning my return to work. I was never offered an alternative position and was told I wouldn't be allowed to return to work without restrictions. It was stated if in the near future the doctor released me without restrictions they would agree to allow me back to work. Still holding out hope I continued submitting lesson plans up until November 2009 when I realized I wasn't going to be able to return the to the position of adaptive education teacher for the semester.

The school district informed me I would be provided an opportunity to remain on temporary disability leave for six additional months without pay. This bought me a little more time, but there were strings attached. If I wasn't able to return to work without restrictions within the specified timeframe I had three choices. I could request a leave of absence without pay for one year, turn in my letter of resignation, or be terminated if they didn't hear from me by February 17, 2010. I was also grateful to know that my disability insurance payments would continue for a little while longer.

The Tenth Sign

When the day finally came and I wasn't able to return to work without restrictions I sank into a deep depression. I don't know why I felt this way after all I knew it was coming but it wasn't easy. To make matters worse and add to that feeling of isolation, in December, 2009 the school district discontinued using GroupWise which had been its major communication system for years. Through this system I was able to keep abreast of all the things going on within the district. The sharing of this information made me feel I still belonged. One vital roll the system played for me was, I had access to all the personal e-mails I sent out as well as received. This system provided me a way to document any communication I had with administration so that I had proof of what was communicated. It wasn't my word against theirs.

To give an example of just how important this communication system was for me, when I received a letter in the mail from, Mr. Scott Elliff, the superintendent of Corpus Christi ISD, stating my letter of resignation had been received and accepted by the school board I was able to dispute those claims because of e-mail documentation. What I actuality requested was a leave of absence without pay. Not only did I send this letter through the U.S. Postal system I also e-mailed it to Mr. Clark Atkinson the administrator that sent me the correspondence which provided me with the choices I had to select from.

Years ago one of my professors, Dr. Jim Walter said, "If it ain't in writing it never happened," and luckily for me I took it to heart and always remembered that. Through e-mails, letters and other forms of written communication my information was well documented.

Given I hadn't worked for the entire school year, when the system switched over I wasn't provided the information necessary to change with the rest of the district's staff. There was one other way I could communicate besides GroupWise, and that was through the district's e-chalk website. The problem was, not many people in the district used this particular site to communicate. School was coming to a close and I decided to try to use the site just to say good-bye to a few of my colleagues since I didn't have phone numbers for them. During that attempt I discovered something interesting. I wasn't expecting to still be listed on the districts e-chalk website and took a chance on entering my old password. To my surprise it still worked. I opened it up and found I was still listed as the teacher of record. What was even more surprising was someone had actually gone into my personal website and completed my lesson plans until the end of the 2009-2010 school year.

To the average person reading this you wouldn't think it was that big of a deal but it really was. Here's the problem. Because Corpus Christi ISD refused to let me return to

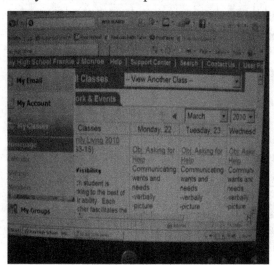

work without restrictions, I didn't receive one dollar for the work I submitted in the beginning of the school year. The district used my certification to prove the class I had been assigned was being conducted with a certified special education teacher in that position. If parents checked the website they would have thought the person working with their child was certified and trained to do so. But in actuality this was not true. Here's were it really becomes a problem for me; because it was stated I was the teacher of record, if something bad had occurred involving this set of students my certification could have been jeopardized.

The Final Sign

I was surprised to get a call from Jonathan. He was the young man that claimed to have contacted me on my home phone when in fact my phone had been disconnected for two weeks. EEOC had managed to confirm a date with Corpus Christi ISD to meet with me and discuss my claims of discrimination based on race, retaliation, and disability. I was sent a letter from Riverside Mediation stating that the meeting would be held on August 26, 2010 at 9:00a.m., in the Corpus Christi City Hall Human Relations department. I think I was a bit shell shocked when I realized the location was only a few blocks from the Corpus Christi ISD administration building. I experienced the same sick feeling I got in the pit of my stomach when Dr. Jesus Chavez was superintendent. Every time I had to go to my attorney's office I would have to pass this building and immediately feel nauseous.

If you remember what I said earlier, I only did this for documentation purposes and had no plans of seeking legal counsel. I was just going to face the school district alone. I shared with my daughter Tina what I planned to do. I told her, "Tina I don't expect to get anything because I know the district has something up their sleeves." Tina replied, "Mom, I know you don't hold out any hope of getting any justice but I think you should take the advice of that lady you talked to. She warned you not to go into any meeting with Corpus Christi ISD without legal counsel." I told her not to worry I would be alright. We finished talking and hung up

A few minutes later the phone rang this time it was Tina's husband Dennis. He rarely gives me any advice on private matters but this time he said he had to get involved. He said, "Hey old lady, Tina just shared with me what you're planning to do in that meeting with Corpus Christi ISD. You know I never get involved in stuff like this but this time I feel I have to speak up. God dropped it in my spirit to tell you not to go without legal counsel. You know that saying that goes something like this, 'A man that represents himself has a fool for a lawyer' well I think you should take it to heart and try to get someone that understands the ins-and-outs of the legal system." I told him I would think about it.

When I told Ed about it he reminded me that he had been saying the same thing all along but I just didn't listen. He said, "Okay that's three other people besides me that told you not to meet with Corpus Christi ISD without legal counsel. Stop being so bullheaded and call somebody."

I broke down about a week before the meeting was to take place and called Mr. Chris McJunkin. He was a tall, blond, serious looking gentleman who had the ability to cut through the red tape and get to the crux of the matter. He was the attorney that presented my case to the appellate courts. Despite his valiant efforts to get the appellate court to let me move forward with my discrimination lawsuit they wouldn't budge and the lower courts decision prevailed.

I wasn't sure he would be willing or able to go with me, but like Momo always said, 'Nothing hurts a failure but a try'. I first thought about Mr. Charles Smith the attorney that originally took on my case and filed a lawsuit against the school district. I remembered all the time I had invested personally in helping get ready for my trial because he had limited staff working with him, at that time, and I just didn't have the energy to do that again. At this juncture I didn't have the time because the meeting was going to take place a few days later.

Mr. McJunkin on the other hand didn't require anything from me when he was preparing my appeal so I decided to call him instead. Initially when I called I got his answering machine and left my name, number and a brief message. I didn't hear anything from him for a few days and resolved that if it was meant to be it would happen but if not I would go with my original plan to do it alone. A day or so later the phone rang and it was Mr. McJunkin. I briefly explained my situation to him and he agreed to go to the meeting with me. We set up a time to meet in his office to discuss everything and hung up. I have to admit after speaking to him I did have a sense of relief just knowing I would have someone else in the meeting besides myself to witness the conversation. Once I met with him I contacted the mediation office to inform them that I had indeed secured an attorney who would sit in on the hearing. I gave his name and phone number. To my surprise and delight they were already familiar with him.

I agreed to e-mail several documents to Mr. McJunkin during our meeting. When I got home I was in defense mode and immediately started going through the hundreds of documents I had when I prepared for the first trial. It had been some time since I had read many of these documents. As I poured through them I began to experience this deep sense of despair. I don't think I expected to relive the pain this intensely. I was hurled back in time and once again pummeled with unbearable emotions of rejection and hurt. I was so overcome I literally started getting physically ill and had to go lay down. I decided not to do anything until the next morning.

After a good nights rest I was better prepared to go through all the paperwork. I decided to construct a letter explaining each document I was going to submit to Mr. McJunkin. I remembered during our meeting he raised some very valid points. Even though I wanted to bring up things that occurred the last time I had gone down this road it was important to stick to the facts involving these particular charges. I could only use information revolving around the job that I had applied for in July 2009. I asked him if the letter Mr. Elliff sent me in late January 2010 stating I had resigned, when I hadn't, was important. I asked this because he didn't mention it during our meeting. He said, even though it was important Corpus Christi ISD could explain it away and the courts would probably accept their explanation.

I also had to be mindful of the time constraints placed on me by state and federal laws. Because I didn't file charges with EEOC until May, 2010 I had missed the 180 day deadline that the state required to contact them so now I had to rely on the federal deadline which was 300 days. I had beaten that particular deadline by about 40 or 50 days so I could include it under the federal guidelines. Upon close examination I began to discover things that I had missed the first time I read the documents. An example of this was when I originally went on-line in July 2009 and applied for the "Special Education Behavior Intervention Specialist" position. I received an e-mail form letter stating that they had received my application. I hadn't seen the sentence that stated that my application would be on file for two years. This confirmed the time frame I had repeatedly told others about but for some reason I had to submit information each time I applied for any position.

By the time I had finished selecting documents that I thought were important for this particular case I had scanned about 50 documents in. I sent the information to Mr. McJunkin and he responded back requesting that I send him just four specific documents he asked for at the meeting. It was just too much information at one time for him to go through. I did as he asked and created another letter and sent him what he specifically asked for. I guess it really would have been nice to have contacted him earlier so he would have had more time to prepare.

I didn't sleep well the night before the meeting was scheduled. I had different documents running through my head. Ed had to go to dialysis and I decided to get up around 5:00 a.m. and turn on the computer. I started printing out copies of a few documents that I hadn't given to Mr. McJunkin and planned to take them with me to the hearing. I took a shower and got dressed. I didn't eat anything because my stomach was a bit queasy and I didn't want to throw-up. Mr. McJunkin called me the night before and told me to meet him around 8:30 a.m. in the Human Relations office so he could give me some additional tips on how we were going to conduct or portion of the meeting. I got there around 8:15 and he arrived about 10 minutes later. He already had his own ID badge, scanned it and showed me into this little room. We sat down and started to talk. I updated him on some additional information I had forgotten to share with him earlier.

It was during the time I was going through information earlier that morning that I ran across documents I had submitted to Corpus Christi ISD risk management office. On three separate occasions Dr. Breeling had provided a physicians statement to the school district releasing me back to work with restrictions and checked off the restrictions. They were dated 5/11/09, 8/01/09 and 8/24/09. Despite this the school district refused to accommodate my disability, which I knew had been done for others in the school district, and was told I would be put on temporary leave of absence without pay for six months. I shared the decision the district had made with Dr. Breeling on my next office visit. He couldn't understand why the school district wouldn't allow me back to work with restrictions especially after I had gotten hurt on the job.

In January 2010 I continued to suffer from lower back, hip, leg and foot pain as well as several other medical problems. The deadline was fast approaching for me to return to work without restrictions and I pleaded with Dr. Breeling to reconsider sending me back to work because I just didn't want to loose my job. But upon examining me he determined that I couldn't return to work at all because of my current medical condition. He took the physicians form I gave him from Corpus Christi ISD, filled it out and indicated that he was taking me off work for the specified year that the school district required or until my current medical problems improved.

I felt Mr. McJunkin definitely needed to know this because it was probably going to come up in the meeting. A few minutes later a gentleman entered the room and introduced himself. It was the mediator that would be facilitating the meeting. He was a handsome, dark haired, younger looking gentleman with a pleasant disposition. He shook both our hands and handed us some forms we needed to fill out. It involved confidentiality. These forms were being used to assure that what was discussed in the meeting and eventually settled on would not go any further. I made a point of asking him if there would be a problem if I included certain information in a book I was writing. He said if we signed off on a settlement agreement I couldn't divulge anything about the terms of the settlement but I could discuss certain aspects of the meeting such as my own personal feelings. I asked him one more time for clarity because I wanted to make sure if this went the way I thought it was going to go I would be free to discuss it. He assured me it would be fine.

He left and came back a few minutes later. It was time to meet. There were three representatives already seated when we entered the conference room. The mediator took a seat at the head of the table. My attorney sat next to him and I sat next to my attorney. Everyone greeted each other and then the meeting started. Mr. McJunkin and I had already decided I wouldn't say anything. The other side explained their side and then Mr.

McJunkin made two statements and we were done with the formalities. This meeting was much nicer than it had been the first time I sat across the table from the school district representatives. In the first meeting their attorney demeaned and belittled me beyond belief.

I guess the school district representatives felt they had my case locked up, tied up and tangled up, because the district's in-house lawyer was present this time not an expensive out-of-town attorney.

There was a settlement offer made which I considered an insult. This offer was even less than the first settlement agreement I signed with them in 2006 and later refused to pay. I had given so much to this district and this is what I had been reduced to doing sitting once again at a bargaining table.

How ironic was this? Just a few weeks earlier I had gone to San Diego, California and represented Corpus Christi ISD at a very prestigious convention where people from all over the world came together to present research they had conducted in the academic arena. I know I didn't have to attend this convention but I wanted to. Not only did I have to borrow money from family members and use my own limited income to register and get the plane tickets, I had to make special arrangements to get a wheelchair to accommodate my physical disabilities that occurred due to my injuries at work.

The decision to attend this convention came about back in the summer of 2009 before I applied for the "Special Education Behavior Intervention Specialist" position. My dissertation chair, Dr.Kamiar Kouzekanani (aka, Dr. K), contacted me and asked if I would be willing to allow him to submit my dissertation abstract to the American Psychological Association (APA) committee. If my dissertation was selected I would present at the APA Convention in San Diego, California in August of 2010. I told him I would be honored to be considered. It was at that time he entered the abstract of my dissertation and put down Corpus Christi ISD as the place of my employment. When I was notified that I had been selected I was quite pleased. I felt if I began saving a little something each month, out of my disability payment, when the time came I would have enough saved up to pay for my plane ticket and registration.

There was one other lady that had been selected to present at the convention as well; her name was Dr. Jacque Hamilton, she was a professor at Texas A & M University. She contacted me by e-mail several months before we were scheduled to present and suggested that we share a room and split the cost. I felt that was an excellent idea. I had been scheduled to present my dissertation on Friday, August 13, 2010. Jacque was scheduled to present hers on Saturday, August 14, 2010. We didn't communicate very much after our initial contact. I guess Jacque got nervous about our arrangements and went ahead and reserved a room at the Manchester Hyatt in San Diego. She wasn't familiar with the area and wanted to make sure she was in walking distance of the convention center just incase I wasn't able to make it. The room was a bit pricy for me. We had to pay $247.00 a night.

As it got closer to the time to for us to go Jacque contacted me by e-mail and told me we might be able to get our room cost supplemented by the university. I was all for that. Eventually she contacted me and told me it had been approved and all I needed to do was come in and sign for it; which I did.

You know! When I first heard I was going to be presenting on Friday the 13th I was quite pleased because normally all kinds of good things happen for me on this day, but this time Murphy's Law kicked in and whatever could go wrong did.

The first thing I should have done before I left on August 12th was touch basis with my partner, Jacque because she worked at the university and knew procedure. I had gone in and signed these papers at the university so they would allow us to use monies set aside for the room expenses, but I never checked to see if everything was in place. Ed kept asking me if I was definite that the hotel room had been taken care of and I kept telling him it had been. I didn't take any credit cards with me. It didn't really matter because I didn't have that much money on them anyway but I did take my debit card. I had even jokingly told Ed if anything went wrong all he had to do was go to my bank and deposit money into my account and I could draw off it. Little did I know; that was exactly what was going to end up happening.

I only took about $300.00 in cash. I felt that would be more than sufficient for what I planned to do for the three days I was scheduled to be in San Diego. I had no intention of shopping, just eating and paying for transportation to and from the convention center. I left on Thursday, August 12, 2010 so I could have a day to rest up before I had to present. It took about 6 hours to get there by plane. There was also about a two-hour difference in the time which I had to contend with. When it was 6:00 o'clock there it was 8:00 o'clock in Texas. My leg and foot were really hurting quite a bit by the time I arrived and a wheelchair was provided for me not only at the airport but at the hotel as well. I caught a cab over to the Manchester Hyatt Hotel where we had reservations. It was understood that I would spend one night alone and Jacque would arrive the day of my presentation. The doorman at the Hyatt called for an attendant to meet me at the cab with a wheelchair and wheel me to the registration desk.

The young lady behind the counter welcomed me and said…. "Hello Dr. Monroe, we have you sharing a room with Dr. Hamilton."….. I smiled and told her yes…… "Well, do you have a credit card we can use to hold the room for three nights?"….. I bet you can only imagine what I looked like. All kinds of things were racing in my head. I knew I didn't have $900.00……. In a panicked voice I said, "The room was suppose to have already been paid for"…… She pecked away on her computer and then glanced up at me with a puzzled look on her face, and said, "No, nothing has been paid……. In a hopeless voice I told her, "All I have is $250.00." I didn't want to have to stay on the streets until the next day so I told her, "I believe my roommate, who is scheduled to share the room with me, probably has a credit card from the university since she works there, but she won't be in until tomorrow." …..The young lady said, "This is what I can do for you Dr. Monroe I'm going to talk to my manager and ask if we can accept your cash of $250 and let you stay the night. What time is your roommate getting in?"…… I told her she was scheduled to arrive around noon....In a perky little voice the young lady said, "That will be good because if she doesn't get in before 2:00 p.m. the room card won't work anymore."

When I handed over the money all I had left was $20 in cash. I was starving by the time I reached the hotel because I hadn't eaten at all that day. I don't generally like to eat when I fly because of nausea. I had planned to order room service but now that was definitely out. Thank goodness I had packed away some grapes, cut up strawberries and pretzels before the flight just incase I got hungry. This became my dinner and breakfast. I was happy they had some bottled water in the room so I didn't have to leave in search of that.

I hardly slept all night because I was worrying about how I was going to pay for this if Jacque didn't come. I called Ed and told him about it and of course he was upset. He yelled on the phone, "You know we are on fixed incomes and I don't have enough money to cover the cost of your room!" I told him to calm down everything was going to work out. I told him, "Don't worry baby, we're both panicking for nothing. I know Jacque is going to make it in time to straighten this all out before the deadline. Anyway, you know God's got this. He hasn't let us down yet! " Ed calmed down and told me to be careful in the hotel by myself and make sure I put the safety latch on the door.

Even though I tried to reassure Ed secretly I was worried. I didn't know how I was going to get back home sooner than the scheduled return time on Sunday. Well, I woke up early the next morning and called my trusty brother Marty. He came through for me and I was able to pay for the room for the three days and had some money left over for my other expenses.

Jacque showed up a little after noon and I explained to her what had happened. She told me she would help out if I didn't have the money but I told her it had already been taken care of. Then she explained to me the way it worked at the university. "You have to pay for everything up front and then submit your bills to be reimbursed." I should have known this because that is what the school district did as well. Not that I had had that much experience with it since special education teachers didn't go on that many out-of-town trips, or maybe I should just speak for myself.

Jacque took a quick shower and got ready to go with me to the convention. I was told it was about 12,000 people at this convention. I had put all of the materials I needed in a big envelope the night before because I didn't want to get into a rush and forget something. Jacque is a wellness instructor at the university and very athletic. She decided she wanted to walk to the convention center which was about a 10 min walk from the hotel and would meet me there. I caught a cab. As we traveled along the busy street different thoughts were running through my mind such as; "I need to take my name tag to the registration booth to be scanned, get this big burlap bag they were giving to all the people attending the convention and then find out where I needed to be to present." When the cab pulled up in front of the convention center I climbed out and the cab pulled off. I felt I was missing something and then realized I was. I had left the envelope with all of my presentation materials in it, on the floor of the cab. I stood there like that kid on *Home*

Alone clinching both of my cheeks with my hands and mouth wide open saying repeatedly, "Oh No! I can't believe I did this" just as Jacque walked up. She asked me what was wrong and I told her I had left everything in the cab. She spotted a cab and took off running. She caught up with it but it was the wrong cab.

I was shaking so hard I could barely stand. I just couldn't believe it. Jacque told me to sit down. She was going to go back to the hotel and see if the cab driver took the envelope back to them. I took a seat next to this little old lady from Vera Cruz, Mexico. Her daughter was also presenting. I told her what I had done and she told me she was going to pray for me. As we sat talking I looked out of the glass doors to the convention center and there driving very slowly pass was the cab driver. He was holding my envelope up in the air and displaying it through the cab window. I jumped up and hobbled to the door, hurt leg and all, and attempted to try and catch him but he never stopped rolling because he wasn't allowed to stop in front of the convention center. I just went in and slumped back down on the bench next to the little old lady feeling totally hopeless.

Jacque showed back up and I told her about the cab driver passing back by. She said she had left her cell phone number with the door attendant and if he brought the envelope back to them he would call her. All I could think about was all the money that had been spent to come on this trip and now it was all for nothing. Jacque kept telling me everything was going to be alright; after all I still had about an hour before I had to present. Just then her phone rang and it was the attendant at the hotel. He told her the cab driver had dropped the envelope back off. She volunteered to go and get the envelope for me. I tried to give her money to catch a cab back but she wanted to walk. She got back just in time for me to register and find out where I had to present. Jacque was the best partner I could have ever gone on a trip with. She was kind, compassionate and definitely patient.

The presentation turned out well. I had a lot of people interested in my dissertation research topic, "The Impact of Uniform Dress Code on Attendance, Discipline and Academic Achievement among Students in A South Texas High School." I met people from Greece, Canada, Australia and England. I thought this was just going to be presentations from universities and colleges in the United States but it turned out this was for universities from all over the world. It really was a big event. I was told I should have been honored to be selected to present and I was.

My attorney spoke and snapped me back to reality. He let me know that regardless to what I had done for the school district in the past it really didn't matter. That was then and this was now. He said, "You do know you've been constructively fired by Corpus Christi ISD." I think I knew it but I had convinced myself I still had a year to return because I had signed the leave of absence without pay which kept the door open to me. I didn't want to admit to myself that I had been fired. I just wasn't ready to give up 20+ years of dedication to something that I loved. But when I heard the words, "You've been fired" spoken out loud it drove the point home. I knew Corpus Christi ISD would definitely not want to take a chance on hiring me back because I would be a threat to their way of running the school district. Even if they had to continue using unfair hiring practices to do it I was definitely not going to be let back in. Despite what I knew here I sat in another mediation meeting trying to get justice.

In reference to the position I applied for in July, 2009, I wanted to know the qualifications of the person that was hired. After all I had been denied the right to compete once again because I was told something was wrong with my application. According to Mrs. Maria Villarreal my application was fine but because only one of my three references had been received before the "Open Until Filled" position closed, and the others were received after that date, she couldn't submit my application to be considered for the position. I later received a rejection letter informing me that someone else had been hired for the position and should some thing else come up I was free to apply for it. I believe if my information had been submitted appropriately I would have qualified for the position because my physician would have felt better about releasing me back to work.

During the mediation meeting I was told the position had never been filled so the district couldn't provide the qualifications of the person that was supposedly hired. It was closed and reopened in February and again in April due to school district budget problems. Because I thought the position had been filled I never checked to see if it was reopened so I didn't know to apply. Had I known; I would have. According to the response letter I was sent my application was suppose to be on file for two years so I felt my references had definitely been received by the new posting dates. Did they wait to reopen it after they knew I wouldn't be able to apply for it? I don't know. It made me feel that way. A few days after this meeting my attorney was contacted by Corpus Christi ISD and told they had made a mistake the position had been filled but they never provided the qualifications of the person that was hired.

When the mediator returned with the school districts representatives, petty nuisance offer, I simply lost it and started sharing everything the school district had done to me over the years. He was nice enough to sit and listen while I ranted and raved for about five minutes. Eventually I stopped and apologized to him saying, "I wasn't arguing with you I just needed to vent." When I finished apologizing I announced to them that the meeting was over and the school district could keep their degrading offer. The mediator wasn't ready to give up so easily. He suggested that I go home and sleep on it. He would be back next Thursday maybe something could be salvaged.

I had surprised myself at how I erupted into this fit of rage. I thought I had gotten passed this but I hadn't. It was as if I had been caught up in this emotional tornado which swept through me, ripping apart every carefully laid barrier I had built up to protect my fragile psyche from the constant bombardment of, hate, rejection, degradation, humiliation, anguish and despair, laying waist to my already devastated and wounded soul. When I walked out of that meeting I knew I wouldn't pursue this in the courts any further it was just too painful and I didn't have the finances to fight them. I also knew the courts would probably side with them anyway.

Mr. McJunkin asked me what I planned to do now, since I had essentially been fired and my disability insurance was going to end in a few months. The disability insurance company sent me a letter informing me they had decided to reclassify my disability. They felt I was no longer suffering from my injuries but I was suffering from the illness that developed because of the injuries. They felt I could work as long as it was sedentary. I told Mr. McJunkin at that point I wasn't sure what I was going to do. I wanted to move beyond the Pre-k thru 12ᵗʰ grade and teach teachers how to teach children with behavior problems. I had dedicated over 25 years of my life to helping children that society deemed un-teachable. What better way to continue to help children than train others the techniques I had used that worked so effectively for me. I informed him that I had applied at several colleges such as the University of Phoenix but had been turned down. I also had written one book and was in the process of getting another one published. Perhaps this would pay off.

I couldn't wait to get home to tell Ed what happened. In a very compassionate voice he said, "I was hoping you would come in with a smile on your face but in my heart-of-hearts I knew this was going to happen. I know you're disappointed but didn't you expect this as well?" Even though I expected things to turn out the way they did, I secretly hoped it would have worked out better.

My nerves were so frayed by the time I got home, after attempting to eat a little something my stomach started churning. I suddenly felt sick to my stomach, rushed to the trash can and started vomiting uncontrollably. I had been having digestive problems and getting nauseous quite frequently for a few weeks. Dr. Breeling had made arrangements for me to see a specialist. I was to have had this endoscopy done about a month earlier but hadn't been contacted. This very problem developed with my stomach the first time I went through this.

Later that day the phone started ringing off the hook but I didn't feel like talking. I needed to recover physically and emotionally from what I had just gone through. As I fixated on the conversations that had taken place during the meeting I felt the only way I could heal my emotionally wounded soul was to expose the culprits that were responsible.

About a week after the meeting all hell broke loose. I noticed water pooling at the end of my driveway. At first I thought someone was washing their car but when I investigated the water was only in front of our house. I immediately knew we had another leak somewhere. It had only been a year since the city worked on our street and broke a water main in front of our house. They told us about it and claimed they had fixed it. Before the incident with the city we hadn't had any plumbing problems. In less than 12 hours after they claimed to have fixed the break in the water main I noticed water running out from under the sink in our kitchen. I contacted the city and they sent some one out. We were told to get a plumber to come and fix it and the city would determine if they were responsible. If they were we would be reimbursed. In the end we had to pay a total of $2500.00 to replace everything that was damaged and install new piping leading from the break to the house. Of course the city didn't pay. Now here we go again with another leak.

After noticing the leak I pulled out of the driveway and headed around the corner and the check engine light came on, on the dashboard of the van. We had been blessed because we hadn't had that many problems with our van. It was six years old and we only had 40,000 miles on it. My husband took it to get it checked out and discovered it was a heat sensor that needed to be fixed. It would cost over $300.00 to repair. We didn't have the money needed to make repairs on anything.

As I sat trying to figure out how we were going to repair what needed to be repaired the phone rang it was my attorney, Mr. McJunkin. He asked if I had thought about the offer the school district made me because they had sent the settlement agreement papers to his office to be signed. He felt given the situation this was probably going to be the best offer I could hope to get. I was confused because at the end of the mediation meeting I had explicitly told them I wasn't willing to accept the offer that had been made. I think they figured once I calmed down I could be convinced this was the best thing for everyone involved. I restated my position to him saying, "Like I said in the meeting I'm not willing to accept that offer." We continued talking about different issues I had with the offer for about 10 minutes and then he asked, "If I can get those issues resolved would you reconsider the offer?" I was hesitant because I felt just like I felt the first time this settlement thing came up. I felt I was being pressured into signing something I didn't agree with and once again the district would be allowed to continue their discriminatory practices. He noticed the hesitancy in my voice and told me, "Let me take your concerns to the district and see if we can resolve some of them."

You don't know how tempted I was to settle. I hadn't worked since my fall at work due to continued medical issues stemming from the injuries I sustained. I hadn't received any payments from workman compensation for over a year and my only source of income was from a private accident insurance policy I had taken out. The disability payment was a little less than half the salary I earned when I worked. So needless to say my finances were very tight. I discussed this with my husband and he said the decision to end this had to be mine and mine alone. He did say I needed to let my consciences and God be my guide. I prayed about this and prayed about this. I thought about the phrase "A bird in the hand is worth two in the bush." Then I talked to my brother and he posed a question that made me think, "If you take this offer what will you have accomplished?"

For several days I mulled over my decision to accept the settlement or not and then I got a call from my attorney. He wanted me to come in to his office to discuss the settlement agreement further. I convinced Ed to go with me. When we arrived Mr. McJunkin invited us to have a seat. Once we were seated he proceeded to tell us he had spoken to the school district's attorney concerning the issues I raised. As he spoke I remembered something that was discussed between my attorney and the mediator concerning another case. Apparently a settlement had been reached between this other gentleman and the company he worked for but a clause had been added in his settlement agreement. It stated if the man accepted the settlement he also had to agree to never apply for a job with that company again. This conversation stuck with me; so once Mr. McJunkin finished talking I asked him if this statement was also added in my settlement agreement. Looking a little surprised at this question, he said, "Yes it is, but you weren't planning to return anyway; were you? I was absolutely livid. How dare Corpus Christi ISD stipulate if I accepted their settlement I could never, ever apply for any other position within the school district! What if I had wanted to retire and come back as a substitute teacher or tutor? A lot of teachers do this to subsidize their retirement. How could a public school district that received federal funding even consider inserting something like this into a discrimination settlement agreement? After all this was suppose to be an equal employment opportunity facility. I was also upset with EEOC for allowing something like this to be inserted into anything they were involved in. I was under the impression this was what they were established to prevent. I thanked Mr. McJunkin for all the work he had done up to this point but I was not going to sign anything. They could keep there offer. He looked a little disappointed but he understood and we left.

About two weeks after this meeting I received a letter from EEOC informing me that due to the impasse that had occurred between myself and the district during the mediation hearing an investigator was going to be assigned to my case. This was what finally provoked me into action. I was determined to expose Corpus Christi ISD for the discriminatory acts they had imposed upon me. I also didn't trust that EEOC would follow through with any kind of true investigation so I wrote a letter expressing my lack of confidence in them and gave an overview of my past history with them and Corpus Christi ISD and my plans to go public with my story. Here is a copy of that letter.

November 8, 2010

Equal Employment Opportunity Commission
801 L Street NW
Washington, D.C. 20507

To Whom It May Concern: RE: EEOC Charge No. 846-2010-41137
                                        Employer: Corpus Christi ISD

My name is Dr. Frankie J. Monroe. I am contacting you in response to the letter I received from your EEOC San Antonio branch office dated November 1, 2010.

I am sending you a copy of the response and booklet I sent to your San Antonio branch office. Because I want the National Branch of the Equal Employment Opportunity Office to be kept abreast of what is transpiring. I'm not sure what the reason, but I feel due to EEOC's inability or unwillingness to investigate my claims of discrimination based on race, age, retaliation, and disability thoroughly, Corpus Christi ISD has been allowed to continue their unfair hiring practices. I filed my initial charges against Corpus Christi ISD in 2004. Since that time many things have surfaced that provided even more proof of my charges of discrimination but for some reason has been ignored by EEOC and the courts. I don't hold out much hope of receiving any assistance from EEOC or the justice system because of previous experiences, but I being the forever optimist try to view the glass as half full rather than half empty.

I'm not the only person that has been experiencing discrimination in Corpus Christi ISD. It is my understanding that EEOC is also working with Ms. Rene Garcia. I had an opportunity to speak with Ms. Garcia several months ago. Though our cases are different we have several similarities. We both are in our 50's. We both taught special education. We both have at least 20 years of experience. We both hold superintendent, principal, and special education certifications. We both were passed over for administrative position that were given to younger people and denied an opportunity to leave the classroom. We both were offered settlements but Ms. Garcia was offered a years salary and I was offered a nuisance settlement. In addition to this a clause was inserted into the agreement I was presented, stating if I accepted the settlement they offered me; I had to also agree I would never again apply for another position in the Corpus Christi Independent School District. Needless to say I was quite distraught after reading this. I had devoted so much of my teaching career to this district and this was the way they treated me. What disturbed me even more was the fact that this mediation meeting was being conducted under the guise of an EEOC representative. How could EEOC even condone a clause like this being inserted into any agreement they were involved with, given this department had been designed to protect employees from this very thing? Could it be because I was valued less and had already been rejected by the courts?

There is a saying "God helps those that help themselves." After a phone conversation I had with someone from EEOC I was told all the information collected from my previous case had been disposed of. I took it upon myself to put together a booklet that includes copies of that information as well as additional information that was requested by the investigator assigned to my case. I feel it is important to include past and present information in order to show there is a pattern of discrimination practiced by Corpus Christi ISD and why I feel I have been "continuously" discriminated against based on *race, age, retaliation and disability.*

I have tried to provide my proof of discrimination as succinctly as possible. This information will include e-mails, letters, my 2005 lawsuit, a Motion of Summary, affidavits, medical records and other documents. After reading this information I hope you will truly investigate my charges to determine for yourself if I was indeed discriminated against and provide remedy to the charges. I also want to inform you that a great deal of the information I am providing you has been included in a book I have written. It has been so exasperating to be continuously ignored by EEOC and the courts I felt perhaps I could get some vindication in the public arena.

Any assistance in this matter will be greatly appreciated.

Sincerely,

Dr. Frankie J. Monroe

Mr. Price called me immediately after receiving a 200 page bound booklet I sent him with all the information I had collected over the years. He told me to ignore the letter he had sent because he was not aware of all the documents I had sent. He stated it would take some time to examine them before a decision could be made.

In the letter, he had prematurely sent me, he alluded to the fact that he had not discovered anything but if I had additional information that would help my case feel free to send it. After reading his letter I decided to respond to it rather than ignore it. Below is a copy of that letter.

November 19, 2010

U. S. Equal Employment Opportunity Commission
5410 Fredericksburg Road, Suite 200
San Antonio, TX 78229-3555

Attention: Mr. Thomas Price   RE: EEOC charge No. 846-2010-41137
                                             Employer: Corpus Christi ISD

I received your letter dated November 15, 2010

I realize during our phone conversation that you stated you were not aware that the
information packet I had sent had arrived and asked that I disregard the letter you sent,
but I felt compelled to address some of the issues raised in your letter. I want to address
each section of your letter one-by-one because it's easy to make statements but when you
dig a little deeper other things will be revealed.

1. Documents which confirmed that Corpus Christi ISD's position that one paper
    reference was returned on or about July 29, 2009. This supported by copy of a
    July 23, 2009 letter from Jacob Perez to you, which shows that at the
    "References" section of this letter, there is a handwritten notation indicating one
    reference was received July 29, 2009. In addition, the WinOcular Query data
    relating to your application shows that none of your references completed the
    online reference form they were electronically sent notice of. Job Posting
    Confirms that three references were required.

Under Defendant's Motion for Summary I provided in the packet I sent you this was
stated.

    a) Page #2 "Defendant CCISD employs a neutral selection process and has
        always hired individuals whose credentials, work experiences, and
        knowledge of both state and federal laws place them at the top of the
        applicant pool"

    b) Page #3 "There is an absence of evidence to support the non-moving
        party's case." Id. At 325. The burden is on the non-moving party to "set
        forth facts showing that there is a genuine issue for trial." Id. At 325"

    c) Page #5 "The only exception to this is if Plaintiff can show there were
        "continuing violations." A continuing violation may be found where there
        is proof of specific ongoing discriminatory policies or practices, or where
        specific and related instance of discrimination are permitted by the
        employer to continue un remedied for so long as to amount to a

48

discriminatory policy or practice. Robinson V. Time Warner Inc., 92 F. Supp.2d 318"

It is now November 2010. Six years have passed since I initially filed charges of discrimination with EEOC against CCISD. For five of those years I continued to apply for different administrative positions. In that time I have not moved beyond classroom teacher. After all court decisions were rendered on my discrimination charges in 2007, in favor of CCISD. I was never sent on another interview by Corpus Christi ISD. *CCISD's Attorney wrote* "The only exception to this is if Plaintiff can show there were "continuing violations." A continuing violation may be found where there is proof of specific ongoing discriminatory policies or practices, or where specific and related instance of discrimination are permitted by the employer to continue un remedied for so long as to amount to a discriminatory policy or practice. Robinson V. Time Warner Inc., 92 F. Supp.2d 318"

I will submit e-mails- and letters I have written to head administrators in CCISD including superintendents voicing my concerns about my application and other information not being submitted so that I could participate in the selection process. This has continued for nearly 10 years. After reviewing my documents would you consider this proof of *"continuing violations"* based on the definition provided by CCISD's attorney? As I address each issue would you please pose the following questions to CCISD?

1) What staff person submitted and signed off on the information presented to them concerning receipt of the paper references? If there response is *Mrs. Maria Villarreal*, please follow my paper trail. On July 10, 2009 I submitted my application on-line and received an automatic response. It also states in that response that application will remain on file for (2) years. I was never contacted and told that I needed to do anything else. When I submitted my letter of interest, in person, on July 16, 2009 and asked was everything in order I was told it was okay. Why did it take until July 23, 2009 to notify me that something was wrong? Due to the fact I didn't believe Mrs. Villarreal was turning in my information in I begin requesting my letter of interest be stamped and dated each time I submitted it in person years ago. I also asked the administrators to monitor her. She didn't like that and has snapped at me when I questioned her concerning different positions on numerous occassions.

2) **Please pay attention to all highlighted dates. You will see pattern**

Remaining true to form on January 26, 2011 I received a Dismissal and Notice of Suits Rights letter from EEOC.

EEOC Form 161 (1/08)

U.S. EQUAL EMPLOYMENT OPPORTUNITY COMMISSION

DISMISSAL AND NOTICE OF RIGHTS

To: Frankie J. Monroe

From: San Antonio Field Office
5410 Fredericksburg Rd
Suite 200
San Antonio, TX 78229

[ ] On behalf of person(s) aggrieved whose identity is CONFIDENTIAL (29 CFR §1601.7(a))

EEOC Charge No.	EEOC Representative	Telephone No.
846-2010-41137 (Amended)	Norma Guzman, Enforcement Supervisor	(210) 281-7617

THE EEOC IS CLOSING ITS FILE ON THIS CHARGE FOR THE FOLLOWING REASON:

[ ] The facts alleged in the charge fail to state a claim under any of the statutes enforced by the EEOC.

[ ] Your allegations did not involve a disability as defined by the Americans With Disabilities Act.

[ ] The Respondent employs less than the required number of employees or is not otherwise covered by the statutes.

[ ] Your charge was not timely filed with EEOC; in other words, you waited too long after the date(s) of the alleged discrimination to file your charge.

[X] The EEOC issues the following determination: Based upon its investigation, the EEOC is unable to conclude that the information obtained establishes violations of the statutes. This does not certify that the respondent is in compliance with the statutes. No finding is made as to any other issues that might be construed as having been raised by this charge.

[ ] The EEOC has adopted the findings of the state or local fair employment practices agency that investigated this charge.

[ ] Other (briefly state)

- NOTICE OF SUIT RIGHTS -
(See the additional information attached to this form.)

Title VII, the Americans with Disabilities Act, and/or the Age Discrimination in Employment Act: This will be the only notice of dismissal and of your right to sue that we will send you. You may file a lawsuit against the respondent(s) under federal law based on this charge in federal or state court. Your lawsuit **must be filed WITHIN 90 DAYS of your receipt of this notice**; or your right to sue based on this charge will be lost. (The time limit for filing suit based on a claim under state law may be different.)

Equal Pay Act (EPA): EPA suits must be filed in federal or state court within 2 years (3 years for willful violations) of the alleged EPA underpayment. This means that **backpay due for any violations that occurred more than 2 years (3 years) before you file suit may not be collectible.**

On behalf of the Commission

_____
Pedro Esquivel, Director

1/21/11
(Date Mailed)

Enclosures(s)

cc:
John J. Janssen, Staff Attorney
Office of Legal Services
Corpus Christi Independent School District
P.O. Box 110
Corpus Christi, Texas 78403

50

Despite all the information I had submitted to them they determined, "Based upon its investigation, the EEOC is unable to conclude that the information obtained established violations of the statutes. This does not certify that the respondent is in compliance with the statutes. No finding is made as to any other issues that might be construed as having been raised by this charge." Now I prepared for battle.

My mother use to tell me to pray the prayer for rescue from my enemies. It was at this time that I prayed the following prayer.

Psalm 35

1. Plead *my cause*, O LORD with them that strive with me: fight against them that fight against me.
2. Take hold of shield and buckler, and stand up for mine help.
3. Draw out also the spear, and stop *the way* against them that persecute me: say unto my soul, I *am* they salvation.
4. Let them be confounded and put to shame that seek after my soul: let them be turned back and brought to confusion that devise my hurt.
5. Let them be as chaff before the wind: and let the angel of the LORD chase *them*.
6. Let their way be dark and slippery: and let the angel of the LORD persecute them.
7. For without cause have they hid for me their net *in* a pit, **which** without cause they have digged for my soul.
8. Let destruction come upon him at unawares; and let his net that he hath hid catch himself: into that very destruction let him fall.
9. And my soul shall be joyful in the LORD: it shall rejoice in his salvation.
10. All my bones shall say, LORD, who *is* like unto thee, which deliverest the poor from him that is too strong for him, yea, the poor and the needy from him that spoileth him?
11. False witnesses did rise up: they laid to my charge *things* that I knew not.
12. They rewarded me evil for good *to* the spoiling of my soul.
13. But as for me, when they were sick, my clothing *was* sackcloth: I humbled my soul with fasting; and my prayer returned into mine own bosom.
14. I behaved myself as though *he had been* my friend *or* brother: I bowed down heavily, as one that mourneth *for his* mother.
15. But in mine adversity they rejoiced, and gathered themselves together: *yea,* the abjects gathered themselves together against me, and I knew *it* not: they did tear *me*, and ceased not:

16. With hypocritical mockers in feasts, they gnashed upon me with their teeth.
17. LORD, how long wilt though look on? Rescue my soul from their destructions, my darling from the lions.
18. I will give thee thanks in the great congregation: I will praise thee among much people
19. Let not them that are mine enemies wrongfully rejoice over me: *neither* let them wink with the eye that hates me without a cause.
20. For they speak not peace: but they devise deceitful matters against *them that are* quiet in the land.
21. Yea, they opened their mouth wide against me, *and* said, Aha, aha, our eye hath seen *it*.
22. *This* thou hast seen, O LORD: keep not silence: O Lord, be not far from me.
23. Stir up thyself, and awake to my judgment *even* unto my cause, my God and my Lord.
24. Judge me, O LORD my God, according to thy righteousness; and let them not rejoice over me.
25. Let them not say in their hearts, Ah, so would we have it: let them not say, We have swallowed him up.
26. Let them be ashamed and brought to confusion together that rejoice at mine hurt: let them be clothed with shame and dishonor that magnify *themselves* against me.
27. Let them shout for, and be glad, that favor my righteous cause: yea, let them say continually, Let the LORD be magnified, which hath pleasure in the prosperity of his servant.
28. And my tongue shall speak of they righteousness *and* of they praise all the day long

Chapter II

Enough is Enough

Have you ever known a woman that has been abused? Family members and friends keep telling her to leave the relationship because it's not right. But she stays there. She believes in her marriage vows for better or worse, in sickness and in health, until death do us part. She stays for the children; after all who would provide for them or her. She stays because she has invested 25 years of her life into this relationship. Who else would want her? Many times she has come to work with sunglasses on and heavy make-up to conceal the bruises. She continuously tries to do things that will make her spouse happy but nothing is ever good enough. She tries a face-lift, breast implants, and weight loss to please her spouse but all for naught. One day out of the blue her spouse just ups and walks out on her leaving her in an emotional upheaval.

Her mind races in search of answers. Hadn't she done everything to make this work? She had sacrificed so much. Why had her spouse done this to her? What was she going to do now? In that moment of frenzy something happens. She hears a scream but it isn't from the outside it is a scream from within. In that moment she realizes something so profound it nearly takes her breath away. The scream she hears is a spiritual scream. God had screamed at her and said, *"ENOUGH IS ENOUGH!"* never again let any man determine your self worth."

I'm sure after reading this you assumed the spouse I was referring to was my husband but that is definitely not the case. My husband has never once abused me in the 31 years we've been together. The spouse I'm referring to is the job I held with Corpus Christi ISD. Yes, I know that sounds ridiculous but I know lots of people married to their jobs. This is just the way I felt about it.

In Newton's Third Law of motion it states, "The mutual forces of action and reaction between two bodies are equal opposite and collinear. In other words to every action there is always an equal and opposite reaction." Everything came to a head in 2004 when I first reached the point of reacting to the school districts actions.

It had been one of those weeks for me. I taught resource language arts, grades 9-12 and had approximately 125 students I was responsible for. On October 27, 2004 around 2:45, which was my planning period, two of my students, Jennifer, a heavy set young lady who loved dressing in tight outfits, and wearing heavy, dark makeup and Linda, her best friend, who had long raven black hair that reached past her knees and loved wearing big gold, earrings, chains and bracelets, came to my class. Jennifer was quite distraught. She had gotten into an argument with her mother and been kicked out of the house. Her family was very dysfunctional.

I wore many hats during my career as an educator teaching children with special needs. I wasn't just their teacher I was their advocate when others treated them unfairly because of their handicaps, surrogate mother, counselor, and disciplinarian when it warranted it.

With tear drenched cheeks and deep sobs Jennifer asked, "Ms what am I going to do? Some of my friends let me stay at their house for a few days but I can't stay with them long. I have nowhere to live." I gave her a tissue and whispered to her, "Calm down sweetie, we're going to figure something out."

While trying to console her, a message flashed across my computer screen. It was from a teacher on campus. She was informing the staff that Briana, one of my other students, was in the hospital in a coma. They didn't know what happened but her brain had begun to swell. Ed was scheduled for surgery the next day, which was a Tuesday, to remove one of the pins out of his ankle because it had worked its way through his ankle and became infected. He had been a heavy equipment operator for the city of Corpus Christi for about 17 years when this happened. One day as he was climbing in his truck, his foot slipped and he fell backwards striking his lower leg and ankle hard on the side step of the truck before landing on his back. The fall caused his ankle to splinter. The doctor was able to reconstruct it and hold it together by putting pins in it, but now another problem had developed. I was going to have to go to the hospital right after school for the next three days to check on him because the doctor wanted to keep him there to monitor the infection. I also had recently been admitted into the doctoral program at Texas A & M University and had a power-point presentation, a report, and reflections due by Monday of the following week. How was I going to get it all done?

This scenario was nothing new for me. I'd faced situations like this on a constant basis for years. Thank God! I was a fairly decent problem solver. First I referred my student to the counselor concerning being homeless. I contacted the teacher that sent the e-mail to inquire about Briana and then called a sub to take over my class for the next day so I could be there during Ed's surgery. I worked on the lesson plans and ran off copies of material for the sub. It took about an hour after school. When I got home I decided to pull an all-nighter to finish the power-point presentation, report and my reflections.

I went back to work Wednesday the day after Ed's surgery and Jennifer was waiting for me. She found out from the counselor she could live on her own because she was 18 years old and had income from her disability. He suggested she go to the Housing Authority and apply for low income housing. She followed his instructions, picked up the application but brought the paperwork to me for help. Jennifer, had dyslexia which caused her to have trouble with reading as well as writing. As I sat talking and assisting her I saw another e-mail flash across the computer. I opened it and found out, Briana, the student that had been in a coma, had passed away. She was in the ninth grade. I hadn't been able to build a close rapport with her. She was a yes or no type student. She did her work but didn't interact much. I felt just awful. I finished helping Jennifer and asked her to leave. Despite how I felt I had to complete several, Individual Education Plans (I.E.P.) for some students because their annual Admit Review and Dismissal (ARD) meetings were going to be held the next day.

As I sat filling out the paperwork for these students another message flashed across the screen and this time it was from Isabel, a young teacher who taught Spanish on the same campus with me. She was a very, cute, petite little thing with a bubbly attitude. She had been teaching for about two or three years and expressed how she had no plans to continue teaching in the classroom. She had big plans. She had mapped it all out. She would teach for a few years and then move into administration.

I didn't really get to know Isabel until the summer of 2004. We were taking an administrative course together. I shared with her how I had held a principal and superintendent certification for a while but hadn't been successful in landing an administrative position. I went on to tell her about the district offering several assistant principal positions for the beginning of the 2004-2005 school year; and how I had applied…. In exasperation I said, "Isabel, I've lost count of how many times I've applied for different administrative positions within the school district since 2001. Maybe with all these positions available this time they'll find it in there hearts to at least send me on an interview."

Isabel sympathized with me and said, "I don't know if I would have the patience you've had. I would've said something by now or left the district." Then she said, "You know, I don't think I'll get it because I don't have enough experience, but I'm going to apply for an assistant principal position as well. Who knows, I might just get a shot at it."

After that conversation I didn't hear from Isabel until after school started in August of 2004. One afternoon, around 4:30 there was a knock at my classroom door. It was Isabel. She asked could she come in and I told her, "Sure." It was the end of the school day and all the students had left. She came over and took a seat next to me as I continued working at the computer. Then she inquisitively asked, "Have you gone on any interviews yet?" I was curious about this line of questioning and stopped working to give her my undivided attention. I told her "No….no one has contacted me but that's nothing new."

A sudden sadness swept over her face and in a trembling voice she began to tell me what happened to her. "I was contacted and told I had been selected for several interviews for assistant principal positions. They were going to be held at the Corpus Christi ISD Administration Office." She went on to describe what she saw when she got there.

"There were about 20 people being interviewed. When it came time for me to interview they took me into this room with several school board members and principals. I wasn't familiar with the interviewing process at first but by the time I got to the third interview I nailed it. I knew what to expect and how the questions were going to be asked. When I left I just knew I was getting an assistant principal position." Then she broke down and started crying. "They had no intention of hiring me they just used me and made it seem like I stood a chance."

As I listened to her talk I thought about something she said and asked, "Did you get these interviews spread out over time?" She said, "no it was all done in the same day."

I scooted my chair next to hers and embraced her as I said, "Look honey! If you had been rejected as many times as I have over the years you'd be crying all the time. All you can do is lick your wounds, pull yourself together, and try again. Like my godmother use to tell me; nothing hurts a failure but a try." She gathered herself together, wiped her eyes and seemed a bit calmer when she left. I couldn't get pass the fact that she had been given not one, not two but three interviews in one day when it had taken me four years to get even one offer.

I didn't hear anything else from Isabel until I saw an e-mail from her. After such a rough week with all the tragic things going on and trying to finish up all the work I needed to complete I decided to take a break and open the e-mail Isabel sent. It wasn't addressed directly to me it was addressed to the Ray High School Staff.

It read….

> *"I just want to say thank you to all of those who have made my stay at Ray High School such a wonderful experience. I am truly blessed to have worked with such an awesome faculty and staff. Please wish me well as I embark on my journey as Assistant Principal at Cunningham Middle School.*
> *Once again, Thanks.*
>
> *Sincerely,*
>
> *Isabel Torrez*
> *Spanish Teacher"*

I sat starring at this message for a few minutes reading it over and over. I was filled with so many mixed emotions. I was happy for Isabel but at the same time I wanted to cry. How did Isabel work only 2 ½ or 3 years in education and zoom past me to become an administrator? I had been in education for 20+ years. Every evaluation I had ever gotten was of exceptional quality. I had a Bachelors degree in Management Administration, Masters in Educational Administration, had a superintendent certification, principal certification, special education certification, vision impaired certification and was working on my doctorate in Educational Leadership. I had pretty much begged different administrators to give me a chance to prove my dedication to them through, phone calls, letters and e-mails but nothing ever came of it. This was the last straw.

I was now infuriated and on a mission. I checked several of the Intercoms, which were monthly employee newsletters. It provided information about what was going on in the district. Usually newly hired people who moved into administrative positions were congratulated in the newsletters. I paid close attention to all the teachers that moved into administrative positions during the months of August-October of 2004, when Isabel was hired. I found out several had been hired from other school districts with no more than I had and some had even less. How had they ranked higher than someone that worked for the district? With the exception of two American surnames, the rest had Spanish surnames. I decided to file charges of discrimination with EEOC on the basis of race, age, and retaliation. This was the only reason I could think of as to why I had never even been provided an interview for any of the entry level management positions I applied for.

Chapter III

Equal Employment Opportunity Commission (EEOC)

I told you earlier I would go into deeper details about EEOC. This is just a personal opinion concerning them. For years I felt the Equal Employment Opportunity Commission (EEOC) was the first line of defense when it came to being discriminated against on the job. I had grown up in the sixties and this was all I ever heard. But now I don't know what purpose they truly serve. Perhaps they were established for a good reason but I think they have outlived their usefulness. I've talked to several people who filed charges with them but not very much happened for them either. They may do alright when it comes to class action lawsuits; but on an individual basis I don't have much faith in them especially after the treatment I received from them not once, not twice but three times. My first personal experience with EEOC occurred in1985 then 2004 and finally 2009.

In 1985 I filed discrimination charges with EEOC when I worked with the Texas Department of Human Services as a Temporary Clerk-Typist II. It all began when I returned to Corpus Christi, Texas, from Gary, Indiana with my bachelor degree in business administration from Indiana University.

From 1974-1976, I worked for the Texas Welfare Department in the food stamp division as a clerk-typist. I enjoyed working there. Everyone felt like family. The only problem I had was the amount of money I earned. I earned about $300 a month. It wasn't so bad at first. I was married and this income was used just for my spending money. After my first husband walked off and left me for another woman this became my only source of income. I had to support not only myself but my two children as well.

I had wanted to become a caseworker for a while because they earned about $800.00 a month which was $500.00 more than I was earning. The only requirement needed to hold this position was to have 60 college credits. A friend of mine, John Wright, whom I called Father John because he once studied for the Catholic priesthood, suggested I apply for a college grant. John was a very compassionate young man who stood about six feet tall, with sandy blond hair, and hazel eyes. He was working his way through college and planned to become a doctor. He saw how I struggled to feed myself and my children after my husband left me.

Near the middle of every month I would approach John and ask to borrow about $40.00 just to make it to the next payday. Once I got paid I would pay him back but stipulate that he hold on to it because I would probably be back before the month was out to borrow it again. He was so kind and considerate he would simply tuck the money away until I came back for it. I think he should have stuck with the priesthood because he encouraged not just me but so many others to further their educations to better themselves. I understood why he left the priesthood though. He fell in love and wanted to get married.

I met John's fiancée, Nancy, a beautiful blue-eyed blond from Hammond, Indiana. She actually grew up about 10 or 15 minutes from my hometown of Gary, Indiana. She had come to Corpus to stay with relatives and go to college. While attending Del Mar she met John and they fell in love. One day Nancy approached me and asked if I would help her conduct a study for her sociology class. She shared with me her idea for the study. She wanted to find out if there was discrimination in housing in Corpus. In one scenario, she wanted John and me to pose as husband and wife; then document the reactions we got as a married, mixed couple. I know in this day and time it's not that big of a deal to see mixed couples but in the early 70's this was still taboo. In another scenario Nancy wanted me to pose as a student in college looking for a place to rent. She had selected several places she wanted me to go. It would have been easy for the potential renters to detect the Black dialect in my voice if I called; so she called in advance to make sure there were places available.

In high school I studied drama and loved it. This was a chance to put those acting skills to use. I was excited to be playing a staring role. I went to Nancy's house to drop off my girls so she could babysit them. John was waiting there so we could leave together. I first went to this little bungalow apartment off Ocean Drive. It was not too far from the beach. The view was breathtaking. You could step right out of your backdoor and see the gulf waters lap onto the shoreline. The landlord asked why I wanted to rent and I told him I was taking some courses at the college and wanted to have a place of my own because I didn't want to be bothered with roommates that loved partying. He smiled and said he would be willing to rent the bungalow to me for about $350.00 a month. That was a bit pricey for the time but understandable because of the location. Then John and I took off for the next location; an apartment complex in the same area. When Nancy called, ahead of time, she had been told they had three apartments available. Once John and I arrived holding hands I saw this little old white couple sitting on a bench. The little old woman sat starring at us with her mouth standing wide open as we passed. Out of the corner of my eye I caught a glimpse of the little old man reaching over and closing her mouth. I just chuckled to myself and followed John into the office.

John approached the counter and introduced me as his wife. He went on to explain to the clerk that we were from Dallas. He worked for this big oil refinery and had been reassigned to Corpus to run one of the subsidiaries here. We would only need to rent a place for about a year and wanted to know if any apartments were available. The clerk kind of sneered and looked us straight in the eyes and said "We don't have anything for rent." Then John told him that his sister had called earlier and was told they had three apartments for rent not more than an hour earlier. The clerk took a deep breath and said, "We might have had apartments available then but they have since been rented out." John thanked him for his time and we left.

Then we went to one more apartment complex in the area. This time we were allowed to see the apartment but there was a glitch there as well. When we entered the lobby of this apartment complex and approached the counter John asked how much it would cost to rent an apartment. We were told it would cost $550.00 a month. John asked to see it. Acting out the role of an adoring wife, I clinched John's hand as we rode up in the elevator then I leaned slightly forward and said to the clerk, "You know I forgot how much you said the apartment would cost." He stared straight ahead and said in this southern drawl, "It'll cost ya'll $750.00. I looked at John and said, "Remember that honey." The elevator doors opened and we walked down the hall to the apartment. We didn't say anything until we got inside. It was very spacious with two huge bedrooms, a one-step kitchen and a large living room. There were French doors located on the back wall of the living room that opened out unto a balcony revealing the Gulf of Mexico in all its glory. I squealed with excitement as I grabbed John's arm and said, "Honey this is absolutely gorgeous. We have to take it." The clerk asked if we had children and I replied, as I stared up at John lovingly, "No not yet, but we've been working on it." Then John asked one more time how much was the apartment. The clerk said under his breath, "$850.00 a month." John said, "Well since my lovely wife wants it so bad we'll take it. Please draw up the contract and give me a call when it's ready," Then he handed the clerk his business card.

We left and went back to Nancy's apartment. Nancy had fixed lunch and we sat down to eat as we laughed at how funny the reactions had been when people first saw John and I together as a couple. I didn't think much about this experience initially because it had all been an act to help out a friend. I never dreamed I would personally be faced with this very injustice later in life. It wasn't so funny then. Oh! by the way Nancy got an "A" for her study.

After several months of helping me out financially; John personally went to Del Mar College and got the paperwork for me to fill out. I went ahead and filled out everything and submitted it to the financial aid office. To my surprise and delight I was given the necessary grant money which allowed me to enter Del Mar College. John suggested I submit my resignation to the welfare office so I could attend college full-time. He said, "You know, you work so hard for the welfare office it's time for them to work for you." In actuality I earned such a small amount of money from my job I qualified for welfare assistance even before I tried to get admitted into college, but because of pride I didn't apply.

If I went to school full-time this would enable me to return to work and become a caseworker sooner. I had no plans of letting welfare be my final destination. I explained to the personnel director, when I submitted my letter of resignation that I had every intention of returning. I was told, at that time, once I completed the necessary education and if positions were available I would definitely be given first choice.

I had every intention of finishing my 60 college hours and returning to work, but after I enrolled into college I decided not to just get an associates degree, which required the 60 college hours I needed to become a caseworker. I decided to get a bachelor degree which took a little longer but would come in handy if a higher paying position availed itself. The entire time I attend school, first at Del Mar College and then at Indiana University were I graduated with my bachelor degree in business administration, I clung to the promise of employment from the welfare department when I returned to Corpus Christi, Texas. As I watched others beating the pavement in search of employment opportunities soon after graduation I felt secure knowing all I had to do was make it back to Texas, or so I thought.

I finally earned enough money as a substitute teacher to return to Corpus in 1984 and discovered there were several caseworker and other administrative positions available at the Texas Department of Human Services which I qualified for. I was thrilled to know this and I applied for several of them. Then I sat back patiently waiting to be contacted. After about a month of not hearing anything I contacted the personnel office and discovered all the positions I had applied for had been filled. I wasn't satisfied with the explanation I was given over the phone and requested a meeting with the personnel director, Mr. Abel Gonzalez, in person. I have never liked being one of those phone people. I prefer face-to-face contact it makes it a little harder to be rejected. During the meeting Mr. Gonzalez told me he was so sorry I hadn't been selected but the people hired had much more experience than I had. I understood this but it still didn't make me happy.

A few weeks later I was contacted by Mr. Gonzales's secretary, Janet Haggle. She knew me personally from years earlier and told me, "Frankie, I know you didn't go to school all those years to return here and only be offered the position of a secretary once again, but I have a Temporary Clerk-Typist II position available if you want it. It will last for about three months. At least you'll have Christmas money for your kids." In a very quiet voice I said to her, "Janet, I'm hurt about everything but I ain't crazy. I need to work. I'll take the temporary position, maybe something else will become available and I'll get hired permanently." Once I accepted the Temporary Clerk-Typist II position Janet felt it was necessary to warned me about the people who had gotten the positions I applied for were going to be in orientation with me.

The day finally arrived for orientation. I walked in the orientation room and found five other people there. Four were White, one Hispanic and then myself the only Black. We were briefed on the policies and procedures of the welfare department and then dismissed for lunch. We all decided to eat lunch together. We shared a few personal things about each other and then the conversation shifted. They started talking about how they got selected for the positions they had been assigned. One young lady stated she was only working for a little while because she needed money for her wedding. After the wedding she was quitting. She went on to say she felt she had gotten her position because she wore a mini skirt and the personnel director was looking at her legs. Then she burst out laughing.

I was crushed and felt the tears welling up in my eyes but I fought them back. Here this young lady was only working to have a wedding and I was trying to work to survive and support my family. I also discovered with the exception of one other newly hired person; none of them had worked in the welfare department. I believe the only reason I was even offered the temporary position was because they felt bad about not hiring me. They knew I had left the food stamp department to pursue my education just so I could return and work for them.

Before I left the food stamp department in 1976, I volunteered to work with several investigators out of Austin as their personal secretary. My duties were to organize the newly formed restitution department. I developed forms, setup up files so charges brought against people who were illegally getting assistance from the Welfare and Food Stamp division could be investigated. I typed up reports and submitted them to the state's attorney in a timely manner. The Temporary Clerk-Typist II position offered to me in 1984 was very similar. I was responsible for setting up and designing forms to collect restitution in the form of reduced food stamps and welfare checks. These clients hadn't done anything wrong they had been given excessive funds because of mistakes their caseworkers made. Restitution was to be set up so the overpayments could be paid back.

The caseworkers I worked for were very happy with my work, at least that's what they told me. They actually collected more restitution than they expected. As fate would have it the Temporary Clerk-Typist II position became permanent and I applied for it. I felt there was no way I wouldn't be hired; after all I was the one that set the division up. There was one thing added to the requirements for the Clerk-Typist II position I didn't expect. Now, in order for me to apply for the position I already held I had to be able to speak fluent Spanish. I questioned this decision. After all, with the exception of three people, including myself, the entire secretarial pool, which consisted of about 12 people, spoke Spanish. Whenever we got a client that couldn't speak English, which wasn't that often during that time, we simply said, "Un momenta pora favor" (forgive the spelling if this is not right) and transferred them to either one of the other Spanish speaking secretaries or caseworkers. This was done the same way in 1976 as well. I didn't let this requirement stop me I went ahead and applied for the position anyway.

As time passed and we hadn't heard anything from personnel, one of the caseworks Daphne, called the personnel director and inquired about the permanent Clerk-Typist II position because the temporary position would be up in a few weeks. I was in her office listening in on the intercom to the conversation as she spoke to Mr. Gonzalez. "Mr. Gonzalez," she said in an inquiring voice, "The Temporary Clerk-Typist II position is almost up and we were wondering if you've made a decision. I want to tell you how pleased we have been at the progress we have made because of Frankie Monroe. Due to all of her hard work we actually collected more money than we expected." As I listened, with a smile on my face, I heard Mr. Gonzalez say, "Frankie! I had no intention of hiring her. You remember Brenda Aleman? She use to work for the department a few years ago and left to work at the Post Office. Well she asked if she could return to the department and I've agreed to re-hire her." I was absolutely devastated. First I had been denied an opportunity to interview for a caseworker position and was offered a Temporary Clerk-Typist II position. I took this position because I needed to work. Then the temporary position became permanent and it was taken away from me as well. To make sure I didn't qualify for the position they threw in another requirement which would pretty much eliminate any chance I had of qualifying by stipulating that whoever applied for the position had to be able to speak fluent Spanish. I had taken two years of Spanish in high school but because I had no one to practice with I forgot most of it.

Daphne picked up the phone receiver quickly and finished her conversation with Mr. Gonzalez in private. I signaled to her that I was leaving. As I left her office my mind was racing and the tears flowed. I went to the restroom and stood in a bathroom stall bawling my eyes out. I started reflecting about my situation as a Black in America, "When my forefathers were captured and forced to leave Africa on slave ships and brought to America they were told they were in America and they better learn to speak English. If they spoke anything other than English they were either beat or killed. We were forced to assimilate into the American culture. English was the dominant language in this country and we learned it to the best of our abilities. As the generations passed we eventually forgot most of our African heritage along with our African languages. Unlike the people from South America and Mexico who came to this country by choice for a better life. I followed the American rules that were set down for my forefathers and now I am told I have to know Spanish if I want to be employed. How was this fair?"

I decided to file charges of discrimination against the Texas Department of Human Services with the Equal Employment Opportunity Commission. I felt I had been denied this position due to the fact I was a minority. About 10 months elapsed and I hadn't heard anything from EEOC so I decided to contact them. When I finally reached them I was told they were sorry but no investigation had taken place because my files had been lost. They went on to say the "Statute of Limitations" was about to run out and the only thing they could do was send me a "Right-to-Sue" letter. When I received the letter I rushed around trying to find an attorney to defend me and finally found someone. His name was Mr. Bill Grimes. He informed me my case would not be presented to a jury. He decided it was best for a judge to make the decision. He told me Judge William Sinclair would hear the case.

When my case finally made it to trial, I noticed on that day the judge was not paying attention. Several people were coming in and out of the hearing while testimonies were being given. The personnel director, Abel Gonzales, even admitted I might have been discriminated against a little bit. As far as I was concerned discrimination was discrimination. I knew Judge Sinclair missed this part of the testimony because when I glanced over at him; he was talking to a young lady that entered the court from a door near his bench. At first I didn't think much of it because I felt the trial would last for a few days and this would give the judge time to read over the testimony later. I also felt if there was a problem my attorney would have said something. Needless to say neither of those things happened. When the testimony was over it was evident the judge had made up his mind even before the trial started. We didn't even take a recess. We were told to stand; as the judge peered over his glasses, looked at us and recited his verdict.

In a rehearsed manner he said, "Ms. Monroe, you stated that you filed discrimination charges against the Texas Welfare Department because you were a minority. I hope you realize the person that was hired in your position was also considered a minority. I do acknowledge that you've been treated badly. A lot of things weren't done correctly and the Texas Department of Human Services needs to do better but I find that you have not been discriminated against. I wish you nothing but the best in your future endeavors." He lowered his gavel, hit the top of his desk and dismissed us. I walked out of court dazed and devastated. After this experience I was determined not to let it happen to me ever again. When the discrimination issue reared its ugly head in my direction again I made sure I crossed my (T's) and dotted my (I's). This time I was more specific. I made sure I filed charges on the basis of race (Black) not minority, because this seemed to have been the pivotal point in the decision the last judge made to throw my case out. From that point on I always kept letters, e-mails and documented notes I felt were important as it related to a job.

Those things that hurt you the most you remember the longest.

Chapter IV

Here We Go Again!

When problems erupted in 2004 I, being the forever optimist, once again took a chance on EEOC. This time I made sure I was prepared. I had all the necessary paperwork ready, I kept up with all the correspondence between the school district and myself as well as letters from EEOC. I was going to stay on top of things and contact them this time and not rely on them contacting me.

For about four years leading up to me filing charges of discrimination with EEOC against Corpus Christi ISD, I contacted one administrator after another asking why I wasn't being allowed to at least be sent out on an interview to get experience in the interviewing process. I once told them in an e-mail, I could even understand if they sent me out on an interview and then decided I just wasn't what they wanted, but to never be sent on an interview was unacceptable. After all I worked hard to do everything necessary to be deemed worthy of advancement in my work career.

I talked to Dr. Jesus Chavez, the Superintendent of Corpus Christi ISD at the time, and asked if he could look into why I hadn't been selected for an interview. He knew me personally because I had completed my superintendent practicum under his tutelage. When I finished my internship Dr. Chavez even agreed to allow me to use him as one of my references when I first started applying for administrative positions through an e-mail request.

I remember in one of the meetings, as an intern for my superintendent practicum, Dr. Chavez shared with the group that he had never been a principal. He worked for about seven years as an assistant principal and then got hired as a superintendent. The reason I bring this up now is because when everything turned bad and I filed discrimination charges with EEOC, Dr. Chavez seemed to have forgotten the fact that he didn't have all the necessary skills to advance in his career but had been afforded the opportunity. In the presence of me, my attorney and the districts in-house attorney, Imelda Martinez he found it necessary to explain to me; as if I wasn't capable of or competent enough to understand; why I wasn't being allowed to advance in my career. He created this scenario, "Frankie, I want to be the CEO of Exxon, I keep applying, and keep applying and keep applying but I don't get the job. Do you know why I don't get the job? It's because I lack the experience therefore causing me not to be qualified." I explained to him, in that same meeting, that I understood that concept. Then I asked if I could ask him a question and was told I could. In an inquiring voice I asked, "Dr. Chavez can you please explain to me how a young Hispanic female, between the ages of 25-30 with 2 ½ to 3 years of teaching experience be hired in an administrative position and I a Black female age 54 with 20+ years of experience not ever even get selected for an interview? He never responded to that question. There was more to this conversation but I will share it later in my story.

I gathered all the e-mails, letters and documentation I had and sent it along with a letter to EEOC in Washington DC in September of 2004. I didn't trust contacting anyone locally especially after what happened in 1985 when they lost my files. I wanted the big guns involved. About a week or so later I received a response from one of their branch offices in San Antonio, Texas. Apparently this was the regional office responsible for handling my case. They sent me several forms instructing me to fill them out so I could officially file discrimination charges of race, age, and retaliation. I was provided a mediation form and asked to check whether I was willing to meet and discuss a settlement agreement. I checked yes and mailed it along with all the other paperwork back to them filled out and signed. I also proceeded to file a grievance with the school district concerning the hiring process.

On November 2, 2004 I contacted Dr. Dawn Dorsey, the principal assigned to my campus that year, by e-mail informing her that I had filed discrimination charges with EEOC against the district. I explained to her I also wanted to file a grievance with the school district and asked if she had the proper forms I needed to do this on in the office. She said they did and invited me to come to her office to explain what was going on. During my planning period I went to her office and waited patiently until she was available to see me. She stepped just outside her office door and said, "Ms. Monroe please come in." We approached her desk and she motioned for me to have a seat. Then she walked around to the other side of her desk and took a seat. I noticed how much neater the office was since Dr. Dorsey took over. When Dr. Scott was principal books were scattered everywhere on the shelves behind him and his desk was cluttered with papers most of the time. The office definitely had improved. I guess a woman's touch was needed to improve the esthetics.

"Now Ms. Monroe please tell me what's going on," Dr. Dorsey said as she eased down into her plush leather chair. I began by saying, "Dr. Dorsey I want to first assure you what's going on right now has nothing to do with you. This was going on long before you took over as principal." I filled her in on my situation and she said she understood. We finished our discussion and I rose to leave. Dr. Dorsey followed me to the door and instructed Tina, her personal secretary, to give me the necessary forms I needed to file the grievance with the district. I thanked her for understanding and left for home.

When I got home and started reading through the grievance form that had been provided; I realized this wasn't the correct form. This was a form for parents to file grievances against the school district not staff. Given I was on a time-line and the grievance had to be submitted by the next day I went on-line searching for the forms through the school district's website but couldn't find anything so I got a generic grievance form I discovered off the internet and submitted it the next day. It was now game time.

Chapter V

Let the Games Begin!

I was contacted several days after submitting my grievance by mail from the school district's new in-house attorney, Ms. Imelda Martinez. In the letter she stated that this wasn't the correct grievance form. I had to submit my grievance on the proper district approved grievance form. The correct form was included in the letter. I completed it and re-submitted it the very next day. Once I re-submitted the form I was sent another letter stating it was too late to file that particular grievance but I could submit another one if something else arose.

Well, by the end of the October I discovered that additional people had been hired as assistant principals and I knew several of them personally. Again I wasn't selected to be sent on an interview. I submitted another grievance complaining about this and was once again contacted by the districts in-house attorney and told this form was not correct either because I hadn't named the correct parties to make these allegations against. I re-submitted another grievance form with a different party named.

The district and I went back and forth over different issues. I was generally a private person and tried to keep my public and private life separate. I guess it was taking a toll on me and I wasn't able to hide it any longer. One day my close friend and colleague, Mary Russell took one look at me and knew something was terribly wrong. She demanded I tell her what was going on and I broke down and told her. I shared with her how I had repeatedly submitted grievance forms to the main office and they had repeatedly rejected them for one reason or another. A puzzled look enveloped her face and then she asked, "Frankie why haven't you gone to the AFT about this?" AFT was one of the local teacher unions in the Corpus Christi school district. I explained to her how I had once belonged to the union back in the 80's. A dispute arose between the personnel director, Mr. Ernesto Barrera and I. I had gone to AFT for help and they simply said they couldn't help me.

Mary had opened herself up to an all out assault concerning my troubles and I bombarded her saying, "Mary, I just don't know. Ever since I returned to Corpus, a city that I absolutely adore, I have had to fight to survive. I've been caught up in one dilemma after another and this is just the latest installment." I proceeded to share my story with her.

The beginnings of my troubles with CCISD

When I returned to Corpus in the early 80s; a problem arose that caused me to file a discrimination lawsuit against the Texas Welfare Department, which I loss. After this ordeal I was able to eventually secure a substitute teaching position with Corpus Christi ISD. I worked in the district for about four years, three years as a substitute teacher and one as a temporary certified teacher. I was allowed to hold my temporary certification as long as I took classes at Corpus Christi State University to secure my permanent teaching certification.

I'm not even sure now how I found out about the very first Special Education Alternative Certification program offered in Corpus Christ. I do remember going to a meeting that was held at the Education Service Center (ESC). During this meeting I learned it would take one year to become certified. At the meeting I was told I could earn a teacher's salary and benefits. They also provided you one-on-one support to make sure you made a smooth transition into the classroom. This was a welcomed relief given I had been in the Special Education Certification program at Corpus Christi State University, which later became Texas A & M University, for almost a year and gotten no such support.

At the university I was expected to attend the Special Education Certification program they offered for approximately three years and was responsible for paying for all my classes. I remember asking Mr. Barrera, the certified personnel director, at the time, who had been involved in getting me admitted into classes at the university, if I was going to get another associates degree or something. I asked him this because not only was it costing me quite a bit to take the classes but it was taking up so much time. He assured me this was the amount of time it would take to complete the program and I would only get a certification, not an Associates degree."

I went on to tell Mary about an experience I remembered having in one of the classes I was required to take at the university. There was this instructor, Mrs. Jensen, who told me she wasn't familiar with the set of special needs students I taught, which were orthopedically handicapped, and mentally challenged. She then asked if I would tell her how I taught them so she could teach me what to do. How absurd was that? I was to pay the university to teach her what I already knew so she could turn around and teach it back to me.

At the end of the meeting I took an application, went home, filled it out and mailed it back to the Education Service Center (ESC). A few weeks later I received a call informing me I had been admitted into the program. I can't explain how happy I was to be accepted. Not only that, I was told I had been their number one choice.

Certain guidelines had been established if you were going to participate in the program. All candidates were required to have a teacher's contract signed, by the district they would be working in, before the new school year began. I went to my campus principal, Mr. Javier Hernandez, and asked if he would be willing to allow me to continue working on the Moody High School campus while I pursued this certification. He said yes, but I had to get approval from Mr. Barrera. I contacted Mr. Barrera by phone and asked if he would allow me to switch programs because I could finish my certification within a year. In a thunderous voice, he yelled at me and said, "We have you where we want you and if you're not going to stay where we put you I suggest you resign. We are **NOT!** interested in this new program and have no intentions of hiring anyone from this program." He was determined not to allow me to switch and actually hung up on me.

I contacted, Mrs. Linda Gehman, the person in charge of the Special Education Alternative Certification Program at ESC. She suggested I go to West Oso ISD and apply. The superintendent had already been informed of my qualifications and was definitely interested in hiring me. I went back to my campus principal, Mr. Hernandez and shared with him what had transpired. He begged me not to do anything until he was able to see if he could convince Mr. Barrera to change his mind. I told him I would give him two weeks. This was the timeframe that had been presented to me by Mr. Ron Howell, the Superintendent of West Oso. He had to have my decision by that time to present to the school board in time for me to be hired for the new school year. Two weeks passed and I hadn't heard anything from Mr. Hernandez so I went to his office.

I loved working on the Moody campus because Mr. Hernandez had an open door policy. If you had any problems he left his door open to all staff to come in and discuss it with him. He was sitting there going over some paperwork when I approached the open door to his office, knocked and asked if it was okay to come in. He stopped and signaled for me to come on in.

"Have a seat Mrs. Monroe," he said as he motioned for me to sit. "I think I know why you're here. I just feel awful because I called in all the favors I had and wasn't able to convince Mr. Barrera to change his mind." As he talked I listen quietly.

Giving up all hope of being able to remain on the campus or in the district I said, "That's okay Mr. Hernandez. I know you did everything you could to keep me. This has been the best experience I've ever had since working for the school district. It's kind of bittersweet. I'm being forced to leave you but I've been welcomed by someone else. If there was any other way I could remain here and complete my certification sooner I would, but I'm not getting any younger and I have a family depending on me to finish this as soon as possible. One year to get certified verses three years, it's not a hard choice."

Mr. Hernandez apologized profusely. I assured him I didn't feel it was his fault and said, "I want to thank you for everything you've done for me and maybe one day, once I get certified, I'll be allowed to return to the district and perhaps your campus." I got up, shook his hand and left.

Immediately after I left Mr. Hernandez's office I contacted AFT by phone. I complained to them about the treatment I had received from Mr. Barrera and how I was being forced to resign because I wanted to get certified in one year rather than three. I would also end up loosing about $3000 annually in salary because the school district that had expressed an interest in me was a smaller school district and paid their teachers less. AFT simply shrugged their shoulders and told me they couldn't help me. I felt if they couldn't intercede in this matter on my behalf why was I paying them nearly a thousand dollars a year in union dues. I decided they served no purpose as far as I was concerned and never joined them or any other teachers union again.

After school ended that day I went straight to West Oso and signed the special education teacher contract which would last for one year.

When the alternative certification program began that summer to prepare us for our teaching assignments in the fall, there were approximately 16 people in attendance. I was the only Black. There were two or three Hispanics and the remaining people where White. We all had signed teaching contracts. I was assigned to West Oso ISD, two others were assigned to Robstown ISD, and one was in Sinton ISD. To my surprise the remaining teachers were assigned to, you guessed it, Corpus Christi ISD. How could this be? I had been told by Mr. Barrera the reason I wasn't going to be allowed to participate in the Special Education Alternative Certification program was because Corpus Christi ISD was *NOT*! interested in it and wouldn't hire anyone from that program. But here sat about 8 to 10 people with contracts, all of them White. Many of them had never taught before. They were accountants, lawyers, or scientist that had tired of their professions or simply wanted to give back to society. I had 5 years of experience in education by this time and was already employed by Corpus Christi ISD when the program was introduced to the city by the Educational Service Center (ESC)."

Mary said she understood and the conversation ended.

Chapter VI

How I Regained Entrance into CCISD

It's important for me to tell you how I regained entrance into Corpus Christi ISD. I completed the Special Education Alternative Certification program within a year and continued working for West Oso ISD. Every year after I became certified I applied for special education positions that were available in Corpus Christi ISD and was never called. I had trained numerous student teachers during my stay at West Oso. Once they completed their student teaching they managed, somehow, to get hired in Corpus Christi ISD. I questioned this but had no recourse.

After the experience I had initially, I'm sure you're wondering why I even wanted to return to Corpus Christi ISD. Well, first of all I didn't hold everyone responsible for the treatment I received. I only held Mr. Ernesto Barrera responsible. Plus the positions I applied for now paid about $5000 more than I was earning annually in West Oso.

By June 1995, after five years of working for West Oso ISD I decided I wanted to start my own daycare business. After a great deal of discussion with my husband, I resigned from West Oso ISD and drew down six years of my retirement.

Years ago I thought about how America was such an elitist society. Not only did we have to live in fancy homes but we also had to house our cars. I could understand why people up north did this because of the harsh winter months of snow and ice but in Corpus we didn't get that kind of weather. So I felt I would put our garage space to use and park our cars on the driveway. Then I went about the business of converting the garage into a childcare facility. I filled out and submitted all the necessary paperwork, attended all the training in order to qualify as a childcare provider, got all necessary health and fire code inspections, advertised the business, and waited. I had no idea when I decided to do this; trouble was on the horizon.

Immediately after we started converting the garage into a daycare Ed ended up not being able to work for almost a year. He injured his toe; which caused gangrene and eventually amputation. Despite this unexpected development I still held out hope the business would take off. But that wasn't the case. Several months passed and I didn't get any responses to my advertisement. I did get a few calls but no one brought their children.

The only one working and bringing in a steady income, at this time, was my daughter, Tamika. She earned only enough to buy a little food and pay her car note. I had drained my bank account and we were three months behind on our mortgage. All the bills started piling up and we had received our first foreclosure notice. I was at my wits end and didn't know what we were going to do. I had gone to many of the community assistance programs in the city, such as Catholic Services and a few others. I was told the only way they could help me was if I had someone living in the house that was under eighteen. The only ones in the house were, Tamika, who was in her 20's, Ed and I.

Slipping into a deep depression, I remember one night around 11:00 p.m. turning my back to Ed, who was sleeping restlessly next to me. As I lay facing the wall and praying very softly so I wouldn't wake Ed, tears welled up in my eyes and trickled down my cheeks. I whispered helplessly, "God! Please help us." The last thing I remember saying as I finished my prayer was **"Lord you know!"**

About 10:30 a.m. the next morning, out of the blue, I received a phone call from Margaret Jones. After you hear what happened I truly believe you will think the way I did; that this was definitely a divine intervention.

Margaret had found my phone number on the back of a napkin which I had given to her at a bingo game, four years earlier; when I worked in West Oso ISD. At that time, I asked her to call me if she heard of any special education teaching positions available in Corpus Christi ISD.

This is what contributed to my re-entrance back into Corpus Christi ISD. Margaret's husband had a massive heart attack and died in bed right next to her four months before she called me. Needless to say it was traumatic. In an effort to try and help Margaret, somewhat, cope with her grief, her mother persuaded her to start clearing some things out of the closets that belonged to her husband. Margaret agreed and started taking boxes down. The very first box she pulled down, right on top, was the napkin I had written four years earlier, with my name, telephone number and address on it. She didn't even remember who I was. She actually thought I was someone her husband knew because I had a male name.

Margaret had been promoted from teacher to assistant principal on the Cunningham Middle School campus since I spoke to her four years earlier. Apparently, all four special education teachers had gotten angry with Janet Vega, the principal on the campus, at the end of the previous school year and decided to get even. Three days before school was to start, they all quit. This left the principal scrambling to fill those positions as quickly as possible. Many of the people that worked in the district knew how difficult it was to work with this particular principal and refused to transfer to the campus. The principal asked Margaret did she know of any special education teachers that were qualified and willing to work on campus. Margaret had taken the napkin with my name on it to her sister Edith and asked if she knew who I was. As they both studied the napkin at the same time they both repeated my name three times Frankie Monroe, Frankie Monroe, Frankie Monroe, and at the same time they said, "That special education teacher from the bingo." The next day she called me.

After I was called and offered a job 12 people called inquiring about my daycare center. I asked Ed what he thought. Should I go with starting the daycare business or I take the job? He said, "A bird in the hand is worth two in the bush. There is always the possibility that parents will decide not to bring their children but if you work for the school district you will be getting a guaranteed pay check." Given how hard we had suffered that year I did what Ed advised and went the next day to sign the teaching contract. Look at how God works things out. My mother use to sing this song, "He may not come when you want him, but He's always, right on time."

Chapter VII

Knowledge Is Power

I worked on the Cunningham Middle School campus with Margaret for about three years before she was offered a promotion as principal on another middle school campus. Soon after she took over as principal on the Martin Middle School campus the Special Education Department Chairperson on her campus was promoted to a higher paying position. This left Margaret needing someone to take over that position. She called and asked me if I would I be interested in taking over. It would be a change for me and an increase in salary. I told her I would be happy to take it.

Not only had Margaret been offered a higher position, Janet Vargas was allowed to transfer, at her request, back to an elementary principal position on another campus. She also asked if I would be willing to go with her but I declined. Margaret contacted the new principal at Cunningham, Mr. Jack Pena, and asked if he would be willing to allow me to move to her campus. He agreed and I took over in October of 1999.

In March of 2001 I was inspired to complete my Masters degree. There was a middle school convention being held in Chicago, Illinois. I couldn't believe it but I was actually invited to attend. Not many special education teachers were ever asked to go to trainings outside of the city. This was always reserved for the general education teachers. They went to conferences in California, Colorado and even Hawaii. I felt this was done because the general education teacher's were deemed more valuable academically because of the student population they served.

Well, while at the convention I had the privilege of listening to, Mr. Edward Olmos, the actor who played Selena's Father in the movie of the same name. He was one of the guest speakers. As he spoke to the educators in the audience he posed the question, "How many of you out there have your Bachelor's degree?" Almost all of the people in the room raised their hands. Then he asked, "How many of you out there have your Master's degree?" Quite a few raised their hands but I couldn't and that bothered me. When we returned home I checked into being re-admitted into Texas A & M University to complete my Masters degree. I had worked on this a few years earlier while still working at West Oso ISD but had to dropout due to the onset of diabetes. The diabetes had caused me to have temporary blindness for almost a year. I could see but when I looked at the printed word it was so blurry I couldn't read anything. Even glasses didn't help. My assistant had to read everything for me.

I talked to one of the counselors at the university and was surprised to discover I had enough credits to finish my degree in one summer. I took 5 classes over the summer and graduated on August 8, 2001 with my Masters in Educational Administration. During that same period I was working on my mid-management certification to move into the administrative side of education. All I had to do was complete my principal practicum and pass the mid-management ExCet exam then I was headed for the big time or so I thought. Then reality set in.

Chapter VIII

You Be My Judge and Jury

As issues arose over the next few years and I discussed them with different groups of people. I got responses such as:

"Are you sure that's what's going on? Not everybody is out to hurt you."
"The first thing Blacks want to do is *Yell Discrimination* if they don't get hired for certain positions."
"They're going to just say you're a disgruntled employee out to damage their reputation"
"If you complain it'll be career suicide. You will definitely be blackballed."
"You're too sensitive, give it time."

After mulling these comments over and over in my mind I thought to myself….

"I first attempted to advance in my career in September of 2001. I've applied for various administrative positions for almost 10 years and haven't been able to move pass classroom teacher. I think that's more than enough time to do right by me."

I feel the school district played every dirty trick in the book in an effort to keep my case from going to trial. I realize this is part of the process. Initially they refused mediation from EEOC but the judge ordered it in pre-trial. They signed a settlement agreement and then rushed to court to have it thrown out and never honored the agreement. They refused to provide all the documentation requested by my attorney. He had to go before the court repeatedly to plead with the judge to order them to submit the requested documents in order to adequately prepare for my case. Some things that were requested were never provided. Many of those things that were provided arrived a few days before my trial was scheduled to begin. When boxes of documents arrived, days before trial at my attorney's office, I asked him, "Why so many boxes, now?" He said, "It's a stalling tactic some law firms use. They want to appear to be in compliance with the courts but at the same time they want to overload the person requesting the information so they won't have enough time to go through everything before trial that may help them."

In their attempt to overload us with documents they actually provided us with the information I needed to prove what I had been saying all the time. "They meant it for my bad, but God meant it for my good."

I will try to present to you in a chronological, succinct manner all the evidence I have and provide you with my interpretation of events as they occurred so that you can get a clear picture of just what transpired leading up to and after charges of discrimination were filed in 2004. This will include information such as; e-mails, letters, personal documentation, my formal lawsuit, affidavits, documents and other correspondence I sent out and received.

I want to also point out that when Corpus Christi ISD first started developing the infrastructure to integrate the internet and communication system throughout the school district they had no confidential disclaimers. Immediately following my lawsuit, once they discovered I had saved and printed out e-mails to prove what I claimed, during the discovery period of my lawsuit, they implemented a disclaimer policy which wouldn't allow people to divulge what was discussed in the e-mails. I was told by my attorney that this disclaimer would not hold up in a court of law, at least during the time of my first charges. I don't know if laws have since been implemented to uphold that disclaimer policy.

If after you have reviewed everything I have and decide the courts were right in making their decision to throw my case out I will lick my wounds as I have done in the past and move on.

But…..

If you decide the courts were wrong in the way they handled my case I will feel vindicated and justified in sharing my story.

What I truly hope will happen is…

This will cause the public and private sector to monitor the employment policies they have in place. I hope this forces them to make sure they aren't guilty of practicing discrimination through their hiring policies and procedures or falsifying documents for the purpose of deceiving the public or federal and state government.

I especially hope to impact the discriminatory hiring practices within Corpus Christ ISD towards me or anyone else who has earned the right to at least get an interview but were repeatedly denied access to the selection process.

Now let my emotional healing process begin.

Chapter IX

The Proof is in the Pudding

I will present my proof in an (Exhibit) format. I don't feel at this point it would be beneficial to divulge the names of those that were allowed to advance in their careers at my expense. They had no part in the selection process but merely benefited from the discriminatory hiring practices that Corpus Christi ISD engaged in. I think they were innocent therefore I will change and or blackout any personal information such as names, addresses and telephone numbers etc. that will identify them. I do ask that you review my documentation in its entirety in order to give a fair assessment to all parties involved. After reviewing my evidence see if you reach the same conclusions I did.

What was done in the dark will be exposed to the light for all to see.

Exhibit 1

I began communicating earnestly with different Corpus Christi ISD administrators in December of 2001; because this was the year I completed my Masters in Educational Administration and secured my temporary mid-management certification. The first administrator I contacted by e-mail was the Director of Special Education, Mr. Robert Garcia.

One of the consultants, Lauren Bedford, had been promoted to a higher position leaving a consultant position open. Once her position was posted I applied. If there was one thing I knew I qualified for it was a Special Education Consultant position. After all I had been involved in special education for about 13 years, at that time. Not only had I taught in the classroom I also worked as the Special Education Department Chairperson, Content Mastery teacher and Collaborative teacher for three of those years. I was very familiar with federal and state laws and district policies concerning children with disabilities.

I didn't hear anything for some time concerning the consultant position and decided to contact the personnel office to see what the status was. I was told the position now required a permanent mid-management certification, which I didn't have. I only had a temporary mid-management certification. I don't believe this requirement was included in the original posting. After much discussion I was told I needed to contact Mr. Garcia's office to see what he said. It was possible he would consider my temporary certification and allow me to be interviewed for the position.

On Dec 17, 2001 I sent an e-mail to Mr. Robert Garcia, inquiring about the Special Education Consultant position. Since I had been told by the personnel office that I had to have a permanent mid-management certification to apply but other considerations might be made; I wanted to know if my temporary mid-management certificate could be accepted instead. After all I was no stranger to the workings of the school district and was well aware of the exceptions that had been made for others in the district. I soon learned what was done for others didn't apply to me.

From:	Frankie Monroe
To:	Robert Garcia
Date:	Mon, Dec 17, 2001 1:15 PM
Subject:	Special Education Consultant Position

Hello Mr. Garcia

I have tried several times to contact you by phone but have been unsucessful. I am very interested in the Special Education Consultant Position that   held. I have submitted my letter of interest. I was told that even though I have all the necessary paper work except I have a Temporary Administrative Certification on file that I would have to contact you to see if this could be used. I was told that It would be up to you to request my files.

I will be taking the Administrative test in February. I am currently working on my Superintendent Certification. I will be working with Dr. Chavez on my Superindency Practicum starting Jan. 2002

Any consideration would be greatly appreciated.

Exhibit 2

Eventually, I spoke to Mr. Garcia on the phone and he told me his office didn't handle the hiring it had to go through personnel. He also informed me district policy had changed and the position I sought now required a mid-management certification. I explained to him that I had just graduated with my masters in Educational Administration and was in the process of taking the ExCet exam for my permanent mid-management certification but I did have my temporary mid-management certification.

It was so exasperating to I know, first hand, about several people in the school district holding only their temporary mid-management certification and were being allowed to hold administrative position for at least five years until they could successfully pass the ExCet exam. These very same people were allowed to earn administrative salaries and benefits. I, on the other hand, was being denied an opportunity to compete for the consulting position because it was now being classified as an administrative position. I didn't say anything at the time, because I didn't want to hurt my chances of advancing in my career later.

I continued applying for positions and didn't get called for any interviews. Needing a change I requested to be transferred back into the classroom and was offered a transfer to the Ray High School Campus as a Resource Language Arts teacher.

I began communicating with Dr. Chavez in 2002 by e-mail concerning my inability to get an interview for any administrative position I applied for. I had worked so hard to reach this point in my career only to be rejected over and over. I felt given the superintendent knew me on a personal level and was familiar with my abilities he wouldn't mind allowing me to use him as a reference. I hoped this feather in my cap would get me noticed. I also complained about the hiring process and the conduct of the intake personnel in this e-mail.

To: Frankie Monroe
From: Jesus Chavez
Subject: Re: Reference
CC:
Date Sent: Monday, May 20, 2002 1:55 PM

Please feel free to use me as a reference.

Jesus H. Chavez

>>> Frankie Monroe 05/20/02 11:51AM >>>
Good Morning Dr. Chavez,

It was good to see you yesterday at the candle light ceremony. I'm sorry I couldn't stay and talk longer but I had another engagement that I had to attend.

You asked me what was I planning to do and it did not dawn on me until I was in the car what you had asked.

I was sent a letter from personnel informing me of some assistant principal positions that were going to be available for the next school year. I needed to send references. It would be a great honor if you would allow me to use you as a reference.

I wanted to let you know that in all the years that I have worked for CCISD I have never gotten a position through the front door. What I mean by that is any time that I have applied for a position I was never called or given an interview. I got hired by CCISD by word of mouth because people were familiar with my work ethic and dedication to my profession. The prinicipal of whatever school that was interested in me would call and request my application be pulled in personnel.

Something else that I think needs to be addressed is the response of the receptionist to the public. I think that they could work on improving their interpersonal skills when dealing with the public. First impressions are lasting impressions. When you go to the window and request things or ask for information many of these people are very abrupt and rude. This has happened to me on several occassions as well as some of my colleagues.

I did not mean to get on my soap box I only wanted to request to use you as a reference. But as you can see dealing with the personnel office is a sore spot for me.

Please let me know as soon as possible if I can use you as a reference because I have to turn this information in on May 21 or 22.

Have A Great Day !

<u>Exhibit 3</u>

As time went on I became more and more suspicious about, Mrs. Maria Villarreal, the person in charge of accepting applications and subsequent information. I felt she wasn't submitting my information to be included in the selection process. Because of my suspicions I began submitting my information in person and started requesting that I get a stamped and dated copy of the information I submitted. This provided proof of the date and time I applied. I don't think Mrs. Villarreal liked this but she did it anyway. I contacted the superintendent, Dr. Jesus Chavez, voiced my concerns once again and asked that he check into it.

From: Frankie Monroe
To: Jesus Chavez
Date: Fri, May 24, 2002 11:36 AM
Subject: Assistant Principal Information

Good Morning Dr. Chavez:

I saw you at Kikos this morning. I was with the Martin group.

I know this is personnel business and you probably do not do this ordinarily but I do not trust them. Could you please just make sure that my application, updated transcript, and resume has been included in with the rest of the applicants for Assistant principal positions.

I promise I will not bother you any more this year. I just want to have a fair chance to at least be interviewed.

Have a great day!

Exhibit 4

Over the course of several months and several additional administrative postings that I applied for I was not selected even once for an interview which prompted me to send another e-mail to Dr. Chavez on Sept 3, 2002 expressing my disappointment.

From: Frankie Monroe
To: Chavez, Jesus
Date: Tue, Sep 3, 2002 12:33 PM
Subject: Superintendent Certification

Hello Dr. Chavez,

I would have written sooner but my Groupwise has just been installed at Ray High School. I left Martin where I was the Special Education Dept Chairperson and went back into the classroom.

I wanted to let you know that I passed my Superintendent ExCet exam and now have a Superintendent Certification.

I was hoping to be contacted over the summer for an interview in one of the assistant principal positions but I was never contacted.

I can understand when I am sent out on an interview and then it is decided that I am not the best candidate for the position but I have never been sent out on any position through the personnel office.

I think it is pretty sad to hold not only a Mid-Management Certification but a Superintendent Certification and not even be considered for an interview in an assistant principal position.

I just wanted to let you know whats going on with me. I hope you have a great year.

Sincerely,

Frankie J. Monroe

Exhibit 5

October was Hispanic Heritage Month and I felt it would be a great surprise for my students, who were mostly Hispanic and at-risk, to meet the superintendent of the school district up close and personal. Many of them didn't even know there were famous Hispanics that impacted society in a positive way in America. This would give them an opportunity to meet someone that had beat the odds and made it. I hoped this would encourage them to work hard, take their education seriously and realize they too could be successful. I especially wanted them to know it didn't matter what race, color or creed they were anything was possible if they put fourth an effort. On Oct 1, 2002 I sent an e-mail to Dr. Chavez requesting he visit my class for Hispanic Heritage Month. I was contacted by his secretary, Imelda Lujan confirming the visit.

From:	Frankie Monroe
To:	Lujan, Imelda
Date:	Tue, Oct 1, 2002 11:21 AM
Subject:	Re: Supt's. Speaking Engagement

Good Morning Imelda,

How have you been doing?

The time that Dr. Chavez has available will be fine. That will indeed cover two classes. Thank Him for me ahead of time.

Have a Great Day!

>>> Imelda Lujan 10/01/02 10:23AM >>>
Good morning Frankie,

Dr. Chavez asked that I contact you to schedule a day when he can speak to your class. In checking the Supt's. calendar, the only day he is clear is on Wednesday, October 9 (between 2 p.m. - 2:45 p.m.) Is it possible for him to speak during this time? Perhaps this will cover two classes. Let me know. Thanks, Imelda

Exhibit 6

After visiting my class on Oct 9, 2002 I e-mailed a thank you note to Dr. Chavez
thanking him for speaking to my class. I once again included in this e-mail that I was hurt
at first because I hadn't been given an interview for several positions that I applied for,
but I now realized that God puts you were he wants you to be for that point in time.

From: Frankie Monroe
To: Chavez, Jesus
Date: Wed, Oct 9, 2002 4:38 PM
Subject: Student Response to Visit

Dr. Chavez I want to take the time to thank you so much for taking the time out of your busy schedule to visit my class room. You made a great impression on my students.

I once had a counselor years ago to tell me that I could not save all of my students. My response to him was," But do I have to loose them all?" The students that you saw were the "Sweat Hogs" of the school. Most of the time they are in trouble. Many are caught up in gang activity. Most have 2nd to 8th grade reading level. They have low self esteem and tend to put themselves down. Everyday I seek to show them a better way to do things. I try to model respect so that they know what it looks like.

When I first came to Ray I did not know what subject I would be teaching. I found out that it was Language Arts. Given that I have taught all subjects it did not matter to me. I did notice that my class was larger than most of the other special population classes. I asked when were these numbers going to stop growing. I was told, " Don't worry! Around the second week of school about half of the students normally stop coming. This had been the pattern. Well I am proud to say that this pattern has been broken. As you could see most of my students were here. I have high expectations and they give me what I want. It's the self fulfilling prohecy.

I was hurt at first because I had not been given an interview for several positions that I had tried for but I now realize that God puts you were He wants you to be for that point in time.

Again thank you so much for sharing your time with my class. It was greatly appreciated.

Exhibit 7

After a lot of begging and pleading with Mr. Briones and Dr. Chavez, I was contacted for the very first time from the personnel office that I would be sent out in January of 2003 for this assistant principal position at King High School. I had been made aware ahead of time by a friend of mine that it was only for interviewing purposes. The part-time assistant principal on that campus was going to be hired and this was merely a formality to interview others. I know, I know I shouldn't have gone on the interview but I didn't want it said that I was finally offered an interview and rejected it.

I didn't hear anything concerning any other administrative positions for the rest of the school year. I contacted Mr. Michael Briones, the school districts Director of Certified Personnel in the summer of 2003. I applied for several administrative positions I knew would be available for the following school year. I had noticed something over the course of time. Whenever I applied for a position I was told I had to update my references and application each time. During that time it had only been required to update references every two years. How do I know this? They told me. We were only required to submit a letter of interest by mail as long as we worked for the school district. The internet infrastructure hadn't been completed throughout the school district, at the time, so everything was submitted in person or through the postal system rather than on-line.

I also complained about the intake personnel once again. I truly believed I was being stopped from moving forward in the interviewing process because of some action or inaction on her part.

From: Frankie Monroe
To: Briones, Michael
Subject: Conversation on phone

Mr. Briones,

I talked to you this summer about several positions that were available for principals, assistant principals and special education consultant. We discussed my qualifications and how I have a mid-management certification and superintendent certification and how up until January 2003 I had only been sent out through the personnel office on one interview. That one position was for an assistant principal position at King. The position was given to someone that already worked at King. I can understand that you should hire from within especially if that person is doing a good job.

Every time that I have applied for a position there has always been something that is not right with my paperwork according to the intake person. I started with CCISD in 1986 as a substitute teacher then special education teacher up until 1989, left the district and worked for West Oso for 5 years and returned to CCISD in 1996.

It was through the request of a principal that knew my work, contacted me and asked if I would return to work at her campus in 1996. Once I agreed to work at her campus she had my application pulled, My application had been on file for 4 years. Every year I would update my information and ask if there were any special education positions available and each year I was being told no but people that I trained in the West Oso District, and had less experience than I were being hired by CCISD.

This time I was told that I had to turn in all new information because the information that had been used just six months earlier to send me on my very first interview ever to King, through the personnel office, needed to be re-done. I was told that if the recommendation information was not sent before the due date I would not be given an opportunity to be sent on an interview. I informed the intake person that it would be hard to contact professors, principals, consultants at that time because they were on summer vacation. I asked why couldn't the recommendations that were on file now , that were used for the interview in January be used now and I would get the others as soon as summer was over I have yet to get a response for that.

You stated that you would check into my concerns and get back with me. I have not heard from you since that time.

Today is August 11, 2003 and I'm almost certain that at this time those positions have been filled. This is the third school year that I have applied for different administrative positions that I knew I qualified for and to this date I have been sent on one through the personnel office. If I am never given an opportunity to be sent on interviews how am I ever going to get the experience that I need.

I am looking forward to your response.

CC: Chavez, Jesus

Exhibit 8

It had now been three years since I began applying for different administrative positions within Corpus Christi ISD and still I remained in the classroom. In 2003 I was in a staff training session and overheard a conversation between a young lady in her mid-to- late 20s, who had been in one of my mid-management classes and another older lady. Apparently the young ladies father had been or was employed with Corpus Christi ISD, or was possibly an administrator of some sort in another district. The older lady stated, "I bet your father is so proud of you for being hired as an assistant principal. You are following in his footsteps" The young lady said, "Yes he is. They are going to have a big party for me. Do you know I didn't even know they were considering hiring me until the principal on my campus told me? I was told to hurry up and go fill out my application so they could make it official. I've got to get there before the week is out so I can make sure everything is updated."

I applied for this same position but was never offered an interview, but this young lady hadn't even submitted an application but was made aware she had gotten an administrative position.

Here is a copy of both our applications. Mr. Briones stated in his sworn affidavit, which you will have an opportunity to review later, that everyone hired had more work experience and was more qualified than I was. This was the reason I had been given, repeatedly over the years when I questioned why I wasn't hired in any administrative positions. My work experience has not moved passed classroom teacher since I first sought to advance in my career. I have also obtained my doctorate in Educational Leadership since submitting this resume to Corpus Christi ISD. I want you to compare our applications and resumes. Would you say this young lady, who was hired as an assistant principal, had more work experience or was better qualified than I was? Corpus Christi ISD did.

Young Ladies Application and Professional Vita

APPLICATION FOR A PROFESSIONAL POSITION
WITH THE
CORPUS CHRISTI INDEPENDENT SCHOOL DISTRICT

RECEIVED
JUN 3 2002
DEPARTMENT FOR HUMAN RESOURCES

Interview Date

Last Name _____ First _____ Middle _____

Current Street Address _____ City/State/Zip Code _____

Work Telephone Number _____ Home Telephone Number _____

Same   ( ) Same

Permanent Home Address   City/State/Zip Code _____ Permanent Home Telephone Number _____

1995 - 2002
Date of Prior Service

Former CCISD Employee? ☑ Yes ☐ No

Social Security Number _____

INDICATE THE POSITION FOR WHICH THIS APPLICATION IS MADE

Title: Elementary _____ Résumé attached ☑ Yes ☐ No

CREDENTIALS

CERTIFICATE/ENDORSEMENT	STATE	DATE	CERTIFICATE/ENDORSEMENT	STATE	DATE
Principal (Elementary)	Tx	05/01			
Professional Development and Appraisal System	Tx	08/99			
Elementary Self-Contained	Tx	01/99			
Elementary Mathematics	Tx	01/99			

Name   *FOR OFFICE USE ONLY*

The Corpus Christi Independent School District does not discriminate in employment
on the basis of race, color, religion, national origin, sex,
age, marital or veteran status, or the presence of a handicap or disability.
AN EQUAL OPPORTUNITY EMPLOYER

PLAINTIFF'S EXHIBIT

94

1. DRIVER LICENSE   State: ___TX___   Type: _Class C_   Number: _____

2. If employed, can you provide proof of citizenship or determination of intent?   ☑ Yes   ☐ No

3. Please indicate the extracurricular activities you are able to direct:

Drill Team, Dance Team, Jump Rope, Student Council, and

Safety Patrol

4. Have you ever been terminated, nonrenewed, discharged, suspended, or asked to resign from a school district or job?   ☐ Yes   ☑ No   If yes, provide name of employer, date, and reason for each occurrence.

5. PROFESSIONAL AND/OR TEACHING EXPERIENCE   Give a record of each employment you have held, omitting student teaching and substitute teaching experience. Start with your current employer and work back.

NAME AND ADDRESS OF SCHOOL/EMPLOYER	PERIOD OF SERVICE (Give exact dates)	GRADES OR SUBJECT/JOB	REASON FOR LEAVING POSITION
Central Park Elem. 3602 McArdle	Aug 1999 - Nov	1st, 2nd, 4th Teacher	

6. May we contact your current employer?   ☑ Yes   ☐ No

7. Conviction of a crime is not an automatic bar to employment. Corpus Christi ISD will consider the nature of the offense, the date of the offense, and the relationship between the offense and the position for which you are applying. A Criminal History Check Authorization and Information form is enclosed with this application. Complete all of the Criminal History Information requested, sign and date the Authorization and Acknowledgment, and include the form when you submit this application to the Department for Human Resources.

FAILURE TO DISCLOSE INFORMATION REGARDING CONVICTION OR DEFERRED PROCEEDINGS FOR ANY OFFENSE MAY BE GROUNDS FOR DISQUALIFICATION OF YOUR APPLICATION FOR CONSIDERATION FOR EMPLOYMENT, OR, IF EMPLOYED, FOR TERMINATION OF YOUR EMPLOYMENT.

8. EDUCATIONAL AND PROFESSIONAL TRAINING

☐ *Please have your College/University Teacher Placement Office send your file to the Director for Certified Personnel.*

INSTITUTION NAME AND ADDRESS	MAJOR	MINOR	DIPLOMA, DEGREE, CERTIFICATE	DATE CONFERRED
Del Mar College - East	A.S.		Interdisciplinary - Reading	August 1997
Texas A+M c.c. 6300 Ocean Dr	B.A.		Interdisciplinary - Math	December 1998
Texas A+M c.c. 6300 Ocean Dr.	M.A.		Educational Administration	December 1999

9. PROFESSIONAL DATA   Please identify your published works, professional memberships and offices held, seminars or workshops conducted, outstanding professional accomplishments.

Member of Association of Texas Professional Educators, Kappa Delta Pi International Honor Society in Educations, and Texas State Reading Association.
Conducted Microsoft Word, Excel, and Power Point inservice, TEKS Survey of Proposed Objective inservice, and Book and Brain inservice

10. REFERENCES   Five (5) references must be supplied and may include superintendents, principals, teachers, university instructors, and former employers. References must have first-hand knowledge of your character, scholarship, teaching ability, and working ability. *Do not list relatives.*

NAME/POSITION	ORGANIZATION	TELEPHONE	ADDRESS/ZIP CODE
Principal	Central Park Elem	878-1714	
Professor	Texas A+M c.c.	825-2662	6300 Ocean Dr, 78412
Professor	Texas A+M c.c.	825-2662	6300 Ocean Dr. 78412
Professor	Texas A+M c.c.	825-2662	6300 Ocean Dr, 78412
Teacher	Travis Elementary	854-6523	6202 Hartack Cr. 78417

11. COMMENTS   Provide any additional information that might qualify you for the position you seek.

Please see attached résumé.

Whom may we contact if we are unable to reach you during the application process?

_____

Name   Address   Telephone Number

If you are employed with the District, whom may we notify in case of emergency?

_____

Name   Relationship   Telephone Number

Are you related, in any way, to any member currently serving on the CCISD School Board?   ☐ Yes   ☑ No

If yes, please explain: _____

AFFIRMATION AND AGREEMENT

I hereby affirm that the information given by me in this application is true and complete to the best of my knowledge and belief. I UNDERSTAND THAT ANY MISREPRESENTATION, FALSIFICATION, OR OMISSION WILL BE SUFFICIENT CAUSE FOR CANCELLATION OR THIS APPLICATION OR DISCHARGE IF I HAVE BEEN EMPLOYED. Furthermore, it is understood that this application becomes the property of the Corpus Christi Independent School District which reserves the right to accept or reject it.

I hereby apply for employment with the Corpus Christi Independent School District, and give the District permission to make inquiries of references and former employers concerning my general character and past performance, including permission to obtain criminal history information from any law enforcement agency (local, state or national) pursuant to Chapter 22, Subchapter C of the Texas Education Code (or as subsequently revised). I hereby give you permission to obtain reference requests furnished by Corpus Christi Independent School District. I further agree that references, placement folder information, and information which becomes a part of this record may be revealed to all persons who participate in the selection of employees. In signing this application, I understand that all references and personal information become part of the application and are considered confidential and will not be revealed to me.

_____
Applicant's Signature

06-03-02
Date

> When a position is advertised (Job Line – 361-886-9000), it is the responsibility of the applicant to inform Human Resources of his/her interest. [Certified – 844-0247; Auxiliary – 886-9076]. This application will remain on file for two years. Please update in writing as needed. You will receive no further reply unless favorable consideration is given to your application.

Return this application and the Criminal History Check Authorization and Information form to:

Department for Human Resources
Office of Certified Personnel
PO Box 110 • 801 Leopard Street
Corpus Christi, Texas 78403-0110

PROFESSIONAL VITA

EDUCATION:

M.A. in Educational Administration,
Texas A&M University Corpus Christi, 1999.

B.S. in Interdisciplinary Studies-Mathematics,
Texas A&M University Corpus Christi, 1998.

A.S in Interdisciplinary Studies-Reading,
Del Mar College, 1997.

LICENSES:

Principal (Elementary) ,Texas, Lic.#
Professional Development and Appraisal System
Texas Teacher Certificate, Texas, Lic#
Elementary self-contained (Grades 01-08) Life
Elementary Mathematics (Grades 01-08) Life

PROFESSIONAL EXPERIENCE:

1999-Present

Central Park Elementary, Corpus Christi, Texas.
1st, 2nd, and 4th grade self-contained teacher.

My duties include all teaching duties, attend inservices, attend
workshops and convocations, conduct inservices entitled
Vocabulary Verbose and *Book and Brain*, work collaboratively
with other campus personnel to develop, implement, evaluate, and
revise a comprehensive campus action plan, work collaboratively
with other campus personnel to plan campus curriculum based on
student learning data, appropriate assessments, emerging issues,
technology, and research, keeping a close communication with
parents, sponsoring drill team, and conducting a health fitness
class.

2000-2001   Central Park Elementary, Corpus Christi, Texas
                   Administrative Intern

                   My duties includes attend assistant principal and principal
                   meetings, assist with TAAS testing, prepare mock test, conduct a
                   Microsoft Word, Excel, and PowerPoint inservice, conduct an
                   inservice on the TEKS Survey of Proposed Objective and TEKS
                   Student Expectations, conduct an A.E.I.S PowerPoint presentation
                   for the parents and community, assist with next year enrollment
                   and staffing projection, participate in the interview process, learn
                   how to enter student data into pentimation, became familiar with
                   OOPS book, principal packet, and budget procedures, conduct
                   morning announcements, conduct All Year Awards Ceremony,
                   establish partnerships with local businesses, organize Fall and
                   Spring festivals, monitor campus daily, become familiar with field
                   trip procedures, assist with text book inventory and distribution of
                   books, and conduct school fixed asset inventory.

1998   Sanders Elementary, Corpus Christi, Texas
                   3rd grade student teacher

1995-1997   Corpus Christi Independent School District
                   Substitute Teacher (Pre-K through 12th in all subjects)

PROFESSIONAL
MEMBERSHIPS: Association of Texas Professional Educators
                   Kappa Delta Pi International Honor Society in Education
                   Texas State Reading Association

PERSONAL
ATTRIBUTES: The following are attributes that I possess that I feel are beneficial
                   to the administrative position.

                   1. Effective Communication and Public Relations Skills.

                   2. Organizing the staff and community to work together in
                       continuing to support an excellent school system.

                   3. Inspiring a well-qualified staff to reach new achievement goals.

                   4. Meeting the high expectations of a goal oriented staff and
                       community.

My Application and Professional Vita

APPLICATION FOR A PROFESSIONAL POSITION
WITH THE
CORPUS CHRISTI INDEPENDENT SCHOOL DISTRICT

RECEIVE

··· - 7 ···

DEPARTMENT FOR HUMAN RESOURC

Interview Date

Monroe   Frankie   Jeon
Last Name   First   Middle

Current Street Address   City/State/Zip Code

(   )
Work Telephone Number   Home Telephone Number

Same as above   (   )
Permanent Home Address City/State/Zip Code   Permanent Home Telephone Number

Former CCISD Employee? ☐ Yes ☑ No   Date of Prior Service

Social Security Number _____

INDICATE THE POSITION FOR WHICH THIS APPLICATION IS MADE

Title: Principal, Assistant Principal, Special Ed School Service Consultant   Résumé attached ☐ Yes ☐

CREDENTIALS

CERTIFICATE/ENDORSEMENT	STATE	DATE	CERTIFICATE/ENDORSEMENT	STATE	DAT
Superintendent	TX	7/15/02			
Principal	TX	2/16/02			
Visual Handicapped	TX	6/14/			
Generic Sp. Ed	TX	7/16/91			

Name

FOR OFFICE USE ONLY

The Corpus Christi Independent School District does not discriminate in employment
on the basis of race, color, religion, national origin, sex,
age, marital or veteran status, or the presence of a handicap or disability.
AN EQUAL OPPORTUNITY EMPLOYER

1. **DRIVER LICENSE** State: _TX_   Type: _Class C_   Number: _____

2. If employed, can you provide proof of citizenship or determination of intent? ☒ Yes ☐ No

3. Please indicate the extracurricular activities you are able to direct:

   _____

   _____

4. Have you ever been terminated, nonrenewed, discharged, suspended, or asked to resign from a school district or job? ☐ Yes ☒ No   If yes, provide name of employer, date, and reason for each occurrence.

   _____

5. **PROFESSIONAL AND/OR TEACHING EXPERIENCE** Give a record of each employment you have held, omitting student teaching and substitute teaching experience. Start with your current employer and work back.

NAME AND ADDRESS OF SCHOOL/EMPLOYER	PERIOD OF SERVICE (Give exact dates)	GRADES OR SUBJECT/JOB	REASON FOR LEAVING POSITION
Ray Highschool	8/02 - Present	9th 10th 11th 12th Lau/H. st Sp Ed	Want to work in administrative position
Martin Middleschool	10/99 - 6/02	Content Mastery Dept. Chair	Wanted to work with older student population
Cunningham Middle school	8/96 - 10/99	Resource math Lau Self cont 7-8	Advance to higher paying position as Sp Ed Dept. chair
West OSO Carl Allen	8/94 - 6/95	Severe 5/6 Profound	started Daycare Business
West OSO Skinner	8/93 - 6/94	Severe Profound 3/4	Wanted to work with Severe profound visually in
West OSO Jr. High	8/90 - 6/93	Resource MR Self cont 7/8	Wanted to work on getting Vision Certification
Moody Highschool	8/87 - 6/90	Orthopedically Handicapped 8-9-10-11-12	Wanted to work on Sp Ed Certification
Moody Hi			

6. May we contact your current employer? ☒ Yes ☐ No

7. Conviction of a crime is not an automatic bar to employment. Corpus Christi ISD will consider the nature of the offense, the date of the offense, and the relationship between the offense and the position for which you are applying. A Criminal History Check Authorization and Information form is enclosed with this application. Complete all of the Criminal History Information requested, sign and date the Authorization and Acknowledgment, and include the form when you submit this application to the Department for Human Resources.

FAILURE TO DISCLOSE INFORMATION REGARDING CONVICTION OR DEFERRED PROCEEDINGS FOR ANY OFFENSE MAY BE GROUNDS FOR DISQUALIFICATION OF YOUR APPLICATION FOR CONSIDERATION FOR EMPLOYMENT, OR, IF EMPLOYED, FOR TERMINATION OF YOUR EMPLOYMENT.

8. EDUCATIONAL AND PROFESSIONAL TRAINING

☐ Please have your College/University Teacher Placement Office send your file to the Director for Certified Personnel.

INSTITUTION NAME AND ADDRESS	MAJOR	MINOR	DIPLOMA, DEGREE, CERTIFICATE	DATE CONFERRED
Texas A&M University	Ed Adm		Master	8/8/00
Indiana University	Busines Adm		B.A.	1/82

9. PROFESSIONAL DATA Please identify your published works, professional memberships and offices held, seminars or workshops conducted, outstanding professional accomplishments.

Life member of Delta Sigma Pi Business Fraternity

Member of Phi Delta Kappa Educational Fraternity

Member of Gulf Coast Counselors

Poetry Published in Newspaper Record Contract.

10. REFERENCES Five (5) references must be supplied and may include superintendents, principals, teachers, university instructors, and former employers. References must have first-hand knowledge of your character, scholarship, teaching ability, and working ability. Do not list relatives.

NAME/POSITION	ORGANIZATION	TELEPHONE	ADDRESS/ZIP CODE
Dr. Jesus Chavez Superintendent	CCISD	886-9200	801 Leopard St. C.C. TX 78408
Principal	CCISD		
Professor	TAMUCC	825-8700	6300 Ocean Dr. CC TX 78412
Counselor	CCISD		
Speech Therapist	CCISD		

11. COMMENTS Provide any additional information that might qualify you for the position you seek.

Whom may we contact if we are unable to reach you during the application process?

Addie L. Standifer

| Name | Address | Telephone Number |

If you are employed with the District, whom may we notify in case of emergency?

Eddie L. Moore   _Husband_

| Name | Relationship | Telephone Number |

Are you related, in any way, to any member currently serving on the CCISD School Board?   ☐ Yes   ☑ No

If yes, please explain: _____

AFFIRMATION AND AGREEMENT

I hereby affirm that the information given by me in this application is true and complete to the best of my knowledge and belief. I UNDERSTAND THAT ANY MISREPRESENTATION, FALSIFICATION, OR OMISSION WILL BE SUFFICIENT CAUSE FOR CANCELLATION OF THIS APPLICATION OR DISCHARGE IF I HAVE BEEN EMPLOYED. Furthermore, it is understood that this application becomes the property of the Corpus Christi Independent School District which reserves the right to accept or reject it.

I hereby apply for employment with the Corpus Christi Independent School District, and give the District permission to make inquiries of references and former employers concerning my general character and past performance, including permission to obtain criminal history information from any law enforcement agency (local, state or national) pursuant to Chapter 22, Subchapter C of the Texas Education Code (or as subsequently revised). I hereby give you permission to obtain reference requests furnished by Corpus Christi Independent School District. I further agree the references, placement folder information, and information which becomes a part of this record may be revealed all persons who participate in the selection of employees. In signing this application, I understand that all reference and personal information become part of the application and are considered confidential and will not be revealed to me.

Addie J. Moore
Applicant's Signature

_7-7-03_
Date

When a position is advertised (Job Line – 361-886-9000), it is
the responsibility of the applicant to inform Human Resources
of his/her interest. (Certified–844-0247; Auxiliary–886-9076).
This application will remain on file for two years. Please update
in writing as needed. You will receive no further reply unless
favorable consideration is given to your application.

Return this application and the Criminal History Check Authorization and Information form to:

Department for Human Resources
Office of Certified Personnel
PO Box 110 • 801 Leopard Street
Corpus Christi, Texas 78403-0110

PROFESSIONAL VITA

Frankie J. Monroe

Career Objective:

To use my analytical skills, ability to communicate ideas, commitment to perform quality work and relevant experience to improve efficiency and enhance my educational knowledge base that impacts student performance.

Education:

2000-02   Texas A & M University   Corpus Christi, TX

- Master of Science in Educational Administration
- Superintendent Certification
- Mid-Management Principal Certification
- Professional Development and Appraisal System Certificate TTAS/PPSA
- Instructional Leadership Training Certificate

1989-91   Education Service Center Region II   Corpus Christ, TX

- Alternative Certification Program
- Teacher Generic Special Education Certificate; Pre-K -12 (Life)
- Vision Impaired Teacher Certificate; Pre-K -12 (Life)

1980-82   Indiana University Northwest   Gary, Indiana

- Bachelor of Science in Management Administration

2004-08   Texas A & M University   Corpus Christi, TX

Enrolled in Educational Leadership Doctoral Program

Relevant Experience:

Corpus Christi Independent School District

2002 - Present: Ray High School   Corpus Christi, TX

Resource Language/Arts teacher 9-12

- Provided Language Arts instruction to Special Education students according to skill level and individual Education Plan

1999 - 2002:   Martin Middle School   Corpus Christi TX

Content Mastery Center Teacher for grades 6-8

- Provided assistance to special education students from general education classroom settings.
- Implemented various teaching methods of instruction to meet needs of individual students
- Assisted teachers with the application of modifications for students who received special services.

1999-2002:   Martin Middle School Corpus Christi, TX

Special Education Department Chairperson

Extensive administrative duties and instructional leadership role on Martin Middle School campus. Set up and conducted all ARD meetings involving 150-200 students annually.
- Reported data regarding special education programs, including reports on enrollment, contact hours, and student/staff schedules as requested by the office of Special Education.
- Disseminated special education information at the campus level.
- Conducted regularly scheduled special education team meetings.
- Worked with the special education staff to assist teachers in improving teaching methods, strategies, and techniques, on request.
- Conducted modification workshops for general education teachers on Martin Middle School Campus.
- Assisted principal in piloting a modified version of the Collaborative Teaching Model of instruction. Martin campus received Recognized rating from TEA after the implementation of this program. The pilot program worked so well that Martins campus implemented the complete collaborative model for the 2001-02 school year. The Inclusion model is now being tested and implemented throughout the district to address (NCLB) No Child Left Behind.
- Cooperative teacher for Texas A & M. Student teachers assigned to me. Was responsible for preparing them to become future teachers of education
- Supervising teacher in Educational Assistant Cooperative program. This program placed high school seniors in the classroom. The students helped assist special needs student in Content Mastery Center.
- Mentor Teacher for several teachers in Educational Service Center Region II (Alternative Special Education Certification program).
- Member of Campus Improvement Plan Committee
- Member of PDM Committee

- Member LPAC Committee
- Member of More Accountable Group Literacy Focus Team

2001-02   Martin Middle School/Ray High School   Corpus Christi, TX

Administrative Assistant Superintendent Internship
- Met with superintendent weekly to discuss community issues.
- Attended board/town hall meetings
- Involved with Vitteta Facilities study. Met with architect and business manager to discuss progress made in addressing infrastructural needs of district. Wrote report of my finds in the study and presented to Superintendent.

2000-01   Martin Middle School   Corpus Christi, TX

Administrative Intern Assistant Principal Internship
- Assisted Counselors in TAAS/SDAA/TAKS preparation
- Participated as a member of the leadership committee contributing to decision making process
- Monitored halls, restrooms, outside corridors during passing periods and did cafeteria duty
- Worked with assistant principal and other teachers on the Behavior Improvement Team

1996-1999:   Cunningham Middle School   Corpus Christi, TX

Resource Math, Language/Art/Personal Management Skills/Texas History Teacher
- Provided instructions to special education students according to skill level and individual education Plan.
- Developed I.E.P goals and Objectives
- Monitored student progress and reported to administrators, counselors, and parents.

West Oso Independent School District

1993-1995:   Skinner and Carl Allen Elementary   Corpus Christi, TX

Severe Profound unit Teacher
- Monitored and kept daily documentation of student's medical problems.
- Implemented the Communication and Life Skills program.
- Taught parents different techniques they could use in helping their children at home. Assisted superintendent and administrators in bringing campuses into compliance by informing them of what was needed according to IDEA such as wheelchair ramps, proper bathroom facilities, easier access to the office, etc.
- Designed a portable building for Carl Allen Campus that was conducive to special needs students learning environment. Before leaving the campus

- Made an instructional video on how to work with the severe profound students that were taught.

1990-1993:   West Oso Middle School grades 7th-8th   Corpus Christi,TX

Resource Reading, Math, Social Studies, Science and Language/Arts and Vision Specialist
- Provided instructions to special education students according to skill level and individual education plan
- Held mini-workshops to assist teachers in modifying student work.
- Taught Braille and other visually impaired strategies to Pre K-12th grade and homebound students.
- Was responsible for all-visual assessments, reports, and attending all ARD meetings.

Corpus Christi Independent School District

1987-1990:   Moody High School   Corpus Christi, TX

Self Contained Language Arts/Math/Independent Life Skills, Word Processing/Keyboarding Teacher

- Provided instructions to special education students according to skill level and individual education plan.
- Responsible for monitoring and documenting any medical problems that students had and informing their caregivers on a daily basis.
- Classroom design was observed and modeled by other high school campuses in the district.

Skills:

Level II Proficiency in Word Processing, IBM, Dell, Apple II computer, Power Point and Excel, Intel Innovations

Additional Experiences:
- E-Chalk Training
- Working together: Tools for Collaborative Teaching
- TELPAS training
- Standards Based Instruction Training
- Literacy Focus
- Walk-through
- SIP
- Behavior Improvement
- University Course Work in
  - Grant Writing
  - Globalization in Education
  - Administrative Technology Class Curriculum Planning

- Campus Finance
- District Finance
- Multicultural Diversity

Additional Information:

- Life member of Delta Sigma Pi Business Fraternity
- Member of Cunningham/ Martin Campus PDM/PTA
- Member of More Accountable Group Literacy Focus funded by Edna McCardle Clark Foundation
- Member of Phi Delta Kappa Educational Fraternity
- Member of Gulf Coast Counseling

:

References are available upon request

Texas Educator Certificate

This certifies that

Frankie Jean Monroe

has fulfilled requirements of state law and regulations of the
State Board for Educator Certification
and is hereby authorized to perform duties as designated below:

STANDARD

Description	Effective Date	Expiration Date	Status
Principal			
Principal	02/16/2002	03/31/2007	Valid
Grades (EC-12)			
Superintendent			
Superintendent	07/13/2002	03/31/2007	Valid
Grades (EC-12)			

TEMPORARY

Description	Effective Date	Expiration Date	Status
Principal	05/11/2001	05/11/2006	Valid
Grades (EC-12)			

PROVISIONAL

Description	Effective Date	Expiration Date	Status
Generic Special Education	07/18/1991	Life	Valid
Grades (PK-12)			
Visually Handicapped	06/19/1993	Life	Valid
Grades (PK-12)			

Official Record of Certification
Wednesday, April 14, 2004
Another Search   Home

https://secure.sbec.state.tx.us/virtcert/virtcertdisplay.asp?spid=618258&mode=C   4/14/04

Exhibit 9

By the end of the 2003-2004 school year I decided to apply once again for several assistant principal positions that were available for the 2004-2005 school year. In April of 2004 I remembered Dr. Chavez had agreed to allow me to use him as a reference and sent him an e-mail inquiring if this offer still held true. I'm pretty sure by this time he was well aware of my feelings about only being selected to go on one interview.

I was privy to a lot of information during the discovery phase of my lawsuit. There was a statement submitted to EEOC from Corpus Christi ISD stating I didn't want to be considered for any elementary assistant principal positions during this timeframe, but as you will see in the following e-mails I stated I was applying for all-level assistant principal positions throughout the school district.

I also sent a follow up e-mail to Mr. Briones and Dr. Chavez in May of 2004. I wanted them to make sure this time my information for the positions I applied for had been received.

On May 11, 2004, I received a confirmation e-mail from Mrs. Maria Villarreal, the intake person for applications. She informed me that all necessary documents had been received. I constantly questioned if my information was being submitted in a timely manner because she was the one responsible for sending information to the selection committee on who had completed all the necessary paperwork. As I stated before for some reason there always seemed to be something wrong with my application. After applying so many times you would think I knew how to complete the necessary forms correctly but according to her I didn't.

To give you additional proof of what I had to contend with over the years on September 1, 2005, I sent an e-mail to Maria Villarreal personally concerning an application I submitted. Despite the concerns I voiced to administration this problem persisted.

From: Frankie Monroe
To: Chavez, Jesus
Date: 4/20/2004 12:14:44 PM
Subject: Re: Reference Letter

Good Afternoon Dr. Chavez,

I am going to be applying for assistant principal positions throughout CCISD for the 2004-05 school year.

You once told me that I could feel free to use you as a reference. Does that offer still stand.

Please let me know so that I can send you a reference form.

Any assistance would be greatly appreciated.

Sincerely

Frankie J. Monroe

Mail Message

N

Close   Previous Next   Delete From   Delete From All   Forward Reply to Sender Reply All   Move Delete   Read Later Properties
                         This Mailbox   Mailboxes

Print View

From: Frankie Monroe
To: Michael Briones
CC: Jesus Chavez
Date: Tuesday - May 11, 2004 12:00 PM
Subject: Assistant Principal Positions

Mr. Briones

I spoke with you last year concerning assistant principal positions that were offered and I was not even given an opportunity to participate in.

I recently submitted my letter of interest along with copies of my Superintendent, and Mid-management certification. I also informed you that I have been admitted to the doctoral program at Texas
A& M in educational administration.

I have asked that my references be sent to the personnel office from people that are familiar with my work ethic. I would like to make sure all necessary documentation is in so that I may be given an opportunity to participate in the selections process this year.

Please let me know as soon as possible if all the paper work is in that you required.

It would be most appreciated.

Have a Great Day!!!

From: Frankie Monroe
To: Villarreal, Maria
Date: Tue, May 11, 2004 4:19 PM
Subject: RE: Assistant Principal - All levels

Thak you for your prompt response

>>> Maria Villarreal 05/11/04 12:57PM >>>
I just wanted to inform you that your file for the above mention position is complete.

****
Maria G. Villarreal
Human Resource Specialist
Phone: 361-886-9075
Fax :   361-886-9057
E-Mail: mgvillarreal@ccisd.us

From: Maria Villarreal
To: Frankie Monroe
Date: 9/1/2005 1:01:36 PM
Subject: Re: Application

Hello Ms. Monroe

The professional application has to be completed again, your previous application is over 2 years old. The highlighted topics format has been changed it is to be addressed in the format given...Please call me if you have any questions.....Just 1 set of documents..........I will place this information in both files (Assistant Principal Middle School and Assistant Principal High School)....

****

Maria G. Villarreal
Human Resource Specialist
Phone: 361-886-9075
Fax :   361-886-9057
E-Mail: mgvillarreal@ccisd.us

>>> Frankie Monroe 09/01/05 12:42 PM >>>
Maria,

I submitted my letter of interest last week for an assistant principal position in the high school and middle school. Yesterday I received two packets in the mail for those positions.

I am questioning why I have to fill this information out again. In July of this year 2005, I was sent on an interview for an assistant principal position. The information that was used to select me then has not changed. I don't understand why I now have to repeat everything that has already been submitted.

Please utilize the information that I have already provided to allow me the opportunity to be included in this selection process for an assistant principal position. As I stated before I updated this information in 2004.

Your cooperation in this matter will be greatly appreciated.

Have a Great!

Exhibit 10

By July of 2004 I was fed up with the status quo and requested Mr. Briones provided me with a list of principals who would need an assistant principal on their campus for the 2004-2005 school year. I informed him I would take it upon myself to speak to them personally on my own behalf. From past experience I knew this was the way the school district handled things. I personally had never gone through the front door of the personnel office to get hired as a teacher. There was always an administrator on a campus that knew of my work ethics who would request my record be pulled in the personnel office so they could hire me. I felt getting hired as an administrator in this manner was no different. Even though Mr. Briones tried to state otherwise, in his response to me; we both knew better. We went back and forth communicating by e-mail and I eventually ended it by saying if nothing was done about this situation the only recourse I felt I had was to file discrimination charges with EEOC.

On July 19, 2004 after this exchange of e-mail messages between Mr. Briones and myself I sent a 14 page letter to EEOC in Washington D.C and hand delivered that same letter to the Corpus Christi ISD superintendent, personnel director and school board. Much of what was mentioned in the letter you already read earlier in my story. I went into greater details in the letter including all of my accomplishments over the span of my career as well as the treatment I received. I want to ask you, after you read the following e-mails; would you consider it a grievance that the school district should have been aware of? Ms. Imelda Martinez, the Corpus Christi ISD in-house attorney, stated in January 2005, when I met her for the very first time that Dr. Chavez was not aware of any problems that I was having.

You see years earlier I was told by a Corpus Christi ISD personnel director, "The school district has you where we wanted you to be", which in this case was to remain in the classroom, "and if you aren't happy where you are you can leave." But not this time. Not without a fight. Dr. Jesus Chavez received a carbon copy each time Mr. Briones and I contacted each other so he was well aware of the conflict that was brewing despite his denial.

Mail Message

N

Close Previous Next   Delete From   Delete From All   Forward Reply to Sender Reply All Move Delete Read Later Properties
                         This Mailbox   Mailboxes

Print View

From: Frankie Monroe
To: Michael Briones
CC: Jesus Chavez
Date: Friday - July 9, 2004 9:24 PM
Subject: Unfair Hiring Practices

Mr. Briones,

I have waited patiently for three years to be given an opportunity to be considered for an assistant principal position. All I ever asked was to be given an opportunity to be considered by being sent on interviews. If after I interviewed and was not accepted I could understand that, but never being given an opportunity to interview at all is not acceptable.

As the years have passed I have seen people hired from outside the district that were teachers in the classroom just like myself. They have been elevated not only to assistant principal but principal positions. Many of these people have had only 3 years of classroom experience and are in their 20s or 30s. I have 17 years of educational experience. I have a Superintendent and Principal certification along with numerous other certificates. I am also in the doctoral program at TAMUCC. I should not have to go outside the district to get a position when there are positions available in the district I work in.

There have been several assistant principal positions open for the 2004-05 school year. I sent a letter of interest at the end of the 2003-04 school year and filled out all the necessary paper work. I have only been sent on one interview and that was because I asked the principal of my school to consider me for a position.

I have applied for several positions with the district over 10 years and in that time I have only been sent on two interviews those happened in the 2003-04 school year. At this point I can only assume that I am not being given an opportunity because I am not in a click, or am not related to someone or simply that I am black.

I want to let you know ahead of time that I plan to go to the media in the very near future with my grievances.

From: Michael Briones
To: Monroe, Frankie
Date: Thu, Jul 15, 2004 4:11 PM
Subject: Re: Unfair Hiring Practices

There are procedures in place to paper screen assistant principal applicants and I am sorry you don't agree with the procedures. The Human Resource department ensures that this procedure is followed by the principals to ensure the best qualified applicants are considered to be interviewed for their campus. The applicants do not decide what interviews they are to be screened for. Once again I am sorry you don't agree with the procedure.

Thank you
Michael Briones
Phone (361) 886-9064
Fax (361) 886-9057
NEW EMAIL ADDRESS mrbriones@ccisd.us

>>> Frankie Monroe 7/15/2004 9:10:35 AM >>>
Mr. Briones the criteria would not help me. A list of the principals that are in need of assistant principals would help me. This way I could make personal contact with them and ask if I could be considered for an interview. I realize that principals can only see so many applicants. But I do think that all the applicants that have the proper qualifications should be sent on more than one interview. If the Department of Human Resources has no part in sending people out on interviews for jobs why are you needed?

>>> Michael Briones 07/13/04 1:33 PM >>>
I will be glad to send you the paper screening process that is used by principals to determine which applicants will be interviewed. I apologize for you not being interviewed for an assistant principal position however that decision is made by the principals not the Department of Human Resources. The process to determine who is paper screened includes a listing of criteria and evidence from the applicant that they have evidence of such.

Please advise of the address you would like for me to send the criteria.

Thank you
Michael Briones
Phone (361) 886-9064
Fax (361) 886-9057
NEW EMAIL ADDRESS mrbriones@ccisd.us

>>> Frankie Monroe 7/9/2004 9:24:05 PM >>>
Mr. Briones,

I have waited patiently for three years to be given an opportunity to be considered for an assistant principal position. All I ever asked was to be given an opportunity to be considered by being sent on interviews. If after I interviewed and was not accepted I could understand that, but never being given an opportunity to interview at all is not acceptable.

As the years have passed I have seen people hired from outside the district that were teachers in the classroom just like myself. They have been elevated not only to assistant principal but principal positions. Many of these people have had only 3 years of classroom experience and are in their 20s or 30s. I have 17 years of educational experience. I have a Superintendent and Principal certification along with numerous other certificates. I am also in the doctoral program at TAMUCC. I should not have to go outside the district to get a position when there are positions available in the district I work in.

There have been several assistant principal positions open for the 2004-05 school year. I sent a letter of interest at the end of the 2003-04 school year and filled out all the necessary paper work. I have only

118

Exhibit 11

In September of 2004 things really heated up. I had already been passed up for several assistant principal positions in 2003 and discovered the young lady whose application you reviewed earlier had been hired as an assistant principal. This time, Isabel, the young Spanish teacher who was in her mid to late 20's and had only 2 ½ to 3 ½ years in education as a teacher, had not only been granted several interviews, she too was hired in an assistant principal position. She shared with me personally that she had not applied for the position until late July or early August of 2004. How many years had I begged and pleaded with administration to provide me opportunities to interview for this very same position? This was the last straw. I was tired and now I was going to take action. I contacted EEOC and requested the forms I needed to fill out so I could file discrimination charges against Corpus Christi ISD.

I filled out the application and sent it out on October 7, 2004

EEOC Form 5 (5/01)

CHARGE OF DISCRIMINATION	Charge Presented To:	Agency(ies) Charge No(s):
This form is affected by the Privacy Act of 1974. See enclosed Privacy Act Statement and other information before completing this form.	☐ FEPA ☒ EEOC	360-2005-00072

Civil Rights Div Texas Workforce Cm	and EEOC

State or local Agency, if any

Name *(Indicate Mr., Ms., Mrs.)*	Home Phone No. (Incl Area Code)	Date of Birth
Ms. Frankie J. Monroe	(361,	
Street Address City, State and ZIP Code		

Named is the Employer, Labor Organization, Employment Agency, Apprenticeship Committee, or State or Local Government Agency That I Believe Discriminated Against Me or Others. *(If more than two, list under PARTICULARS below.)*

Name	No. Employees, Members	Phone No. (Include Area Code)
CORPUS CHRISTI I.S.D.	15 - 100	(512) 888-7911
Street Address City, State and ZIP Code		
801 Leopard, Corpus Christi, TX 78401		
Name	No. Employees, Members	Phone No. (Include Area Code)
Street Address City, State and ZIP Code		

DISCRIMINATION BASED ON *(Check appropriate box(es).)*	DATE(S) DISCRIMINATION TOOK PLACE
☒ RACE ☐ COLOR ☐ SEX ☐ RELIGION ☐ NATIONAL ORIGIN ☒ RETALIATION ☒ AGE ☐ DISABILITY ☐ OTHER *(Specify below.)*	Earliest: 01-01-2000 Latest: 09-07-2004 ☐ CONTINUING ACTION

THE PARTICULARS ARE *(If additional paper is needed, attach extra sheet(s)):*

During the period from the year 2000 up to and including at least September 7, 2004, I have applied and I have not been hired for the following positions for which I am qualified, within the Corpus Christi I.S.D, i.e., Executive Director for Human Resources, Special Education School Services Consultant, Principal or Assistant Principal. I have complained about the unfair hiring practices within this school district.

I believe that I have been discriminated against because of my race, Black and for complaining about unfair hiring practices (retaliation), in violation of Title VII of the Civil Rights Act of 1964, as amended, and because of my age (DOB 03/29/52), in violation of the Age Discrimination in Employment Act of 1967, as amended.

I want this charge filed with both the EEOC and the State or local Agency, if any. I will advise the agencies if I change my address or phone number and I will cooperate fully with them in the processing of my charge in accordance with their procedures.	NOTARY – When necessary for State and Local Agency Requirements
I declare under penalty of perjury that the above is true and correct.	I swear or affirm that I have read the above charge and that it is true to the best of my knowledge, information and belief. SIGNATURE OF COMPLAINANT
X 10-7-04 X *Frankie J. Monroe* Date Charging Party Signature	SUBSCRIBED AND SWORN TO BEFORE ME THIS DATE *(month, day, year)*

Exhibit 12

I mentioned this e-mail earlier but this is the actual e-mail Isabel sent out on October 29, 2004 contacting the campus to inform them she had been hired as an assistant principal.

Frankie Monroe - Thank You   Page 1

From:
To: Ray HS Staff
Date: 10/29/2004 4:18:33 PM
Subject: Thank You

I just want to say **thank you** to all of those who have made my stay at Ray High School such a wonderful experience. I am truly blessed to have worked with such an awesome faculty and staff. Please wish me well as I embark on my journey as Assistant Principal at Cunningham Middle School.
Once again, Thanks.
Sincerely

Spanish Teacher

Exhibit 13

On November 8, 2004 I received another letter from EEOC headquarters informing me that Corpus Christi ISD had refused mediation. Because of the school districts actions I was told an immediate investigation would be launched into my allegations within five business days from the date posted on the letter

U.S. EQUAL EMPLOYMENT OPPORTUNITY COMMISSION
San Antonio District Office

5410 Fredericksburg Road, Suite 200
San Antonio, TX 78229-3555
(210) 281-7600
TTY (210) 281-7610
FAX (210) 281-2512

Charge Number: **360-2005-00072**

Dear Charging Party,

As a follow up to our previous mediation notice to you, the San Antonio District Office of the US Equal Employment Opportunity Commission (EEOC) is unable to schedule mediation for this charge because the other party did not agree to mediate. Although our focus from this point on will be to investigate the allegations raised in the charge, settlement will remain a resolution option throughout our processing the charge.

Within a week from the postmark date of this notice the charge will be assigned to an investigator in our office. At that time you may obtain the investigator's name and telephone number by calling (210) 281-7600 and providing the above charge number to the receptionist. If you need to speak with someone from our office before then, you may contact Rodney Klein, Charge Receipt Supervisor, at (210) 281-7621. Thank you.

Pedro Esquivel
Director, San Antonio District

Exhibit 14

I applied for yet another assistant principal position in September 2004, but was once again rejected. It appeared to me Mr. Briones was in such a rush to inform me that I had been rejected he didn't even notice the date hadn't been finished at the top of the letter before he signed it.

**Corpus Christi
Independent
School
District**   801 Leopard • PO Box 110 Corpus Christi, Texas 78404-0110

10/28/200

Frankie Monroe

Dear Ms. Monroe

Thank you for expressing interest in employment with the Corpus Christi Independent School District (CCISD). Your application for Assistant Principal - All Levels was considered along with others. Another applicant has been selected for the position.

Should another vacancy be advertised for which you wish to be considered, you are welcome to reactivate your file by submitting a new letter of interest to the Office of Certified Personnel.

Best wishes in your future endeavors.

Sincerely,

Michael Briones, Director
for Certified Personnel

Exhibit 15

On November 1, after receiving my rejection notice I contacted Dr. Chavez and requested that he have Mr. Briones send me another rejection letter with a complete date because I saved my rejections letters. When I discussed this in the meeting I had with Dr. Chavez and our attorney's present he merely chuckled.

From: Frankie Monroe
To: Jesus Chavez
Date: 11/1/2004 8:49:29 AM
Subject: Date on Form letter

Good Morning Dr. Chavez,

I want to ask you to have Mr. Briones send me another form letter letting me know that all the Assistant principal positions have been filled and if another position should become available for me to please feel free to apply. The letter implied that the best qualified people for the job had been hired.

The letter that I received on Friday appeared to have been done in such a hurry to let me know that they forgot to put the year on the letter. I have been saving my rejection letters and I need to have the dates in order.

I want to also ask you why you think I should not file a discrimination lawsuit.

Have a Great Day!

Exhibit 16

Not only did I let the district know of my plans to file discrimination charges I also let the principal of the campus I had been assigned to know my intentions and requested a grievance form. On Nov 2, 2004 I sent an e-mail to Dr. Dorsey, my campus principal, requesting grievance forms which I was told she had. I was given the wrong grievance forms by mistake. The forms given were for parents to file a complaint against the school district. So I went on the internet, found a generic copy of one, printed it and filled it out. On Nov 5, 2004 I hand delivered the letter and grievance not only to the superintendent's office but provided copies for the school board president, who I thought was Harry Williams but was later told by the secretary that it was Larry Elizondo and was instructed by the secretary to cross Mr. Williams' name out and write in Mr. Elizondo's name. I also provided Michael Briones, the certified personnel director, a copy and had it stamped and dated by the superintendent's secretary.

From: Dawn Dorsey
To: Frankie Monroe
Date: Tue, Nov 2, 2004 8:44 AM
Subject: Re: Grievance Forms

We have the formal complaint forms. Please ask Tina. May I ask what this is about?

>>> Frankie Monroe 11/2/2004 8:29:33 AM >>>
Good Morning Dr. Dorsey,

I want to let you know that I have filed charges of discrimination with EEOC and I am filing a grievance against the district. In the handbook it states that I must file this grievance within 30 days of the of the alleged violation of law or Board Policy.

It also stated that the campus should have the form that I need to file this grievance on. Can this form be made available to me through your office or do I need to request this from the main office.

I have already informed the Superintendent of my intentions. I want to also let you know that this has nothing directly do with you.

November 3, 2004

Corpus Christi ISD
School Board President
801 Leopard Street
Corpus Christi, TX 78403-0110
                         -Larry Elizondo
Attention: Mr. ~~Harry Williams~~   Re: Grievance

Enclosed is a completed grievance form that is required by the district to be tuned in within 30 days identifying an alleged violation of law or board policy.

Sincerely,

Frankie J. Monroe

Frankie J. Monroe

RECEIVED

NOV 0 5 2004

OFFICE OF SUPERINTENDENT
CORPUS CHRISTI ISD

130

RECEIVED
NOV 2004
DEPARTMENT FOR

November 3, 2004

Corpus Christi ISD
Department of Human Resource
801 Leopard Street
Corpus Christi, TX 78403-0110

Attention: Mr. Michael Briones   Re: Grievance

Enclosed is a completed grievance form that is required by the district to be tuned in within 30 days identifying an alleged violation of law or board policy.

Sincerely,

Frankie J. Monroe

Frankie J. Monroe

RECEIVED

NOV 0 5 2004

OFFICE OF SUPERINTENDENT
CORPUS CHRISTI ISD

DGBA-E- PERSONNEL MANAGEMENT RELATIONS: EMPLOYEE COMPLAINT

1. NAME: **FRANKIE J. MONROE**

2. POSITION/DEPT: **TEACHER/SPECIAL EDUCATION DEPARTMENT**

3. PLEASE STATE DATE OF THE EVENT, OR SERIES OF EVENTS, CAUSING THE COMPLAINT:

The last event occurred on 10-28-04. I received a letter from the Corpus Christi ISD Personnel Department signed by Mr. Michael Briones, informing me that all assistant principal positions had been filled and should another opening become available I was welcome to apply. The letter was typed so hastily that part of the date was left off. This letter implied that the people hired had much more experience and was better qualified to hold this position. I have a Superintendent Certification, Mid-Management Certification, Vision Certification, and Special Education Certification; and currently enrolled in the Educational Leadership Doctoral program at TAMUCC, along with 20 years of teaching experience.

4. PLEASE STATE YOUR COMPLAINT, INCLUDING RELEVANT AND SPECIFIC SUPPORTING FACTS, INCLUDING HOW YOU BELIEVE THE ACTION (S) YOU ARE COMPLAINING ABOUT WAS/IS HARMFUL TO YOU.

I have applied for different administrative positions since 2000. I have all the rejection notices to prove that. In that time I have contacted Dr. Jesus Chavez and Mr. Michael Briones about my concerns of not being given an opportunity to be sent out on interviews. I could understand if after being interviewed it was felt that perhaps I was not the best candidate for the job but not being sent out was unfair. I received an e-mail from a young Hispanic woman stating that she had been hired as an assistant principal. She had approximately two and half to three years of teaching experience. I know a Hispanic male who did not hold a mid-management certification for five years but was afforded the opportunity to work as a full time assistant principal. I was denied that same opportunity. I know people that were hired outside the district as assistant principals. I have given almost 13 years of dedication to CCISD and not been afforded the opportunity to advance in am being discriminated against based on my race (black), my age, and retaliation.

5. PLEASE STATE THE SPECIFIC REMEDY YOU ARE SEEKING, INCLUDING A REQUEST FOR WHAT YOU WHAT TO HAPPEN:

I contacted Mr. Briones in July of 2004 and asked if I would be given an opportunity to be interviewed because I knew that several AP positions would be available. After our conversation I informed Mr. Briones, Dr. Chavez, and the School Board through a letter that I did not want to sue the district because it would not help the children that I serve. I have all of this communication. In light of what has happened on 10-28-04 I want restitution for all of the money I have paid upgrading my skills for advancement per your requirement and an administrative position. I have also filed a complaint with EEOC.

Fennfie J. Monroe   _11-3-04_
Signature   Date

Any employee who wishes to file a complaint must fill out this form completely and submit it in accordance with Level One and Two Instructions in <u>DGBA</u>. All complaints will be processed in accordance with <u>DGBA</u>.

Adopted: 6/29/81

Amended: 9/27/91, 11/18/92, 8/1/97, 5/28/03

Reviewed: 3/25/94

http://www.tsbvi.edu/policy/dgba-e.htm   11/3/04

133

Exhibit 17

I now believe the school district was beginning to get the message. I had filed charges of discrimination with EEOC and submitted what I felt was a sufficient grievance notice to them. On Nov 11, 2004 I received a letter from the school district. I didn't receive this letter on the date it implied in the body of the letter. I received this letter at a later date from Imelda Martinez telling me my grievance was timely filed. No where does she mention in this letter that I had filed the grievance on the wrong form. She did say my grievance didn't meet the prerequisite because no informal conference was held. How could an informal conference be held; when I was continuously ignored despite the fact I sent a 14 page letter to Dr. Jesus Chavez, the Superintendent, School Board President, Larry Elizondo, and the Human Resource Director, Michael Briones in July of 2004?

OFFICE OF LEGAL SERVICES
361-886-9067   FAX: 361-844-0283

**Corpus Christi
Independent
School
District**   801 Leopard ∘ PO Box 110   Corpus Christi, Texas 78403-0110

November 11, 2004

Ms. Frankie J. Monroe

RE: Grievance dated 11-03-04

Dear Ms. Monroe:

This will acknowledge receipt of your grievance filed with the Superintendent on or about November 3, 2004. Please note that although your grievance was timely filed, according to Board Policy DGBA (Local), your grievance does not meet the prerequisites of a formal grievance in that no informal conference was held nor was a specific individual named as the Respondent. Board Policy DGBA (Local) requires that "prior to the time the employee files his Grievance, the parties shall attempt to resolve the problem informally." Additionally, with regard to the naming of a Respondent, Board Policy DGBA (Local) defines Respondent as "the employee of the District who has been charged by the Grievant with a Grievance." According to your grievance, you have failed to specifically name a CCISD employee as the Respondent.

If you desire to re-file this grievance, please comply with the District's Board Policy regarding specific timelines (i.e., "filed within 30 days of the time when the employee first knew, or should have known, of the decision or action causing the grievance or dissatisfaction, exclusive of the time spent in seeking informal resolution"). For your reference, I have enclosed a copy of Board Policy DGBA (Local) and (Exhibit).

Please feel free to call my office if you have any questions.

Sincerely,

Imelda Martinez, Attorney at Law
Office of Legal Services

mas

Enclosure

cc: Dr. Jesús H. Chávez, Superintendent of Schools

Exhibit 18

I filed another grievance on December 15, 2004 after returning from a family emergency meeting out of town on Nov- 29-04 (mother hospitalized). When I returned to Corpus I discovered Mr. Jason Carver, a (Black teacher) from West OSO ISD had been hired as an assistant principal. He was assigned to work on the Driscoll Middle School campus. I knew Mr. Carver personally. I ran into him a month or so before he was hired and he shared with me that he had been trying to get hired in Corpus Christi ISD for several years but been unsuccessful. He told me he was totally surprised when he was contacted and offered an interview. He went on to say during the hiring blitz the district put on he looked for me, because he just knew I was going to be there. He described the same scene Isabel had described when she discussed her interviewing experience.

I felt this move by Corpus Christi ISD served two purposes. First it was an attempt to cover up the fact they hadn't hired many Blacks in administrative positions for several years and EEOC was coming. Second it was to show me they were going to hire some Blacks, but I wasn't going to be one of them because I had the audacity to challenge their hiring practices and bring the federal government into it (Retaliation).

CORPUS CHRISTI ISD
178904

PERSONNEL-MANAGEMENT RELATIONS: DGBA(E-2)
EMPLOYEE GRIEVANCES AND COMPLAINTS   (LOCAL)

GRIEVANCE REPORT FORM

RECEIVED

DEC 1 5 2004

OFFICE OF SUPERINTENDEN
CORPUS CHRISTI ISD

Date of incident or event giving rise to grievance: __11-29-04 and 10/28/04__

Informal resolution meeting or conference date(s):_____

Filing Date ____12/15/04____ (Must be filed in writing within 30 days of the time the employee knew, or should have known, of the decision or action causing the grievance or dissatisfaction, exclusive of the time spent in seeking informal resolution.)

Name of Grievant _____Frankie J. Monroe_____

Name of Respondent ___Corpus Christi Independent School District, Dr. Jesus Chavez, and Michael Briones___

Principal/Immediate Supervisor ___Dr. Dawn Dorsey_____

School/Department ___Ray High School_____ Work Phone ___(361) 806-5300__

Home Address ███████████████████████ Home Phone ██████████████

Statement of Facts upon which the Grievance is predicated, including the names of any persons involved, the date of the event or incident giving rise to the Grievance, and a description of the event or incident: (See DGBA (Local), Prerequisites, page 3. Attach additional page(s), if necessary, and supporting documentation, if any.)

I have applied for different administrative positions with CCISD since 2000. In that time I have contacted Dr. Jesus Chavez and Mr. Michael Briones about my concerned for not being given an opportunity to be sent on interviews. I could understand if after being interviewed it was felt that perhaps I was not the best candidate for the job but not being sent out at all was unfair. I feel that I have not been afforded an opportunity to compete.

I base my charges of discrimination (race, age, and retaliation) on the following incidents that have occurred. I discovered on 11-29-04, after returning out of town on a family emergency, that Mr. █████ ██████ had been hired at Driscoll Middle School as an assistant principal (black). He worked at West Oso as a teacher. About a month before being hired with the district █████████ had shared with me the fact that he had tried several times to get interviewed with CCISD but had been rejected. After I filed charges of discrimination with EEOC he was hired. (Retaliation)

On 10/28/ 04 an e-mail was sent out to Ray staff from Miss ██████████████ stating that she had been hired as an assistant principal at Cunningham Middle School. Miss ███████ had shared with me that she had applied in late August for an assistant principal position. I applied in early April and received one interview, which I requested from Dr. Dorsey. By September Miss █████ had received not one but three interviews. She was not hired on the first set of interviews but by the second round of interviews she was. Miss ██████ has approximately 2 1/2 years of teaching experience and is in her mid-to-late twenties. I have almost 20 years of teaching experience in education. (Age discrimination)

ADOPTED: 04/28/89   AMENDED: 06/09/97   1 of 4
NEWLOC

SEE E- MAIL ATTACHMENTS TO MR. MICHAEL BRIONES AND CC TO DR. JESUS
CHAVEZ IN JULY 2004 AND A BRIEF HISTORY OF NOT BEING AFFORDED

Witnesses of whom the Grievant is aware who may have any information related to the Grievance:

     Dr. Dawn Dorsey

Law alleged to have been violated or the dissatisfaction raised by the Grievant, and the alleged harm or damage caused by such violation of dissatisfaction:

     Discrimination and Civil Rights violation: Race (Black), Age and Retaliation.

Steps taken to resolve Grievance informally:

Discussed this matter with Mr. Michael Briones and Dr. Jesus Chavez several times via e-mail and phone. A copy of e-mail conversations attached.

Remedy sought:

     Restitution for emotional and mental anguish.

Frudie J. Monroe   12-15-04
Grievant's Signature   Date

Accepted/Rejected by Superintendent:
   (Circle one)

_____
Superintendent's Signature   Date

ADOPTED: 04/28/89   AMENDED: 06/09/97   2 of 4
NEWLOC

Exhibit 19

Immediately after school ended I left and dropped my grievance off at the main office, on December 15, 2004. Then I arrived home to the news that my mother in Gary, Indiana and aunt in Grand Rapid, Michigan both passed away within hours of each other. I wanted to try to finish out the semester which ended the very next day, on December 16, 2004, but was too distraught to finish the day out and sent an e-mail to my principal, Dr. Dorsey informing her of my intention to leave school at 12:40 p.m. She understood and called a sub for me.

From: Frankie Monroe
To: Dorsey, Dawn
Date: Thu, Dec 16, 2004 7:47 AM
Subject: Deaths in the family

Good Morning Dr. Dorsey,

I want to inform you that my mother passed away yesterday as well as my husbands aunt. I will be leaving for Indiana the first thing in the morning.
I will try to get through today with testing but I will leave at 12:40. How should I handle testing for tomorrow. Should I call a sub in for half a day or do I call one in for the whole day?

Thank you for all your understanding.

Exhibit 20

The school district realized I wasn't going to stop filing grievances and eventually, Mrs. Imelda Martinez, the districts in-house attorney, contacted me by e-mail requesting a meeting. The problem was she didn't make an effort to contact me until December 16, 2004 the last day before winter break and the day I left early to prepare to leave for my mother's funeral. I didn't check my e-mails until I returned from my mother's funeral on December 31, 2004 and contacted her to set up the meeting.

From: Frankie Monroe
To: IMMartinez1@ccisd.us
Date: Fri, Dec 31, 2004 9:44 PM
Subject: Re: Dear Ms. Monroe,

Mrs. Martinez,

My mother and husband's aunt passed away on December 15, 2004 in Gary Indiana. I just returned today December 31, 2004. I would like to meet with you after we return from the winter break. I will contact you as soon as it is convenient.

>>> Imelda Martinez 12/16/04 4:23 PM >>>
Dear Ms. Monroe,
My name is Imelda Martinez and I'm the new attorney and Title IX Officer for the district. Previously, I was an attorney for the Texas Education Agency for eight years.

I've read the grievance you submitted and I'd like to meet with you to discuss the source of your grievance. I have one appointment from 11:00 to 12:00 tomorrow but I'm free before and after that meeting. If it's more convenient for you, we can meet after the holidays. Let me know.

Imelda Martinez

Imelda Martinez
Legal Services
IMMartinez1@CCISD.us
(361) 886-9067

Exhibit 21

After contacting Mrs. Martinez on Dec. 31, 2004 informing her that my mother and aunt had passed away and setting the meeting up for Jan 6, 2005 she sent this letter date January 3, 2005 stating that my grievance from November 29, 2004 was no longer valid. The problem was I didn't submit a grievance for that date. I stated in the grievance I filed on Dec 15, I heard about someone getting hired around that time. I believe board policy stated I had to submit my grievance within 30 days after learning of a problem. Only 15 days had passed so I was in compliance.

**Corpus Christi
Independent
School
District**

OFFICE OF LEGAL SERVICES
361-886-9067   FAX: 361-844-0283

801 Leopard • PO Box 110   Corpus Christi, Texas 78403-0110

January 3, 2005

<u>Via CM:RRR – 7002-2030-0005-8293-2364</u>
<u>and Regular Mail</u>
Ms. Frankie J. Monroe
▮▮▮▮▮▮▮▮
Corpus Christi, Texas 78415

RE: Grievance dated 12-15-04

Dear Ms. Monroe:

This will acknowledge receipt of your Grievance Report Form filed with the Superintendent on December 15, 2004. Please note that, pursuant to the correspondence sent to you on or about November 11, 2004, your November 29, 2004 grievance is no longer valid as it was not timely re-filed within the 30-day time limit as reflected in Board Policy DGBA (Local).

Additionally, with regard to your December 15, 2004 grievance, although it was timely filed a nd o n the p roper grievance r eport f orm, you a gain failed t o m eet the f ollowing prerequisites according to Board Policy DGBA (Local):

- Your grievance does not meet the prerequisites of a formal grievance in that no informal conference was held nor was a specific individual named as the Respondent. Board Policy DGBA (Local) requires that "prior to the time the employee files his Grievance, the parties shall attempt to resolve the problem informally."

- With regard to the naming of a Respondent, Board Policy DGBA (Local) defines Respondent as "the employee of the District who has been charged by the Grievant w ith a G rievance." According t o your g rievance, you h ave f ailed t o specifically name a (one individual rather than two separate individuals and CCISD) CCISD employee as the Respondent.

If you desire to re-file this grievance, please comply with the District's Board Policy regarding specific timelines (i.e., "filed within 30 days of the time when the employee first knew, or should have known, of the decision or action causing the grievance or dissatisfaction, exclusive of the time spent in seeking informal resolution"). Please note that if properly re-filed and after all prerequisites have been met within the 30-day time limit, only the December 15, 2005 grievance will be heard. For your reference, I have enclosed another copy of Board Policy DGBA (Local) and (Exhibit).

144

Please feel free to call my office if you have any questions.

Sincerely,

Imelda Martinez, Attorney at Law
Office of Legal Services

mas

Enclosure

cc: Dr. Jesús H. Chávez, Superintendent of Schools

Exhibit 22

After being sent the letter on January 3, 2005; I became even more suspicious and didn't trust meeting without some form of documentation. I hadn't secured an attorney but my brother, Pen, suggested I send a summary of the meeting by e-mail for documentation purposes after the meeting.

I met with Mrs. Martinez on January 6, 2005 after school. No one was in attendance during this meeting but the two of us. It had taken 3 months from the time I began filing grievances until the district finally acknowledged there might be a problem and set up a meeting. Was this done according to board policy? After reviewing the board policy form that was sent to me it stated that a grievance would be addressed within 5 business days.

On January 11, 2005 after the meeting I sent a summary of our visit to Mrs. Martinez via e-mail. In the e-mail I requested that Mrs. Martinez provide feed back if any part of the events stated in the letter weren't correct. She responded and didn't dispute any parts of the letter. In fact she thanked me for the summary of the meeting. There was no mention whatsoever that anything in the letter was not factual. Dr. Chavez was also sent a carbon copy.

From: Imelda Martinez
To: Frankie Monroe
Date: Tue, Jan 11, 2005 11:22 AM
Subject: Re: Follow up letter to Meeting with CCISD Lawyer

Thanks, I did receive the attachment with your first email.

Imelda Martinez
Legal Services
IMMartinez1@CCISD.us
(361) 886-9067

>>> Frankie Monroe 1/11/2005 6:58:30 AM >>>
Ms. Martinez I am not sure the attachment was sent so here is another cop.y

To: Ms. Imelda Martinez
From: Frankie J. Monroe
Date: 1-10-05

Ms. Martinez this letter is a follow up to our meeting that was held on 1-6-05 at approximately 4:25 in your office at CCISD main office located at 801 Leopard Street. CCTX.

I was greeted by Ms. Martinez and escorted to her office. We discussed the loss of my relatives, our families, our ages and then proceeded to discuss my grievance. She stated that Dr. Chavez had asked her to review my files and investigate why I had not been provided an opportunity to interview for the many positions that had been available. She explained that sometimes others feel that the boss does not need to know what's going on and takes it upon themselves to deal with issues. She informed me that she had questioned Mr. Michael Briones and asked him about my complaint. I told her that I had asked Mr. Briones if the personnel department had nothing to do with the selection process what purpose did that department serve in an e-mail conversation we had over the summer.

Ms. Martinez explained that Mr. Briones was merely the person that took the applications in and had nothing to do with the selection process. I explained to her about my history with the district and never coming through the front door. She asked me what did I mean. I explained that I had only gotten hired to sub after being rejected at the beginning of the school year in 1986 because CCISD was short on subs when I went in a few months later to request my college transcript back. I was offered positions after that because my reputation proceeded me. People knew what I was capable of and was always wanting me to work for them. I discussed how I had been forced to leave the district because I wanted to pursue an alternative special education certification through the Educational Service Center, which would have only taken me one year rather than continue at the university where it would take me three years. After being forced to leave I discovered that CCISD hired about eight people from the same program that I had been admitted in. I had to take a $3000.00 cut in pay to go to another district.

She went on to say that she had reviewed my files and had not found one blemish on my record. She commented on how rare that was when someone had nearly 20 years of educational experience. She had reviewed all of my evaluations and they were exceptional. She gave me some hints about preparing my application so that it would stand out when I was in a pool of applicants. She had always attached her evaluations and this seemed to have given her the edge she needed. She had almost always been given interviews using this tactic.

I requested a copy of my entire file and offered to pay if that was necessary. She told me that there was no way she would charge me for my file. She had me write a note on the bottom of a yollow note pad requesting my files and sign and date it

I discussed the many people that I knew personally that had been promoted and had much less experience than myself. I also discussed the fact that I had opted to go for assistant principal positions because many people did not want a black person over them plus I wanted to get a little experience under my belt. Ms. Martinez stated that she understood exactly what I was talking about being a minority herself.

Ms. Martinez stated that she personally could not understand why I had not been provided an opportunity to be interviewed but expressed that perhaps it was because of the job that I did, working with special needs children, they did not want to let me go. After all they were getting the work of four to five people done from me. I was cheap labor. I responded by telling her that I did not feel it was fair to penalize me for a job well done. I had not gone to school all of these years to remain in the same position. She commented that she was going to do everything she could to get me promoted. She stated that I was a very patient person. She questioned me about what I had done after graduation in 1982 until I moved to Corpus Christi, TX in 1984. I told her that I had substitute taught in Gary, Indiana. She also asked about all of my degrees, and certifications. Our meeting ended at approximately 5:15. Ms. Martinez walked with me out of the building because it was dusk outside and there was a transient problem in the area. As we walked to my car I informed her that I had contact EEOC and filed charges against the district. I had done this out of frustration and I was tired of begging to be given an opportunity to compete. I warned Dr. Chavez and Mr. Briones of this through an e-mail and letter that I sent. I liked Dr. Chavez but he never responded to my plea for help. EEOC was willing to provide mediation but the district refused and EEOC stated that they would begin to investigate the district immediately. She asked when did I receive this letter I told her a little before the break. She stated that this was district policy. She did not understand it but she had dealt with OCR before.

Ms. Martinez this is what transpired during our meeting. In the event that something was stated on this letter that you do not agree with please feel free to give me feedback.

Sincerely,

Frankie J. Monroe

P. S. Ms. Martinez you stated that you were going to see what you could do to get me a promoted during our meeting. This is part of what I requested in my initial grievance to Dr. Chavez on 11/03/04. I want to also include the remaining remedy that I stated I am seeking in that grievance. I want restitution for all of the money I have invested to advance my education; per CCISD requirements. I want a year's salary for each position that I have applied for but not been afford the opportunity to compete. I also want an administrative position.

From: Imelda Martinez
To: Frankie Monroe
Date: Tue, Jan 11, 2005 11:21 AM
Subject: Re: Follow-up letter to meeting with Attorney

Ms. Monroe,

Thank you for the summary of our meeting of January 6th. I remain committed to supporting your efforts in seeking an administrative position in Corpus Christi ISD.

Respectfully,
Imelda Martinez

Imelda Martinez
Legal Services
IMMartinez1@CCISD.us
(361) 886-9067

>>> Frankie Monroe 1/11/2005 12:30:43 AM >>>
Attached is a follow -up letter to the meeting I had with the school Attoney. Ms. Imelda Martinez.

CC: Jesus Chavez; Karen Soehnge

Exhibit 23

On Jan 13, 2005 after meeting on Jan 6, 2005 I was not satisfied with the discussion that transpired. Especially when Mrs. Martinez stated Dr. Chavez did not know I hadn't been given opportunities to interview for administrative positions. After Mrs. Martinez said my records were of exceptional quality and she had never seen a record like mine; where a person had worked for 20+ years but didn't have even one bad note in their files. I decided to get a copy of my records. I contacted Mrs. Martinez to see when would be a good time to pick up my files. I offered to pay for the copies during the January 6, 2005 meeting and was told by Mrs. Martinez; there was no way she would charge me. All I had to do was write the request for my records on a yellow legal pad she had and she would see that I got them. I contacted Monica, Ms. Martinez's secretary, and asked if my files were ready to be picked up.

After securing my files I walked straight over to the superintendent's office and submitted another grievance. This time I named Dr. Chavez as the guilty party.

From: Imelda Martinez
To: Frankie Monroe
Date: Thu, Jan 13, 2005 12:47 PM
Subject: Re: Copy of File

That would be fine. Please contact Monica Salinas to coordinate your arrival at central office.

Imelda Martinez
Legal Services
IMMartinez1@CCISD.us
(361) 886-9067

>>> Frankie Monroe 1/13/2005 10:56:28 AM >>>
Good Morning Ms. Martinez,

I would like to pick up a copy of my file at the end of school today. Would that be possible?

From: Monica Salinas
To: Frankie Monroe
Date: Thu, Jan 13, 2005 2:47 PM
Subject: Re: File Copy

That will be fine.

>>> Frankie Monroe 1/13/2005 2:22:43 PM >>>
Ms. Salinas,

Ms. Imelda Martinez instructed me to contact you to set up the time that I would arrive to pick up the copy of my file. I will leave campus at 4:05. It should take me approximately 15-20 minutes to get there. I should arrive around 4:30 baring any bad traffic jams.

CORPUS CHRISTI ISD
178904

RECEIVED

IAN 1 3 2005

OFFICE OF SUPERINTENDENT
CORPUS CHRISTI ISD

PERSONNEL-MANAGEMENT RELATIONS: DGBA(E-2)
EMPLOYEE GRIEVANCES AND COMPLAINTS   (LOCAL)

GRIEVANCE REPORT FORM

Date of incident or event giving rise to grievance: **11-29-04 and 10/28/04**

Informal resolution meeting or conference date(s): **1-6-05**

Filing Date **1-13-05** *(Must be filed in writing within 30 days of the time the employee knew, or should have known, of the decision or action causing the grievance or dissatisfaction, exclusive of the time spent in seeking informal resolution.)*

Name of Grievant **Frankie J. Monroe**

Name of Respondent **Dr. Jesus Chavez**

Principal/Immediate Supervisor **Dr. Dawn Dorsey**

School/Department **Ray High School**   Work Phone **(361) 806-5300**

Home Address ███████████████████   Home Phone ███████████

Statement of Facts upon which the Grievance is predicated, including the names of any persons involved, the date of the event or incident giving rise to the Grievance, and a description of the event or incident: *(See DGBA (Local), Prerequisites, page 3. Attach additional page(s), if necessary, and supporting documentation, if any.)*

I have applied for different administrative positions with CCISD since 2000. In that time I have contacted Dr. Jesus Chavez and Mr. Michael Briones about my concerned for not being given an opportunity to be sent on interviews. I could understand if after being interviewed it was felt that perhaps I was not the best candidate for the job but not being sent out at all was unfair. I feel that I have not been afforded an opportunity to compete.

I base my charges of discrimination (race, age, and retaliation) on the following incidents that have occurred. I discovered on 11-29-04, after returning out of town on a family emergency, that Mr. ██ ████ had been hired at Driscoll Middle School as an assistant principal (black). He worked at West Oso as a teacher. About a month before being hired with the district Mr. ██████ had shared with me the fact that he had tried several times to get interviewed with CCISD but had been rejected. After I filed charges of discrimination with EEOC he was hired. (Retaliation)

On 10/28/ 04 an e-mail was sent out to Ray staff from Miss ██████████ stating that she had been hired as an assistant principal at Cunningham Middle School. Miss ████ had shared with me that she had applied in late August for an assistant principal position. I applied in early April and received one interview, which I requested from Dr. Dorsey. By September Miss ████ had received not one but three interviews. She was not hired on the first set of interviews but by the second round of interviews she was. Miss ████ has approximately 2 1/2 years of teaching experience and is in her mid-to-late twenties. I have almost 20 years of teaching experience in education. (Age discrimination)

ADOPTED: 04/28/89   AMENDED: 06/09/97   1 of 4

NEWLOC

SEE E- MAIL ATTACHMENTS TO MR. MICHAEL BRIONES AND CC TO DR. JESUS
CHAVEZ IN JULY 2004 AND A BRIEF HISTORY OF NOT BEING AFFORDED

Witnesses of whom the Grievant is aware who may have any information related to the Grievance:

Dr. Dawn Dorsey

Law alleged to have been violated or the dissatisfaction raised by the Grievant, and the alleged harm or damage caused by such violation of dissatisfaction:

Discrimination and Civil Rights violation: Race (Black), Age and Retaliation.

Steps taken to resolve Grievance informally:

Discussed this with Mr. Michael Briones and Dr. Jesus Chavez several times via e-mail and phone. Met with school district attorney Ms. Imelda Martinez on 1-6-05. She stated that she would do everything she could to help me get promoted but never mention any other restitution. I informed Ms. Martinez in a summary letter that I sent her about the previous grievance I had filed.

Remedy sought:

I want restitution for emotional and mental anguish. I want all the money I have invested to advance my education, per CCISD requirements. I want a year's salary for each position that I have applied for but not been afforded the opportunity to compete. I also want an administrative position.

Frankie J. Monroe 1-13-05
Grievant's Signature   Date

Accepted/Rejected by Superintendent:
    (Circle one)

_____
Superintendent's Signature   Date

Exhibit 24

Something else was also said in the initial meeting I had with Mrs. Martinez on January 6, 2005 that made me question whether EEOC was investigating my case. Mrs. Imelda Martinez stated that the district had had no further contact with EEOC since they had refused mediation which was district policy. She didn't understand it but that was the way it was. On January 25, 2005 I started trying to find out why EEOC hadn't contacted Corpus Christi ISD. After all it was stated in the letter I received from them back in November of 2004 that an investigation was in progress. I tried to contact the person I was told was my assigned investigator (Ms. Mary Esther Jimenez). After numerous attempts to contact her and got no response; I was told to speak to her boss. After speaking to him she contacted me.

On February 1, 2005 after having a conversation with Ms. Mary Esther Jimenez my suspicions were heightened even further that something was amiss. She told me she could not move forward with my case until she got the mediation report back which indicated to me that no investigation had taken place by EEOC. I had been contacted back on November 16, 2004 by EEOC stating that mediation had been refused by Corpus Christi ISD. I requested to be sent that response. She began complaining that there was no way she could send me all the records that had been sent to them by Corpus Christi ISD. I stopped her right there and told her I only wanted the response nothing more. I also informed her I was sending additional information I had collected. This began to feel like 1986 all over again so I sent a letter to the San Antonio office requesting to be assigned to another investigator...

February 1, 2005

EEOC
San Antonio District Office
5410 Fredericksburg Road – Suite 200
San Antonio TX 78229-3555

Mr. Thomas Price:

Charge No.: 360-2005 00072 (Unperfected)
Respondent: Corpus Christi I.S.D

I received a letter from the San Antonio EEOC office postmarked October 28, 2004. In that letter it stated the following "(EEOC) is unable to schedule mediation for this charge because the other party did not agree to mediate. Although our focus from this point on will be to investigate the allegations raised in the charge, settlement will remain a resolution option throughout our processing the charge.

Within a week from the postmark date of this notice the charge will be assigned to an investigator in our office. At that time you may obtain the investigator's name and telephone number by calling (210) 281-7600 and providing the above charge number to the receptionist. I you need to speak with someone from our office before then, you may contact Rodney Klein, Charge Receipt Supervisor, at (210) 281-7621. Thank You.

Pedro Esquivel
Director, San Antonio District."

Documentation of the phone conversation I (Frankie J. Monroe) had with EEOC investigator Ms. Mary Ester Jimenez at approximately 4:25 PM on January 25, 2005.

I attempted to contact Ms. Jimenez approximately 10 times after finding out that she had been assigned to my case by Mr. Thomas Price. It was not until I called Mr. Price and his superior that I was told to contact Mr. Guillermo Zamora, her immediate supervisor, that Ms. Jimenez finally contacted me. She explained that they were allowed to work out of their house on Fridays and that she had been ill.

I explained to her why I had been trying so desperately to contact her about CCISD stating that they had not heard from any investigator after declining mediation. She started off by stating that EEOC did not handle cases that extended beyond 360 days. I informed her that what she was reading was merely a synopsis of my history with the district over the years and that I had reached the boiling point which prompted me to file these charges of discrimination. She stated that she had read the districts response to my charges and that based on what they had said I had not been qualified for the positions that I sought because I did not have enough experience.

My response to her was that now there lay the problem. How was I ever going to get the experience if I was never allowed the opportunity to compete? I also informed her of the other teachers that had been hired right out of the classroom and catapulted into administration with only 2 ½ years of teaching experience and ages 26-30 I was a 52 year old black woman. I had 20 years of educational experience, held a Masters degree, and was a doctoral student. I also held a mid-management certification as well as a superintendent certification and had not been afforded that same opportunity.

Ms. Jimenez asked me what my salary with the school district was. I told her a little over $40,000. I am not sure why she asked that question. She asked me had there been any blacks hired. I told her that I only knew of one that was hired after I informed the district about me filing charges of discrimination with EEOC. I informed Ms Jimenez that there had been anywhere from 20-30 administrative positions available at the end of the 2003-04 school year and the only time I had interviewed was when I personally talked to the principal and requested that they give me an opportunity to be interviewed. I was never sent by the CCISD personnel office from April-October 2004 which was the time that many of these positions were available.

I told Ms. Jimenez that I was going to send her more of the information that had transpired between the CCISD attorney and me since I had sent the initial information. She told me to send her this information.

I realize that this is just a first impression and that Ms Jimenez was ill but I don't want my case to get lost until my time is over and nothing gets done with my case. I don't feel that Ms. Jimenez will act in my best interest and I would like to request that another case worker be assigned to my case at this time.

It is now February 1, 2005 and the clock is ticking.

I am also enclosing the following updated information so that you can review it. I feel that this solidifies my claim that I have been discriminated against.

I look forward to hearing from you in the very near future concerning this matter. My phone number is (361) and my cell phone number is (361) don't answer please leave a message and will contact you as soon as I check it.

Thank you for your prompt attention.

Sincerely,

Frankie J. Monroe

CC: Pedro Esquivel
Director, San Antonio District

Exhibit 25

On February 1, 2005 I also submitted another grievance to Corpus Christi ISD. I thought I had filled out the January 13, 2005 grievance forms incorrectly again because I hadn't heard anything. Each time I had filed in the past there always seemed to be something wrong with it. I changed the respondent from Dr. Chavez to Corpus Christi ISD and filed it again. In this grievance I included information I had obtained from EEOC.

PERSONNEL-MANAGEMENT RELATIONS: DGBA(E-2)
EMPLOYEE GRIEVANCES AND COMPLAINTS   (LOCAL)

GRIEVANCE REPORT FORM

Date of incident or event giving rise to grievance: 1-27-05

Informal resolution meeting or conference date(s): __1-6-05__

Filing Date ___2-1-05___ *(Must be filed in writing within 30 days of the time the employee knew, or should have known, of the decision or action causing the grievance or dissatisfaction, exclusive of the time spent in seeking informal resolution.)*

Name of Grievant _____Frankie J. Monroe_____

Name of Respondent _____Corpus Christi ISD_____

Principal/Immediate Supervisor _____Dr. Dawn Dorsey_____

School/Department ___Ray High School___   Work Phone _(361) 806-5300_

Home Address ████████████████   Home Phone ██████████

Statement of Facts upon which the Grievance is predicated, including the names of any persons involved, the date of the event or incident giving rise to the Grievance, and a description of the event or incident: *(See DGBA (Local), Prerequisites, page 3. Attach additional page(s), if necessary, and supporting documentation, if any.)*

I spoke with EEOC investigator and discovered that CCISD had refused mediation request that I had agreed to. It was stated that the district was refusing mediation because after investigating my claim it was decided that I was not qualified for any of the positions I applied for due to lack of experience. I am well aware of all of the teachers that were hired in the district. Many of them were hired from teaching positions. I have Mid-management and Superintendent Certifications as well as nearly 20 years of education experience. I am also a doctoral student enrolled at Texas A & M in educational administration.

Attached is a brief synopsis of my experience with the district.

ADOPTED: 04/28/89   AMENDED: 06/09/97   1 of 4

NEWLOC

SEE E- MAIL ATTACHMENTS TO MR. MICHAEL BRIONES AND CC TO DR. JESUS
CHAVEZ IN JULY 2004 AND A BRIEF HISTORY OF NOT BEING AFFORDED

PERSONNEL-MANAGEMENT RELATIONS:
EMPLOYEE GRIEVANCES AND COMPLAINTS

DGBA(E-2)
(LOCAL)

Witnesses of whom the Grievant is aware who may have any information related to the Grievance:

Dr. Dawn Dorsey

Law alleged to have been violated or the dissatisfaction raised by the Grievant, and the alleged harm or damage caused by such violation of dissatisfaction:

Discrimination and Civil Rights violation: Race (Black), Age and Retaliation.

Steps taken to resolve Grievance informally:

Discussed this with Mr. Michael Briones and Dr. Jesus Chavez several times via e-mail and phone. Met with school district attorney Ms. Imelda Martinez on 1-6-05. She stated that she would do everything she could to help me get promoted but never mention any other restitution. I informed Ms. Martinez in a summary letter that I sent her about the previous grievance I had filed.

Remedy sought:

I want restitution for emotional and mental anguish. I want all the money I have invested to advance my education, per CCISD requirements. I want a year's salary for each position that I have applied for but not been afforded the opportunity to compete. I also want an administrative position.

Frudie J. Monroe   2-1-05
Grievant's Signature   Date

Accepted/Rejected by Superintendent:
 (Circle one)

_____
Superintendent's Signature   Date

NEWLOC   ADOPTED: 04/28/89   AMENDED: 06/09/97   2 of 4

From: Monica Salinas
To: Frankie Monroe
Date: Thu, Feb 3, 2005 11:18 AM
Subject: 02-01-05 Grievance Report Form

Please call me. Thank you.

Monica
CCISD Office of Legal Services
886-9067

Exhibit 27

On Feb 7, 2005 after the conversation I had with Monica, Mrs. Imelda Martinez immediately contacted me via e-mail and requested a meeting at my earliest convenience. Initially I believe Dr. Chavez hadn't been aware that I had been walking my grievances in and getting them stamped. Once he realized this he wanted a meeting set up to discuss this as soon as possible. There was also another problem. It had been announced on television that Dr. Chavez had applied at Fort Worth ISD to become its superintendant, but someone else was hired. With me filing charges of discrimination against him it wouldn't have been good for his career. It would also look bad to the Corpus Christi ISD school board if this came to light. It would definitely be a black-eye on the district. I was planning to meet with them but I still hadn't sought legal representation.

From: Frankie Monroe
To: Martinez, Imelda
Date: Mon, Feb 7, 2005 10:54 AM
Subject: Re: Ms. Monroe,

Ms. Martinez,

I have class this evening at the University at 4:30. I am working on my doctoral degree. I will be available tomorrow after school. Is 4:30 Okay with you?

>>> Imelda Martinez 2/7/2005 10:30:55 AM >>>
Ms. Monroe,
I would like to meet with you at your earliest convenience. Please let me know.
Imelda

Imelda Martinez
Legal Services
IMMartinez1@CCISD.us
(361) 886-9067

Exhibit 28

Feb 8, 2005 I spoke to Dr. Dorsey and she suggested that I not meet with anyone unless I had legal representation so I cancelled the meeting via e-mail.

From: Imelda Martinez
To: Frankie Monroe
Date: Tue, Feb 8, 2005 4:13 PM
Subject: Re: Meeting

That's fine, just let me know if you have an alternate date and time.

Imelda Martinez
Legal Services
IMMartinez1@CCISD.us
(361) 886-9067

>>> Frankie Monroe 2/8/2005 4:11:04 PM >>>
Mrs. Martinez,

I am sorry that I will not be able to meet with you today. I will have to schedule another time.

Exhibit 29

I later became aware of some additional information after I filed my lawsuit. My attorney requested all information exchanged between Corpus Christi ISD and EEOC be submitted to him. As we poured through the information I came across a letter from my EEOC investigator, Mary Esther Jimenez. It had been sent to Corpus Christi ISD on Feb 8, 2005. She thanked Mrs. Martinez for supplying the information to EEOC on November 16, 2005. As far as I was concerned this confirmed what I had said all along about nothing being done on my case by EEOC until I contacted them in February 2005 even though I had been told that an immediate investigation would take place in October, 2004.

I had sent letters to Washington DC and San Antonio headquarters requesting a new investigator because I didn't feel Ms. Jimenez had my best interest at heart because of the tone she had taken with me during our first conversation. Here was the proof.

Now all the puzzle pieces started to come together and I had a clearer picture of what was happening. I understood why Ms. Martinez was playing games with me now. She wasn't only trying to protect Dr. Chavez's career she also had to prove to EEOC that the school district had made several attempts to meet with me since, I filled charges of discrimination, but I was being uncooperative.

U.S. EQUAL EMPLOYMENT OPPORTUNITY COMMISSION
San Antonio District Office

5410 Fredericksburg Road, Suite 200
San Antonio, TX 78229-3555
(210) 281-7600
TTY (210) 281-7610
FAX (210) 281-7606

Imelda Martinez
Staff Atty
Office of Legal Services
P.O. Box 110
Corpus Christi Independent School District
Corpus Christi, Texas 78403-0110

RECEIVED

FEB 0 8 2005

CCISD OFFICE OF
LEGAL SERVICES

Ref: Charge No.: 360-2005-00072
Respondent: Corpus Christ ISD

Dear Ms. Martinez:

This is to thank you and to acknowledge receipt of Respondent's position statement which was received in our office on November 16, 2004. The following additional information is being requested and is due in our office on February 21, 2005.

1. Provide a list of all individuals that were selected to Assistant Principals and Principals from June 2003 to present to include the employee's name, race, date of birth, and the reason the employee's selection.

2. Provide a list of the candidates who were selected for the seven (7) job opening which Charging Party met the requirements to include, the selectee's name, race, date of birth and the reason for the candidates selection. Provide the reason Charging Party was not selected for the seven (7) job opening she was qualified for.

3. Provide copies of the selectees' original job application, resume, and qualifications for the selected candidates who were not of the same race and under 40 years of age.

4. Provide the dates Charging Party reported or complained about discrimination based on her race or age; to include the name, race, and date of birth of the management official she reported the discrimination. What action was taken by the Respondent?

Thank you for your cooperation. You may call me at 210-281-7663, if you have any questions.

Sincerely,

Mary Esther Jimenez
Mary Esther Jimenez
Federal Investigator

2/5/05
Date

Exhibit 30

On Feb 10, 2005, I submitted another grievance telling what had occurred concerning the concealment of the January 13, 2005 grievance which named Dr. Chavez as the respondent.

CORPUS CHRISTI ISD
178904

PERSONNEL-MANAGEMENT RELATIONS: DGBA(E-2)
EMPLOYEE GRIEVANCES AND COMPLAINTS   (LOCAL)

GRIEVANCE REPORT FORM

RECEIVE
FEB 10 200!
OFFICE OF SUPERINTEN
CORPUS CHRISTI IS!

Date of incident or event giving rise to grievance: _____2-3-05_____

Informal resolution meeting or conference date(s): _____1-6-05_____

Filing Date _____2-10-05_____ *(Must be filed in writing within 30 days of the time the employee knew, or should have known, of the decision or action causing the grievance or dissatisfaction, exclusive of the time spent in seeking informal resolution.)*

Name of Grievant _____Frankie J. Monroe_____

Name of Respondent _____Dr. Jesus Chavez, Superintendent_____

Principal/Immediate Supervisor _____Dr. Dawn Dorsey_____

School/Department _____Ray High School_____   Work Phone _____(361) 806-5300_____

Home Address _____[redacted]_____   Home Phone _____[redacted]_____

Statement of Facts upon which the Grievance is predicated, including the names of any persons involved, the date of the event or incident giving rise to the Grievance, and a description of the event or incident: *(See DGBA (Local), Prerequisites, page 3. Attach additional page(s), if necessary, and supporting documentation, if any.)*

On February 3, 2005 around 11:15, I received an e-mail from Ms Monica Salinas, the secretary in the legal department, asking me to contact her as soon as possible concerning the 2-1-05 grievance that I had filed. I contacted her during my lunch hour at which time she informed me that I had once again filled the Grievance Report Form out incorrectly. This had been my fourth attempt.

In the last grievance that I filed I informed the district of a conversation that I had had with EEOC. I reported that I had spoke with an EEOC investigator and discovered that CCISD had refused mediation request that I had agreed to. It was stated that the district was refusing mediation because after investigating my claim it was decided that I was not qualified for any of the positions that I applied for due to lack of experience. I am well aware of all of the teachers that were hired in the district. Many of them were hired from teaching positions. I have Mid-management and Superintendent Certifications as well as nearly 20 years of education experience. I am also a doctoral student enrolled at Texas A & M in educational administration.

CONTINUE ON NEXT PAGE

ADOPTED: 04/28/89   AMENDED: 06/09/97   1 of 4

NEWLOC

SEE E-MAIL ATTACHMENTS TO MR. MICHAEL BRIONES AND CC TO DR. JESUS
CHAVEZ IN JULY 2004 AND A BRIEF HISTORY OF NOT BEING AFFORDED

Ms. Salinas stated that I could not file a grievance against the district. It had to be against a specific person. In my initial filing I listed (CCISD, Dr. Jesus Chavez, and Mr. Michael Briones) as the respondent. I told her that I had selected a single person, when I resubmitted my grievance on 1-13-05. I informed her that I had put Dr. Jesus Chavez down as the respondent.

She gave me all the grievance dates that she had in front of her and there was no grievance date for 1-13-05 with Dr. Jesus Chavez's named as the Respondent on it. I told her that after I had met with Ms. Martinez, the CCISD school attorney on 1-06-05. I turned in my grievance form on January 13, 2005. She repeated that she did not see that particular grievance form but that she would go and look for it. At that point I told her if she could not find the copy I could send her a copy of mine which had the date stamped on it.

Ms. Salinas proceeded to tell me the procedures that had to be followed when filing a grievance. If the grievance were filed against a school employee for instance Mr. Michael Briones, one of my initial respondents listed on my grievance, I would need to have a meeting with him and his superior Mr. Noriega. If I were still not happy with the decisions that were reached then I would go to step two meet with Dr. Chavez, the Superintendent, concerning the matter. But if I were filing charges against the Superintendent I would skip all other stages and go to stage 3 meeting with the school board.

I informed her that I had only talked personally with Mrs. Imelda Martinez, the school attorney concerning this matter and had not been offered any other meetings. At that point we ended the conversation with me assuring her that I would get her a copy of the Grievance Report that I filed on January 13, 2005.

ATTACHED ARE TWO COPIES OF PREVIOUS ATTEMPTS TO FILE GRIEVANCE WITH THE DISTRICT.

PERSONNEL-MANAGEMENT RELATIONS: DGBA(E-2)
EMPLOYEE GRIEVANCES AND COMPLAINTS   (LOCAL)

Witnesses of whom the Grievant is aware who may have any information related to the
Grievance:

       Dr. Dawn Dorsey

Law alleged to have been violated or the dissatisfaction raised by the Grievant, and the
alleged harm or damage caused by such violation of dissatisfaction:

      Discrimination and Civil Rights violation: Race (Black), Age and Retaliation.

Steps taken to resolve Grievance informally:

Discussed this with Mr. Michael Briones and Dr. Jesus Chavez several times via e-mail and phone. Met with school district attorney Ms. Imelda Martinez on 1-6-05.
She stated that she would do everything she could to help me get promoted but
never mention any other restitution. I informed Ms. Martinez in a summary letter
that I sent her about the previous grievance I had filed.

Remedy sought:

I want restitution for emotional and mental anguish. I want all the money I have
invested to advance my education, per CCISD requirements. I want a year's salary
for each position that I have applied for but not been afforded the opportunity to
compete. I also want an administrative position.

Frankie J. Monroe   2-10-05
Grievant's Signature   Date

Accepted/Rejected by Superintendent:
   (Circle one)

_____
Superintendent's Signature   Date

     ADOPTED: 04/28/89   AMENDED: 06/09/97   2 of 4
NEWLOC

Exhibit 31

On Feb 14, 2005 I received a letter from EEOC in response to the letter I sent on February 1, 2005. I expressed my concern to Ms Jimenez's supervisor about the treatment I had received from Ms. Jimenez in my initial phone conversation with her and requested a new investigator because I did not feel Ms. Jimenez had my best interest at heart. In that letter I also included the request to have response letter from Corpus Christi ISD sent to me on the reason they refused mediation.

In the letter dated November 16, 2004 sent to EEOC from Mrs. Imelda Martinez, Corpus Christi ISD's in-house-attorney it states that I only qualified for 7 of the 16 positions I applied for. In May, 2006, Mr. Michael Briones, the Certified Personnel Director, testified under oath during in his deposition that several people in the district had been allowed to hold administrative positions for at least 5 years with the same temporary mid-management certification that I was denied the right to apply for. He also swore under oath that all the people hired had more work experience than I did. In previous documents that I have submitted this has been proven not to be the case.

Mrs. Martiniez states in the letter that 'at no time is an applicant's race, color, sex, religion, national origin, age, disability or status of an EEOC complaint reflected or available to the screening and interview committee.' This was proven to be a false statement during discovery. All applicants that were screened had their names appear at the very top of each screening sheet. On several of the screening sheets notes were hand written in indicating I was only interested in secondary grade levels which include grades 6-12. As you have seen in several of the e-mails I sent out I requested to be considered for all levels. After reviewing several of the screening forms I also discovered I knew almost everyone on the interviewing committee and they knew me personally.

After reviewing this information I sent another letter dated February 16, 2005 to Mr. Pedro Esquivel, Director of EEOC San Antonio district office refuting some statements he made concerning information about Ms. Jimenez.

U.S. EQUAL EMPLOYMENT OPPORTUNITY COMMISSION
San Antonio District Office

5410 Fredericksburg Road, Suite 200
San Antonio, TX 78229-3555
(210) 281-7600
TTY (210) 281-7610
FAX (210) 281-7606

Frankie J. Monroe

Ref: Charge No.: 360-2005-00072
Respondent: Corpus Christi ISD

Dear Ms. Monroe:

This is to acknowledge receipt of your letter to our office dated February 1, 2005.

Initially, please accept my apology for the times that Ms. Jimenez failed to return your telephone calls of January 24, 2005. She was ill and as such was away from the office. A close review of the file indicates that Ms. Jimenez did call you back twice on January 25, 2005, and left you a message on your cell telephone and with your daughter. Upon speaking to you Ms. Jimenez did inform you that she was in the process of requesting information from Corpus Christi ISD to address the issues raised in your charge of discrimination.

We also acknowledge receipt of the additional information you provided to us and to Mr. Price. It was received in our office on February 5, 2005. Please be assured that your charge will be processed in accordance with our policies and procedures and that it will receive the attention given to every charge handled by our office. Since Ms. Jimenez is the Investigator assigned to your charge we ask that you direct your correspondence and telephone calls to her attention. A copy of Corpus Christi ISD's position statement is enclosed per your request.

Sincerely,

Guillermo Zamora
Enforcement Supervisor

2.14.05
Date

Corpus Christi
Independent
School
District

OFFICE OF LEGAL SERVICES
361-695-9067   FAX: 361-844-0283

801 Leopard • PO Box 110   Corpus Christi, Texas 78403-0110

November 16, 2004

<u>Via CM:RRR – 7003-2260-0003-9948-1848</u>
<u>And Facsimile: (210) 281-2522</u>
Mr. Rodney R. Klein
Supervising Investigator
U. S. Equal Employment Opportunity Commission
San Antonio District Office
5410 Fredericksburg Road, Suite 200
San Antonio, Texas 78229

RE: EEOC Charge No. 360-2005-00072
        Frankie J. Monroe

Dear Mr. Klein:

This is in response to the Notice of Charge of Discrimination dated October 18, 2004 regarding Ms. Frankie J. Monroe. The Corpus Christi Independent School District (CCISD) categorically denies all charges of discrimination submitted by Ms. Monroe. During the period of November 6, 2000 through June 4, 2004, Ms. Monroe applied for sixteen positions of which nine positions she did not meet the job description requirements.
                                Of the remaining seven positions, her application was reviewed by the respective supervisors during the process of selecting candidates for interviews.

The selection process for professional staff in CCISD requires that the Office of Secondary Certified Personnel review and screen all timely submitted applications for compliance with the minimal requirements established by the job position.   Principal and assistant principal applicants are then scored by a committee according to years of experience, training, performance, certifications, etc. The score sheets are then presented to the interview committee for their review and ultimate selection of candidates for interviews. Once the interviews have been conducted, the supervisor submits the name of the applicant selected for the position to the personnel department for further background checks.

It is important to note, that at no time during the selection process is an applicant's race, color, sex, religion, national origin, age, disability, or status of an EEOC complaint reflected or available to the screening and interview committees. To date, CCISD employs 61 principals and 88 assistant principals at 61 campuses. The makeup of this group of administrators is varied and uniquely diverse as indicated below.

174

Ethnicity		Gender		Age	
White	34.2 %	Female	72.5 %	Under 29	1.3 %
Black	8.1 %	Male	27.5 %	30 to 39	20.8 %
Hispanic	57.7 %			40 to 49	37.6 %
Other	.0 %			50 to 59	35.6 %
				60 to 69	4.7 %

In each of the seven job openings in which Ms. Monroe met the requirements of the job description, other applicants were recommended without regards to Ms. Monroe's race, color, sex, religion, national origin, age, disability, retaliation, or status of an EEOC complaint. It is entirely possible that most members of the interview committee never personally met Ms. Monroe or were aware of her concerns.

In summary, the CCISD has not engaged in any discriminatory actions or decisions regarding Ms. Monroe and her pursuit of an administrative position with the district. Simply put, CCISD selected and continues to select individuals whose credentials, work experiences, and knowledge of both state and federal laws placed them at the top of the applicant pool. CCISD encourages Ms. Monroe to apply for any open positions posted by CCISD in which she feels she has the required qualifications. If you have any questions, I may be reached at (361) 886-9163.

Respectfully,

Imelda Martinez

Imelda Martinez
Staff Attorney

CORPUS CHRISTI INDEPENDENT SCHOOL DISTRICT
Corpus Christi, Texas

Assistant Principal
Paper Screening Rating Form

Candidate: Frankie Monroe   Date: 7/14/04

Criteria		Rating
1. Success in restructuring programs and/or schools.	(Max 10 points)	_____
2. Success in improving student achievement.	(Max 10 points)	_____
3. Knowledge of curriculum.	(Max 10 points)	_____
4. Knowledge of effective teaching practices.	(Max 10 points)	_____
5. Diversity and depth of experience (positions/assignments/committees).	(Max 10 points)	_____
6. Knowledge/Experience in budget management.	(Max 10 points)	_____
7. Successful collaboration in community efforts and decision making.	(Max 10 points)	_____
8. Positive references.	(Max 10 points)	_____
9. Administrative experience or equivalent.	(Max 10 points)	_____
	TOTAL	_____

Rating by: _____

Date: 7/14/04

Secondary emphasis

mgv

(Please note: make copies of this form as necessary for each candidate)

(Attachment 1)

Asst Principal-Selection Process Info-Letter-Moody w-complete pkt 4-8-04

3

176

FAX

CORPUS CHRISTI INDEPENDENT SCHOOL DISTRICT
Corpus Christi, Texas

Assistant Principal
Paper Screening Rating Form

Candidate: _Frankie Monroe_   Date: _7/14/04_

Criteria		Rating
1. Success in restructuring programs and/or schools.	(Max 10 points)	_____
2. Success in improving student achievement.	(Max 10 points)	_____
3. Knowledge of curriculum.	(Max 10 points)	_____
4. Knowledge of effective teaching practices.	(Max 10 points)	_____
5. Diversity and depth of experience (positions/assignments/committees).	(Max 10 points)	_____
6. Knowledge/Experience in budget management.	(Max 10 points)	_____
7. Successful collaboration in community efforts and decision making.	(Max 10 points)	_____
8. Positive references.	(Max 10 points)	_____
9. Administrative experience or equivalent.	(Max 10 points)	_____
	TOTAL	_____

Rating by: _D. Mone_
Date: _7/14/04_

mgv   _fee. emphasis only_

(Please note: make copies of this form as necessary for each candidate)

(Attachment 1)

EXHIBIT

February 16, 2005

EEOC
San Antonio District Office
Pedro Esquivel, Director, San Antonio District
5410 Fredericksburg Road – Suite 200
San Antonio TX 78229-3555

Mr. Pedro Esquivel:

Charge No.: 360-2005 00072 (Unperfected)
Respondent: Corpus Christi I.S.D

Mr. Esquivel I beg to differ with you on the contact date and the discussion that took place. Ms. Jimenez did not inform me that she was contacting CCISD until 2-8-05. This was after I called and left a message with Mr. Thomas Price.

Documentation of conversation I had with Ms. Mary Ester Jimenez on 2-8-05.

Ms. Jimenez contacted me at home around 4:45 p.m. She stated that she had just been e-mailed by Mr. Thomas price informing her that I had called concerning a copy of the statement that had been sent to EEOC from CCISD declining mediation. She stated that she could tell me what was said but she could not send me all of the attachments. I told her that I did not want the attachments I only wanted a copy of the statement. I told her that if necessary I would be willing to send money for the copy.

She proceeded to stress the fact that Mr. Price was not the person that I should be contacting concerning my case she was. He was merely the person that had received the initial information.

I told her that I realized that Mr. Price was the intake person but the only time that I had gotten any information was through him. No matter when I contacted him he always got back with me and directed me to who I needed to talk to. He had told me that you were my investigator. When I tried to contact you, you never responded so I reverted back to the person that had been responsive to me.

She went on to tell me that she had sent a letter to CCISD. They had 10-15 days to respond. She stated that nothing could proceed until EEOC had gotten something from the mediation team. I told her that I had received a letter back on October 28, 2004 telling me that CCISD had been contacted concerning mediation and they had declined mediation. The letter went on to say based on that information they would proceed within five days of the post date on the letter to investigate. Ms. Jimenez stated that she did not get my case until October. I told her that I had sent a letter to Washington in July 2004. I was contacted by the regional EEOC in San Antonio in September 2004 and sent the necessary paperwork to fill out to file official charges of discrimination. Everything

178

had been completed by October. I told her that it was now four months later and apparently no investigation had taken place.

She then reverted back to stating that EEOC did not go back any further than three hundred days. This was the same conversation we had had on January 25, 2005 during my initial contact with her for the first time. For some reason Ms. Jimenez can not understand that what I had done was to create a time-line to show that the treatment I had experienced had not just started it had been going on and I had reached my boiling point by September. It is also apparent that Ms. Jimenez has not read through any of the documentation that I sent her or she would not continue to cover the same ground over and over.

I informed Ms. Jimenez that I had filed another grievance with the district on February 1, 2005. On February 3, 2005 around 11:15 a.m., I received an e-mail from Ms. Monica Salinas, the secretary in the legal department, asking me to contact her as soon as possible concerning the 2-1-05 grievance that I had filed. I contacted her during my lunch hour at which time she informed me that I had once again filled the Grievance Report Form out incorrectly. This had been my fourth attempt.

In the last grievance that I filed I informed the district of a conversation that I had had with EEOC. I reported that I had spoke with an EEOC investigator and discovered that CCISD had refused mediation because after investigating my claim it was decided that I was not qualified for any of the positions that I applied for due to lack of experience. I told her that I had a Mid-management and Superintendent Certification as well as nearly 20 years of education experience. I was also a doctoral student enrolled at Texas A&M in educational administration.

Ms. Salinas stated that I could not file a grievance against the district. It had to be against a specific person. In my initial filing I listed (CCISD, Dr. Jesus Chavez, and Mr. Michael Briones) as the respondent. I told her that I had selected a singled person, when I resubmitted my grievance on 1-13-05. I informed her that I had put Dr. Jesus Chavez down as the respondent.

She gave me all the grievance dates that she had in front of her and there was no grievance date for 1-13-05 with Dr. Jesus Chavez's name as the Respondent on it. I told her that after I had met with Ms. Martinez, the CCISD school attorney on 1-6-05. I turned in my grievance form on January 13, 2005. She repeated that she did not see that particular grievance form but that she would go and look for it. At that point I told her if she could not find the copy I could send her a copy of mine which had the date stamped on it.

Ms. Salinas proceeded to tell me the procedures that had to be followed when filing a grievance. If the grievance were filed against a school employee for instance Mr. Michael Briones, one of my initial respondents listed on my grievance, I would need to have a meeting with him and his superior Mr. Noriega. If I were still not happy with the decisions that were reached then I would go to step two, meet with Dr. Chavez, the superintendent, concerning the matter. But if I were filing charges against the superintendent I would skip all other stages and go to stage three meeting with the school board.

I informed her that I had only talked personally with Mrs. Imelda Martinez; the school attorney concerning this matter and had not been offered any other meetings. At that point we ended the conversation with me assuring her that I would get her a copy of the Grievance Report that I filed on January 13, 2005.

I went on to inform Ms. Jimenez that I did not feel that she had my best interest at heart. I had requested another investigator. She stated that I could contact her supervisor concerning this matter. I also told her that I had experienced this same treatment with EEOC 20 years ago. My complaint was lost for an entire year and nothing was ever done. I never met with anyone for mediation or anything else. The statute of limitations were implemented and nothing ever happened. I refused to fall through the cracks this time.

Enclosed you will find a copy of a letter I sent on February 1, 2005. At this time I would like to request another investigator.

Your cooperation will be greatly appreciated

Sincerely,

Frankie J. Monroe

Frankie J. Monroe

Exhibit 32

On Feb 14, 2005 I also received an e-mail from Ms. Imelda Martinez requesting to reschedule meeting that she had tried to set up a week before but I cancelled.

Mail Message

N

Close   Previous   Next   Forward   Reply to Sender   Reply All   Move   Delete   Read Later   Properties

Print View

From: Imelda Martinez
To: Frankie Monroe
Date: Monday - February 14, 2005 3:32 PM
Subject: Ms. Monroe,

Ms. Monroe,
I'm just checking to see if we can re-schedule our meeting from last week. We can meet at your campus, if that's more convenient. Please let me know the dates you are available.
Imelda Martinez

Imelda Martinez
Legal Services
IMMartinez1@CCISD.us
(361) 886-9067

Exhibit 33

On Feb 15, 2005 I sent e-mail to Dr. Dorsey informing her of an e-mail I received from Mrs. Imelda Martinez, to meet on campus. I didn't want to meet her alone so I asked Dr. Dorsey to be a witness to our conversation. She agreed to be present during the meeting.

From: Frankie Monroe
To: Dorsey, Dawn
Date: Tue, Feb 15, 2005 1:09 PM
Subject: School Attorney

Dr. Dorsey,

Ms. Imelda Martinez has requested that I meet with her even if it is on campus. Should I decide to meet with her would you be available to attend this meeting. I would like to have it in your office. I will understand if you don't want to get involved. But if you do please let me know when you would be available. I will schedule it around you.

Exhibit 34

On Feb 17, 2005 Dr. Dorsey came to class and informed me she had gotten a strange e-mail from Imelda Martinez. It was a letter written to me but it was e-mailed to her dated Feb 16, 2005. She stated she would forward it to me so that I could see what it was. I received that same letter at my home address when I got home that evening. Nowhere in this letter does it say that the meeting site is to be changed from campus to main office.

From:	Dawn Dorsey
To:	Frankie Monroe
Date:	Thu, Feb 17, 2005 1:11 PM
Subject:	Fwd: Letter dated 02-16-05

fyi

Dawn E. Dorsey, Ph.D.
Prinicpal
W.B. Ray High School
1002 Texan Trail
Corpus Christi, Texas 78411
(361) 806-5300 ext 240
(361-852-6528 fax
dedorsey@ccisd.us

TRULY TEXAN
each mind - each body - each spirit - each day

>>> Monica Salinas 2/17/2005 9:53:22 AM >>>
Please see attached letter. Thank you.

186

**Corpus Christi
Independent
School
District**

801 Leopard • PO Box 110   Corpus Christi, Texas 78403-0110

February 16, 2005

Ms. Frankie J. Monroe

RE: Grievances

Dear Ms. Monroe:

I have attempted to contact you via e-mail to schedule a date and time to meet and discuss the various grievances you have filed within the last four months. However, I would appreciate meeting with you on Friday, February 18, 2005, at 8:30 a.m. to discuss your grievances.

Additionally, please note that we will contact your principal to insure that a substitute teacher will cover your class during this time.

Please feel free to call my office if you have any questions.

Sincerely,

Imelda Martinez

Imelda Martinez, In-House Counsel
Office of Legal Services

mas

cc: Dr. Jesús H. Chávez, Superintendent of Schools
        Dr. Dawn Dorsey, Principal, Ray High School

Exhibit 35

On Feb 18, 2005 I documented what occurred from Feb 16-18, 2005.

On February 16, 2005 Dr. Dorsey came to my class and informed me that she had gotten this strange letter from Imelda Martinez. It was a letter that had been addressed to me but sent to her via e-mail. She wasn't sure what was going on but she would forward the letter to me. In the letter Ms. Martinez stated she had attempted to contact me via e-mail to schedule a date and time to meet and discuss my grievances for the last four months. (Previously submitted letter) She didn't attempt to set these meetings up until she realized I had been bringing these grievances into the office and getting them stamped. She then proceeded to try and force me to meet.

She set up a meeting for February 18, 2005 at 8:30 a.m. and told Dr. Dorsey to get me a sub. Dr. Dorsey told me she had talked to Mrs. Martinez the day before the meeting and asked how long the meeting would last and if she needed to be present. She was told it would last about 30 minutes and she didn't need to be present. I requested Dr. Dorsey attend the meeting so I would have a witness to the conversation. Because Dr. Dorsey called inquiring about the meeting I believe Ms. Martinez decided to change the meeting site but she never told Dr. Dorsey this. She didn't want any witnesses to the conversation because this would defeat the purpose to twist whatever I might say to help cover the district.

On February 18, 2005 at 8:30 I prepared to meet with Mrs. Martinez along with Dr. Dorsey. At 8:45 Dr. Dorsey came to my class and asked if I had heard from Ms. Martinez. I told her I hadn't heard from her. I told her maybe something came up and she couldn't meet after all. Around 11:34 I received an e-mail from Ms. Martinez. She stated that she was sorry for the confusion regarding the location of our meeting. She intended for the meeting to take place in her office. That was why she had requested a substitute teacher to cover my classes until I returned to Ray. She wanted me to let her know when I could reschedule the meeting next week.

Exhibit 36

On Feb 18, 2005 e-mail from Ms Imelda Martinez attempting to explain why meeting didn't take place.

From: Imelda Martinez
To: Frankie Monroe
Date: Fri, Feb 18, 2005 11:34 AM
Subject: Meeting

Ms. Monroe,
I am sorry for the confusion regarding the location of our meeting today. It was my intention that we would meet in my office. That was the reason for requesting a substitute teacher to cover your classes until you returned to Ray H.S. Please accept my apologies to both you and Dr. Dorsey.

I would like to re-schedule this meeting with you soon. Please let me know when you are available early next week.

Thanks,
Imelda

Imelda Martinez
Legal Services
IMMartinez1@CCISD.us
(361) 886-9067

CC: Dawn Dorsey

Exhibit 37

February 18, 2005: Letter to Washington D.C. I wasn't pleased with the way the San Antonio EEOC branch had been investigating my case and I wanted the national headquarters to get involved. After all; this very thing had caused me to loose a similar case almost 20 years earlier. EEOC was suppose to investigate my case but lost my file for almost a year. When I contacted them concerning my case they sent me a Right-to-Sue letter because it was too late to do anything else. I was going to be proactive this time and stay on top of things.

.

February 18, 2005

Equal Employment Opportunity Commission
1801 L Street, NW
Washington, DC 20507

Charge No: 360 2005 00072 (Unperfected)
Respondent: Corpus Christi I.S.D

To Whom It May Concern:

On or about July 19, 2004 I wrote a letter to the EEOC office in Washington D.C
informing you about the discriminatory acts that were being practiced within Corpus
Christi Independent School District against myself and several others.

I was contacted over the phone by Mr. Thomas Price an investigator from San Antonio,
TX, EEOC regional office at the end of September 2004. He stated that I had to follow
protocol. I needed to first file my complaint through the regional office and provided all
necessary documentation to substantiate my claim. He informed me that he would be
sending me all the necessary paper work to fill out. Then he instructed me to send a letter
along with the forms outlining what had transpired between myself and the district that
prompted me to file these charges in the order that the incidents occurred.

I received all the paperwork on or around October 6, 2004. Upon receipt of these
documents I immediately filled out all the paperwork and sent it back.

On or about October 14, 2004 I received a Charge of Discrimination Form which stated
the following: During the period from the year 2000 up and including at least September
7, 2004, I have applied and I have not been hired for the following positions for which I
am qualified, within the Corpus Christi I.S.D i.e., Executive Director of Human
Resources, Special Education School Services Consultant, Principal or Assistant
Principal. I have complained about the unfair hiring practices within this school district.

I believe that I have been discriminated against because of race, Black and for
complaining about unfair hiring practices (retaliation), in violation of Title VII of the
Civil Rights Act of 1964, as amended, and because of my age (DOB 03/29/52), in
violation of Age Discrimination in Employment Act of 1967, as amended.

In the initial documents that I filled out I was asked would I be willing to mediate with
Corpus Christi Independent School District. I filled out and signed yes I would be willing
to. On or about October 28, 2004 I received a letter from EEOC regional office stating
the following:

Dear Charging Party,

As a follow up to our previous mediation notice to you, The San Antonio District Office of the US Equal Employment Opportunity Commission (EEOC) is unable to schedule mediation for this charge because the other party did not agree to mediate. Although our focus from this point on will be to investigate the allegations raised in the charge, settlement will remain a resolution option throughout our processing the charge.

Within a week from the postmark date of this notice the charge will be assigned to an investigator in our office. At that time you may obtain the investigator's name and telephone number by calling (210) 281-7600 and providing the above charge number to the receptionist. If you need to speak with someone from our office before then, you may contact Rodney Klein, Charge Receipt Supervisor, at (210) 28107621.

Thank You.

Pedro Esquivel
Director, San Antonio District.

I had no more contact with EEOC San Antonio Office until I initiated it in January 2005 prompted by a statement from Corpus Christi Independent School District attorney Ms. Imelda Martinez. She stated that the district had not had any further contact with EEOC since they had refused mediation. She stated that this was standard practice within the district not to mediate.

I called Mr. Price and was told that Mary Ester Jimenez was my assigned investigator.

The finding is I have yet been assisted by these agencies to bring resolution to my claim. I am requesting that my claim be investigated by your Federal agency. I want to show that the district is not working on a level playing field. In response to charges of discrimination Corpus Christi Independent School District manipulated data by only addressing charges from November 2000- June of 2004. The charges were from 2000 to at least September 2004. It was stated that they never received any grievance dated 1-13-05 charging Dr. Jesus Chavez as the respondent. I was denied a hearing by the school board per their protocol within a timely manner. They violated their own rules of protocol. On February 14, 2005 it was discovered through the news media that the Superintendent Dr. Jesus Chavez had applied for and was in the running for another superintendent position with the Fortworth Independent School District. He knowingly withheld this information so that he would not appear to be unethical. He has been allowed to advance in his career and I have not been afforded that same opportunity.

I would hope that someone at your federal agency would grant me an audience to discuss my grievance with the Corpus Christi Independent School District and my state EEOC agency.

Please respond in a timely manner so that resolution can be brought to this matter as soon as possible.

Your assistance in this matter is greatly appreciated

Sincerely,

Frankie J. Monroe

Exhibit 38

Feb 21, 2005: After what I suspected was a ploy to twist what I said I e-mailed Ms. Martinez and told her that I had spoken to legal counsel and been advised not to meet with them. In actuality I hadn't spoken an attorney but I had talked to my brother in Minnesota who had gone through something similar. Later I found out it was a ploy but not what I thought it was. As you notice in this e-mail Ms. Martinez now states she never told me this meeting was to discuss my OCR complaints. What she stated in the Feb 16, 2005 letters was that she was trying to discuss my grievances.

From:　　　Imelda Martinez
To:　　　　Frankie Monroe
Date:　　　Mon, Feb 21, 2005 10:44 AM
Subject:　　Re: No Further Contact

I'll respect your wishes. However, I never indicated that the meeting was regarding your OCR complaint.
Imelda

Imelda Martinez
Legal Services
IMMartinez1@CCISD.us
(361) 886-9067

>>> Frankie Monroe 2/21/2005 10:34:52 AM >>>
February 21, 2005

Ms. Imelda Martinez
801 Leopard Street
Corpus Christi, TX. 78404

Attention Ms. Martinez,

After consulting with legal counsel I have been advised not to meet with you regarding the matter that I
filed with EEOC against Corpus Christi Independent School District.

At this time please refrain from contacting me via e-mail, phone, letter or personally regarding this matter
until we have dealt with all legal parameters being covered. Perhaps at a later date we will be able to meet
to bring resolution to this matter.

Sincerely,

Frankie J. Monroe

CC:　　　　Jesus Chavez; Monica Salinas

Exhibit 39

On February 23, 2005 it was announced that Dr. Jesus Chavez didn't get the position of Superintendent of Fort Worth ISD that he had secretly applied for.

On February 24, 2005 I received a call from Dr. Chavez's secretary informing me that Dr. Chavez would like to set up a time to meet. This was the first contact Dr. Chavez initiated personally with me since 2002. I had sent him e-mails repeatedly over the years concerning my grievances and never gotten a response. Whenever I complained about my concerns to other people in authority I would send a carbon copy to him but nothing ever happened. I feel after he didn't get the position in Fort Worth he decided I could be a threat to his career and then he decided to contact me.

Ms. Mary Russell the teacher from next door came to deliver the message. I wanted to document this attempted contact after requesting no further contact by the district so I sent an e-mail to his secretary.

From:	Frankie Monroe
To:	Chavez, Jesus
Date:	Thu, Feb 24, 2005 11:08 AM
Subject:	Concerning Meeting

Dr. Chavez,

Would you please have your secretary provide me with a number to reach you in reference to meeting you requested.

Thank You

Exhibit 40

On March 2, 2005 I had gone to run copies for my class., when I arrived back to class Ms. Russell came to my room to tell me that Dr. Chavez himself had called. She told him I was not in my room. If there was a message he wanted to leave she would be happy to give it to me. She stated he told her that was okay. I wanted to document this attempt with an e-mail.

On March 9, 2005 I received a response to letter I sent on February 16, 2005 from EEOC Enforcement Supervisor, Mr. Guillermo Zamora. He wanted to explain policies and procedures to me and assure me that everything was being done to the letter of the law.

From: Frankie Monroe
To: Chavez, Jesus
Date: Wed, Mar 2, 2005 8:08 AM
Subject: Meeting

Good Morning Dr. Chavez,

As I indicated in a previous letter to Ms. Imelda Martinez the school attorney as well as sent a carbon copy to you, I had been instructed by legal counsel not to have any further contact concerning the charges of discrimination that I had filed against the district.

I did receive the message from your secretary Ms. Gonzales, at around 3:55 p.m. on 2/28/05 asking that I contact you to either call you or set up a meeting time to discuss this issue.

I contacted my legal counsel to see if I should meet with you and they advised me not to unless I had legal representation present. My legal counsel is out of town handling another case at this time but as soon as they are available I will be happy to sit down and discuss this matter with legal representation present.

Have A Good Day!

U.S. EQUAL EMPLOYMENT OPPORTUNITY COMMISSION
San Antonio District Office

5410 Fredericksburg Road, Suite 200
San Antonio, TX 78229-3555
(210) 281-7600
TTY (210) 281-7610
FAX (210) 281-7606

Frankie J. Monroe

Re: Charge No.: 360-2005-00072
    Respondent: Corpus Christi I.S.D.

Dear Ms. Monroe:

This is to acknowledge receipt of your February 16, 2005, letter addressed to our District Director, Mr. Pedro Esquivel.

The intent of this letter is not to dispute the facts that you provided in your letter of February 16, 2005, but to reassure you that the investigation of your charge will be conducted in accordance with Commission policies and procedures and that all the issues will be properly addressed.

Soon after a charge is filed, both parties are invited to participate in Mediation in an attempt to resolve the charge quickly. In order for a charge to go through Mediation both parties must agree to participate. As you are aware CCISD declined to participate in Mediation and thus the file was assigned to an Investigative Unit in Enforcement. We received an initial response to your charge from CCISD on November 11, 2004. Following a review of the information provided by CCISD, Ms. Jimenez requested additional information on February 7, 2005. That information will be reviewed upon receipt and we will provide you with a summary of the evidence at that point. While we realize your charge was actually received in our office in October 2004, the process sometimes takes several months due to the details included. The information you provided with respect to your grievance filed with CCISD will be made part of your file. The form from CCISD declining mediation is part of the investigative file and not disclosable during the investigation.

Let me assure you that I will closely monitor the processing of your charge while it is being investigated. Ms. Jimenez will remain as the Investigator assigned to your charge as it is the Commission's practice not to reassign charges at the request of the Charging Party or the Respondent in question. I can be reached at 210/281-7644.

Sincerely,

Guillermo Zamora
Enforcement Supervisor

3.9.05
Date

202

Exhibit 41

On May 9, 2005 I received a letter from EEOC. I was finally able to secure an Attorney Mr. Charles Smith who had requested that EEOC provide information on the status of my case.

Ms Jimenez out-and-out lied. She stated she had sent information to me on her findings, which was a lie. She stated that I had not wanted to be considered for an elementary position on October 6, 2004. I showed you in a letter of interest I sent to personnel stating that I wanted to be considered for all level assistant principal positions.

Until my attorney requested this information I had no idea EEOC had even visited the district on March 30, 2005. It would have been nice to have had a face-to-face meeting with them. She stated that paper screenings were conducted in August 11, 2004. In the paperwork submitted to my attorney by the district's attorney to get my lawsuit dismissed they state that the only position I could claim was June 4, 2004.

After reading this report you could almost assume Ms. Jimenez was employed by Corpus Christi ISD rather than EEOC, the way she defended them.

Mr. Smith wanted me to rebuttal each thing I didn't agree with and submit it to him so he could catch-up on what was happening in my case. You better believe I gave him a complete summary of things happening up to the point I hired him.

I was so upset by the time I finished reading these lies I wanted to contact the media. I had already tried to talk to our local media, in person and by the U.S. Postal Service, but gotten no response at all so I e-mailed John Stossel at ABC news and The Houston Chronicle hoping they would respond to my plight. Nothing ever came of that either.

U.S. EQUAL EMPLOYMENT OPPORTUNITY COMMISSION
San Antonio District Office

5410 Fredericksburg Road, Suite 200
San Antonio, TX 78229-3555
(210) 281-7600
TTY (210) 281-7610
FAX (210) 281-7606

Charles C. Smith
Attorney at Law
615 N. Upper Broadway, Ste. 510
Corpus Christi, Texas 78477

Re: Charge No.: 360-2005-00072
    Respondent: Corpus Christi Independent School District (CCISD)

Dear Mr. Smith:

This is in response to your letter dated May 5, 2005, which was received in our office
on May 9, 2005. The following is the status on the above cited charge of discrimination.

We have gathered information from CCISD to address the issues raised by your client,
Frankie Monroe. Prior to your being retained to represent her, we had mailed a letter to
Ms. Monroe which summarized the evidence we have obtained. Ms. Monroe was also
informed that any vacancies that occurred more than 300 days from the filing date were
not timely and could not be investigated. An on site visit to CCISD was also conducted
on March 30, 2005, to review other files and documents. The on site investigation
revealed the following:

Records show that Ms. Monroe applied for Assistant Principal - All Levels on April 8,
2004, her application was paper screened and it was considered complete. Candidate
regardless of their race or age whose application file was incomplete were not
considered for further paper screening.

Records show that for the April 8, 2004, vacancies, R did not conduct paper screening
or interviews, and the posting for Assistant Principal - All Levels was re-advertised on
May 28, 2004.

Respondent had more than 100 applications for Assistant Principal - All Levels for eight
to nine vacancies. All the applications were paper screened by a 45-year old employee
in the Office of Secondary Certified Personnel. On August 11, 2004, the applications
for Assistant Principals were then screened by two to three principals to establish the
paper screening committee. The committee then scored the applications and based on
the total scores the applicants were then ranked from the highest to the lowest. The
eight to ten highest ranked candidates would be the first to be recommended for
interviews.

Records show that on the Respondent's Paper Screening Result Form for Secondary
Assistant Principal dated August 11, 2004, Ms. Monroe ranked #36 out of 38
candidates. On the Paper Screening Rating Results Form for All Levels- Assistant

Principal dated August 12, 2004, Ms, Monroe was ranked #65 out of 70 candidates.

There were also some candidates who ranked higher than Ms. Monroe, regardless of their age or race, were also not interviewed or selected for Assistant Principals.

Paper Screening Rating Results Form for Elementary Assistant Principal, dated October 6, 2004, did not include Ms. Monroe because she did not want to be considered for Elementary Assistant Principal. Ms. Monroe only wanted to be considered for Secondary Assistant Principal. The evidence clearly indicated that Blacks, non-Blacks, and candidates in the protected and non protected age group have been selected for Assistant Principals.

The information obtained shows that on July 15, 2004, Ms. Monroe informed Michael Briones, Director of Certified Personnel, that she planned to contact EEOC due to unfair hiring practices. Mr. Briones tried to explain to Ms. Monroe that he did not make the selections on who would be interviewed or selected and offered her a packet on Guidelines for Selection of Assistant Principal so she would be informed of the process.

After the filing of the charge of discrimination Superintendent Chavez and Respondent's attorney have tried to work with Ms. Monroe but she has refused.

You may submit a written rebuttal letter to the above summary or provide me with additional documentation to further support Ms. Monroe's allegations to me by May 23, 2005.

If you have any questions, you may call me at 210-281-7663.

Sincerely,

Mary Esther Jimenez
Federal Investigator

5/10/05
Date

May 14, 2005

Mr. Smith I am going to attempt to go through this letter step by step. It is apparent once again that Mrs. Jimenez is sleeping on the job and just drawing a paycheck.

The only two correspondences I received from EEOC after my initial filing and CCISD refusal to mediate was in response to a letter I wrote Mr. Pedro Esquivel, the EEOC Director, out of San Antonio, on February 1, 2005 and February 9, 2005.

Mr. Guillermo Zamora, whom I had been told by Mr. Thomas price, was Ms. Jimenez's immediate supervisor, responded to both letters. In the letter I wrote on February 9, 2005 it stated that they had received my letter on February 14, 2005. I had requested another investigator after a conversation that I had had with Mary J. Jimenez, the investigator that had been assigned to my case.

After talking with her I realized that she did not have my best interest at heart. Based on her conversation and the tone she took with me it appeared that she had already made up her mind that what the district had said was good enough and she did not need to pursue the matter any further. She had never talked to me before I initiated contact. In this same letter I requested a copy of the response the district had sent them in reference to my charges of discrimination. She proceeded to tell me that could not send me everything that the district had sent her. I responded by telling her that I only want the letter not everything else. I also offered to pay for the copying fee of that letter if she wanted me too.

After denying any charges of derelict of duty on Mrs. Jimenez's behalf, I was sent a copy of the response from the district. In the next letter I received from Mr. Zamora he stated that he could not send me any information concerning the investigation. I thought this was strange because he had already provided me the letter from the school district. I am almost positive that if I had not initiated contact nothing further would have been done with my case.

In her letter to you Ms. Jimenez stated that they had gathered information from CCISD to address the issues raised by me. She stated that prior to you being retained I was mailed a letter summarizing the evidence that they

206

obtained. The only letter I received was a letter that I requested from EEOC in January 2005 by phone from Ms. Jimenez. I wanted to know what CCISD had sent them in response to my charges. I had not been contacted by EEOC concerning anything that had transpired between the district and them since October 6, 2004 when I was told that the district had declined mediation and they would immediately start investigating within 5 days from the post date of that letter.

For some strange reason this woman has gotten stuck in a time warp. She keeps harping on this 300 day filing date and that my claims could not be investigated because I had passed the deadline. I have repeatedly told her by phone and in writing that what I had written was just a synopsis of what had been going on over time to solidify my claims of discrimination. In the response from the district it stated that they denied any charges during the period of November 6, 2000 through June 4, 2004. It stated that I had applied for sixteen positions of which nine positions I did not meet the job description requirements. If Mrs. Jimenez had noted the time line of my charges was from November 6, 2000 to at least September 7, 2004 she would have been able to tell that the district was manipulating the data. I did not contact the district until July 15, 2004. Putting the cut off date at June 4, 2004 they are able to deny discrimination. What happened from July 15, 2004 - September 7, 2004? Why didn't the district address this time frame?

It was stated in that response that " The selection process for professional staff in CCISD requires that the Office of Secondary Certified Personnel review and screen all timely submitted applications for compliance with the minimal requirements established by the job position. Principal and assistant principal applicants are then scored by a committee according to years of experience, training, performance, certifications etc.

Well if this selection process included years of experience, training and performance. How was a 26-year-old Hispanic woman that had 2 1/2 years of teaching experience hired as an assistant principal? How did she score hirer than I did and not only get interviewed several times but get hired as and assistant principal at a middle school in September?

Mrs. Jimenez claims that an on-site visit was conducted on March 30, 2005 to the district to review other files and documents. If EEOC took the time to come to town and investigate I feel that I could have been at least notified by them that this was their intention especially since I had filed the charges. I realize that they didn't have to contact me, but I feel that as a courtesy they could have at least made me feel they were concerned.

In going through this letter it is obvious that Ms. Jimenez has taken information that the district sent her on November 16, 2004 and pieced it together to respond to your letter.

Mrs. Jimenez states in her letter to you that" Records show that Ms. Monroe applied for Assistant Principal - All levels on April 8, 2004, Her application was paper screened and it was considered complete. She failed to mention that in my letter of interest I had requested to be considered for all level assistant principal positions for the 2004-05 school year. That covered any positions that were offered for the entire school year.

She goes on the say that candidate regardless of their race or age whose application file was incomplete were not considered for further paper screening. This does not make since. She already stated that I had completed my application.

Ms. Jimenez jumped from April 8, 2004 to August 11, 2004 she proceed to quote some type of paper screening results for secondary assistant principal dated August 11, 2004. She neglected to include the one interview that I was granted because I had requested to be considered by the principal on my campus. If I ranked so low why was I granted that one interview. Based on what Ms. Jimenez is implying I was not good enough to be given any interviews.

She then jumps back to July 15, 2004, in a letter that I e-mailed Mr. Michael Briones, director of certified personnel. I had also cced Dr. Jesus Chavez the superintendent. At this point it is obvious that she is reviewing the information that I supplied her in my defense and she decided to use it against me. If she had read this information with an open mind she would have been able to see that I wrote this e-mail out of frustration because another year had passed and I was once again being looked over. Evidently my threats went unheeded because I was not called in or offered an interview after July 15, 2004. I did not file charges until October 2004 giving the district ample opportunity to interview me for some of the many positions they had available during that time frame. A young lady, 26 years old, with 2 1/2 years of teaching experience, that worked on the campus that I taught on was not only interviewed several times but hired as an assistant principal. She informed me that she had applied in early August and had gotten interviewed by the beginning of September. I had applied in April.

Ms. Jimenez stated that after the filing of the charge of discrimination Superintendent Chavez and the school district attorney had tried to work with me but I had refused. From the initial charge that I filed with EEOC in October 2004 and the district refusal to mediate I was never contacted by the district.

I attempted to file a total of 3 grievances between October and December with the school board and was repeatedly told that I had not filed it correctly. When I would resubmit I was told that I had not filed in a timely manner so the grievance could not be considered. When it became apparent that I was not going to give up I was contacted by e-mail on December 16, 2004 by the school district attorney Ms. Imelda Martinez to meet with her. My mother and aunt had passed away on December 15, 2004 and I was not available to respond to that e-mail until I returned from Indiana on January 3, 2005. I checked my e-mail over the web-mail and setup a meeting at that time with Mrs. Martinez. I did meet with Mrs. Martinez on January 6, 2005. I have a summary of that meeting and what was discussed.

During that meeting Mrs. Martinez did promise to assist me in getting an administrative position as soon as possible, but I did not hear from Mrs. Martinez again until I had a phone conversation with Monica Salinas on February 3, 2005. Ms. Monica Salinas the secretary in the legal department, had e-mailed me around 11:15 and asked me to contact her as soon as possible concerning the February 1, 2005 grievance that I had filed.

I contacted her during my lunch hour by phone. She informed me that once again I had filled the grievance report form out incorrectly. In the last grievance that I filed I informed the district of a conversation that I had had with EEOC. I reported that I had spoke with an EEOC investigator and discovered that CCISD had refused mediation request that I had agreed to. It was stated that the district was refusing mediation because after investigating my claim it was decided that I was not qualified for any of the positions that I applied for due to lack of experience. I told Ms. Salinas that I was well aware of all the teachers that were hired in the district. Many of them were hired from teaching positions. I told her I had Mid-management and Superintendent Certifications as well as nearly 20 years of educational experience. I was also a doctoral student enrolled at Texas A & M in educational administration.

Ms. Salinas stated that I could not file a grievance against the district. It had to be against a specific person. In my initial filing I listed (CCISD, Dr. Jesus Chavez, and Mr. Michael Briones) as the respondent. I told her that I had selected a single person. When I re-submitted my grievance on January 13, 2005 I informed her that I had put Dr. Jesus Chavez down as the respondent.

She gave all the grievance dates that she had in front of her and there was no grievance date for January 13, 2005 with Dr. Jesus Chavez Superintendent named as the respondent on it.

I think that the reason this grievance was not processed was because Dr. Chavez was seeking employment with the Fortworth Independent School district and could not have this type of claim filed against him personally. Especially when I had evidence of the charges filed against him. It would imply that he condoned discrimination and was breaking the Federal Law and could possibly have federal funding pulled.

I told her that after I had met with Mrs. Martinez, the CCISD school attorney on January 6, 2005, I turned in my grievance form on January 13, 2005. She repeated that she did not see that particular grievance form but that she would go and look for it. At that point I told her if she could not find the copy I would send her a copy of mine which had the date stamped on it.

Ms. Salinas proceeded to tell me the procedures that had to be followed when filing a grievance. If the grievance were filed against a school employee, for instance Mr. Michael Briones, one of my initial respondents listed on my grievance, I would need to have a meeting with him and his superior Mr. Noriega. If I were still not happy with the decisions that were reached then I would go to step two, meet with Dr. Chavez, the Superintendent, concerning the matter. But If I were filing charges against the Superintendent I would skip all other stages and go to stage 3 meeting with the school board.

I informed her that I had only talked personally with Mrs. Imelda Martinez; the school attorney concerning this matter and had not been offered any other meetings. At that point we ended the conversation with me assuring her that I would get her a copy of the Grievance Report that I filed on

January 13, 2005. I provided that copy in the form of another grievance on February 10, 2005.

I researched information on Texas State Laws concerning grievances I discovered that, any discussion of grievances immediately implicates both a provision of the Texas Constitution and Section 617.005 of the Government Code, which, allows employees to present grievances. The constitutional provision is **Article I, section 27**, which in one form or another has been part of the Texas Constitution since 1845. It provides that **"the citizens shall have the right, in a peaceable manner, to apply to those invested with the powers of government for redress of grievances, by petition, address, or remonstrance,"**

I also discovered that in 1984, Attorney General Jim Mattox was asked about the scope of employee grievances under Texas Law. Specifically, the attorney general was asked to outline " conditions of work" which was the proper subject of a grievance. Mattox opined that the term **"conditions of work" could not be construed to "restrict, limit, narrow, or exclude" any aspect of the employment relationship from the grievance process.** Mattox concluded his opinion { Att'y. Gen. Op. JM -I77}: the term " **conditions of work" should be construed broadly to include any areas of wages, hours, or conditions of employment, and any other matter which is appropriate for communications from employees to employer concerning an aspect of their relationship.**

After speaking to Monica I researched CCISD employee grievance policy it states there is a standard procedure that must be followed in filing a grievance with the district which is as follows:

      A. Grievant/Respondent - Informal Conference with Supervisor
      B. Grievance -Must be filed within 30 days in writing on District's Grievance form Superintendent notifies Respondent and appoints hearing officer
      C. Level One - Hearing held within 5 working days of notice of hearing Decision rendered within 5 working days of hearing
      D. Appeal - May appeal within 5 Working days after receipt of decision

E. Level Two - Hearing scheduled within 5 working days of notice of hearing. Hearing must take place within 5 working days of the date of the notice. Decision rendered within 5 working days of hearing.

F. Appeal - May appeal to the board within 10 working days after receipt of the Level Two decision

G. Level Three - This is only a review of the Level Two decision. Board schedules hearing during calendaring session at next board meeting

H. Board may communicate its decision orally at the conclusion of the hearing or in writing to the parties within 15 days following the hearing

I. Decision of the Board is final

I also researched the case, Thomas *E. Malone v. Houston ISD,* heard by the Commissioner of Education in the State of Texas. In that case it sited Art. I Section 27 of the Texas Constitution in a similar case on the duty of the person in a position of authority under art. 5154c, Section 6Beverly v. City of Dallas, 292 S. W.2d 172(Tex. Civ. App. El Paso 1956, writ ref'd n.r.e.), The Court held that "The presentation of a grievance is in effect a unilateral procedure. " Further, the Attorney General wrote that although "the right to present grievances necessarily implies that someone in a position of authority is required to hear them," such an authority "is under no legal compulsion to take any action to rectify them." Op. Tex. Att'y Gen. No. H-422(1974).

It is evident that Dr. Chavez intentionally violated school board policy in reference to the grievance that I filed on January 13, 2005. I was not contacted concerning this particular grievance until February 7, 2005, which was out of compliance with the district's guidelines. My grievance was not addressed in a timely manner and therefore I was denied due process in accordance to their own district policy.

After the conversation I had with Monica I received an e-mail from Mrs. Martinez on February 7, 2005 requesting that I meet with her at my earliest convenience. I responded back telling her that I had evening classes at the University at 4:30 and I had agreed to meet with her the following day.

From the previous letter that I had received from Mrs. Martinez she implied that she was going to meet me on campus. When she realized that there was the possibility of Dr. Dorsey being included in this meeting she decided against meeting on campus. The other possibility is that this was an obvious ploy to create a paper trail in an attempt to make it seem that I had not been cooperative. She had no intention of meeting with me.

After these shenanigans I contacted Mrs. Martinez on Monday February 21, 2005 via- e-mail with the following letter.

>>> Frankie Monroe 2/21/2005 10:34:52 AM >>>
February 21, 2005

Ms. Imelda Martinez
801 Leopard Street
Corpus Christi, TX. 78404

Attention Ms. Martinez,

After consulting with legal counsel I have been advised not to meet with you regarding the matter that I filed with EEOC against Corpus Christi Independent School District.

At this time please refrain from contacting me via e-mail, phone, letter or personally regarding this matter until we have dealt with all legal parameters being covered. Perhaps at a later date we will be able to meet to bring resolution to this matter.

Sincerely,

Frankie J. Monroe

She e-mailed me back with the following response.

Date: Mon, 21 Feb 2005 10:44:23 -0600
From: "Imelda Martinez" <IMMartinez1@ccisd.us>
To: "Frankie Monroe" <FJMonroe@ccisd.us>

On February 8.2005 before meeting with her I contacted legal counsel and was advised not to meet unless I had my lawyer present. I e-mailed her a little after 4:00 and told her I could not meet with her.

On Monday February 14, 2005 Mrs. Martinez contacted me again stating that she wanted to reschedule the meeting from the previous week. She stated that she would be willing to meet on campus, if that was more convenient. She just wanted me to let her know the date. I did not respond.

When I talked to Ms. Jimenez she stated that she had sent a letter to CCISD requesting additional information and they had 30 days to respond.

On February 16, 2005 Dr. Dorsey came to my class and informed me that she had gotten this strange letter from Imelda Martinez. It was a letter that had been addressed to me but sent to her via e-mail. She was not sure what was going on but she would forward the letter to me. In the letter Ms. Martinez stated that she had attempted to contact me via e-mail to schedule a date and time to meet and discuss my grievances for the last four months. She did not attempt to set these meetings up until she realized I had been bringing these grievances into the office and getting them stamped. She then proceeded to try and force me to meet.

She set up a meeting for February 18, 2005 at 8:30 a.m. and told Dr. Dorsey to get me a sub. Dr. Dorsey told me that she had talked to Mrs. Martinez and asked how long would the meeting last and if she needed to be present. She was told it would last about 30 minutes and she did not need to be present. I requested that Dr. Dorsey attend the meeting so that I had a witness to the conversation.

On February 18 at 8:30 I prepared to meet with Mrs. Martinez along with Dr. Dorsey. At 8:45 Dr. Dorsey came to my class and asked if I had heard from Ms. Martinez. I told her I had not heard from her. I told her maybe something came up and she could not meet after all. Around 11:34 I received an e-mail from Ms. Martinez. She stated that she was sorry for the confusion regarding the location of our meeting. She intended for the meeting to take place in her office. That was why she had requested a substitute teacher to cover my classes until I returned to Ray. She wanted me to let her know when I could reschedule the meeting next week.

CC: "Jesus Chavez" <JHChavez@ccisd.us>, "Monica Salinas"
        <MASalinas@ccisd.us>
Subject: Re: No Further Contact
I'll respect your wishes. However, I never indicated that the meeting
was regarding your OCR complaint.
Imelda

I did not know what she was referring to when she stated she wanted to meet
regarding OCR. I now know it was EEOC. She had told me once before that
she had worked with EEOC and was not worried about them when it came
to charges being filed claiming discrimination.

In the letter on February 16 she stated that she wanted to discuss the
grievances I had filed for the last four months. She was now was writing me
to tell me she wanted to discuss my EEOC Charges.

Given that the district had already declined mediation I don't understand
why Ms. Jimenez was now trying to contact them and get them to respond
again. During our phone conversation she kept telling me that she was
waiting for the letter from mediation before she could proceeded with her
investigation. I told her that the district had decline mediation in October
2004. And I had been told that an immediate investigation was going to take
place within five days. Based on what she was telling me now no
investigation had taken place and we were already in February.

However Mrs. Martinez never contacted me again after February 21, 2005.

On February 23, 2005 it was announced that Dr. Jesus Chavez did not get
the position of Superintendent of Fortworth ISD. On February 24 I received
a call from Dr. Jesus Chavez's secretary informing me that Dr. Chavez
would like to set up a time to meet. This was the first contact Dr. Chavez
initiated personally.

I had sent e-mails to him repeatedly over the years concerning my
grievances and never gotten a response. Whenever I complained about my
concerns to other people in authority I cc him but nothing every happened. I
feel that after he did not get the position he decided that I could be a threat to
his career and then he decided to contact me. I didn't have the number on

hand so I e-mailed him and ask If he could have his secretary provide me with the number to reach him.

Date: Thu, 24 Feb 2005 11:08:32 -0600
From: "Frankie Monroe" <FJMonroe@ccisd.us>
To: "Jesus Chavez" <JHChavez@ccisd.us>
Subject: Concerning Meeting
Dr. Chavez,

Would you please have your secretary provide me with a number to reach? you in reference to meeting you requested.

Thank You

On February 28, 2005 Mrs. Mary Russell the teacher next door brought me a telephone number where I could reach Dr. Chavez. I did not respond that day.

On Wednesday March 2, 2005, I e-mailed Dr. Chavez and informed him that I could not meet with him on the advise of legal counsel.

Date: Wed, 02 Mar 2005 08:08:04 -0600
From: "Frankie Monroe" <FJMonroe@ccisd.us>
To: "Jesus Chavez" <JHChavez@ccisd.us>
Subject: Meeting
Good Morning Dr. Chavez,

As I indicated in a previous letter to Ms. Imelda Martinez the school attorney as well as sent a carbon copy to you, I had been instructed by legal counsel not to have any further contact concerning the charges of discrimination that I had filed against the district.

I did receive the message from your secretary Ms. Gonzales, at around 3:55 p.m. on 2/28/05 asking that I contact you to either call you or set up a meeting time to discuss this issue.

I contacted my legal counsel to see if I should meet with you and they advised me not to unless I had legal representation present. My legal counsel is out of town handling another case at this time but as soon as they are available I will be happy to sit down and discuss this matter with legal representation present.

I am not sure what Mrs. Jimenez was trying to accomplish with this hodgepodge of information. I think it is obvious what I have been stating all along. She did not have my best interest at heart. She may be retaliating against me for reporting her to her superiors. I requested an Investigation be conducted by Washington D.C. EEOC but they never responded. Perhaps I should be allowed to take this public.

Mr. Smith I hope this helps you defend my case.

Thank you so much for your time.

Sincerely,

Frankie J. Monroe

SENDER: COMPLETE THIS SECTION

■ Complete items 1, 2, and 3. Also complete item 4 if Restricted Delivery is desired.
■ Print your name and address on the reverse so that we can return the card to you.
■ Attach this card to the back of the mailpiece, or on the front if space permits.

1. Article Addressed to:

Corpus Christi, Caller times
820 N. Lower Broadway
Corpus Christi, TX. 78401

COMPLETE THIS SECTION ON DELIVERY

A. Signature

X _____ ☐ Agent
                        ☐ Addressee

B. Received by (Printed Name)   C. Date of Delivery
                                  11/17/04

D. Is delivery address different from item 1? ☐ Yes
   If YES, enter delivery address below: ☐ No

3. Service Type
   ☒ Certified Mail   ☐ Express Mail
   ☐ Registered   ☐ Return Receipt for Merchandise
   ☐ Insured Mail   ☐ C.O.D.

4. Restricted Delivery? (Extra Fee)   ☐ Yes

2. Article Number
   (Transfer from   7004 2510 0002 9359 1477

PS Form 3811, February 2004   Domestic Return Receipt   102595-02-M-1540

SENDER: COMPLETE THIS SECTION

■ Complete items 1, 2, and 3. Also complete item 4 if Restricted Delivery is desired.
■ Print your name and address on the reverse so that we can return the card to you.
■ Attach this card to the back of the mailpiece, or on the front if space permits.

1. Article Addressed to:

KRIS TV
409 S. Staples St.
Corpus Christi, TX 78401

COMPLETE THIS SECTION ON DELIVERY

A. Signature

X _____ ☐ Agent
                        ☐ Addressee

B. Received by (Printed Name)   C. Date of Delivery
Daniella Zuniga   11/12/04

D. Is delivery address different from item 1? ☐ Yes
   If YES, enter delivery address below: ☐ No

3. Service Type
   ☒ Certified Mail   ☐ Express Mail
   ☐ Registered   ☐ Return Receipt for Merchandise
   ☐ Insured Mail   ☐ C.O.D.

4. Restricted Delivery? (Extra Fee)   ☐ Yes

2. Article Number
   (Transfer from se   7004 2510 0002 9359 1460

PS Form 3811, February 2004   Domestic Return Receipt   102595-02-M-1540

218

From: "Eddie Moore"
To: <JohnStossel@abcnews.com>
Sent: Friday, June 03, 2005 9:15 PM
Subject: Local Scandal in Corpus Christi ISD

If your paper received a letter like the letter that I am going to post below woul
it at least peek your curiosity enough to investigate?

May 17, 2005

To Whom I May Concern:

Scandal, conspiracy, cover-up, discriminatory practices, deceit, injustice, immoral
degradation, turpitude, distrust, lack of integrity.

Should these words be synonymous with Corpus Christi ISD? Well they are.

I feel Corpus Christi ISD has indulged in each one of these practices and gotten
away with it up until now. I have decided to let the chips fall where they may.

I have taught in CCISD for almost 15 years. I have knowingly been discriminated
against and Dr. Jesus Chavez, Superintendent, as well as members of the school
board have known about it and done nothing.

I waited until the end of the school year because I did not want this to interfere
with my students and their education. Read my story and see if you feel I am
justified in my claims.

My name is Frankie J. Monroe. You can contact me at

Sincerely,

Frankie J. Monroe

I sent this letter along with a story about the school district that I work in to
our local newspaper as well as the local TV stations ABC & NBC. Not one local news
media contacted me.

Did you know that black is the new invisible color in Corpus Christi, TX? Perhaps
it is because I am a black upstanding citizen. If I were an uneducated black
criminal type I would be all over the news. But because I am complaining about a
serious issue I am ignored.

I e-mailed the Houston Chronicle to see If they would write my story. It is a shame
that I had to go to another city to see if I could get justice.

I have a strange feeling if you tell my story the locals will become interested in
something that is occurring in their backyards.

If you are interested please e-mail me at  I will

Eddie Moore

Thank you for contacting The Houston Chronicle. Your message has been forwarded to our News Department.

Sincerely,
The Houston Chronicle.

-----Original Message-----
From: Eddie Moore ███████████████
Posted At: Friday, June 03, 2005 8:50 PM
Posted To: HCI / Online / Register
Conversation: Local Scandal of Corpus Christi ISD
Subject: Local Scandal of Corpus Christi ISD

If your paper received a letter like the letter that I am going to post below would it at least peek your curiosity enough to investigate?

May 17, 2005

To Whom I May Concern:

Scandal, conspiracy, cover-up, discriminatory practices, deceit, injustice, immoral, degradation, turpitude, distrust, lack of integrity. Should these words be synonymous with Corpus Christi ISD? Well they are. I feel Corpus Christi ISD has indulged in each one of these practices and gotten away with it up until now. I have decided to let the chips fall where they may.

I have taught in CCISD for almost 15 years. I have knowingly been discriminated against and Dr. Jesus Chavez, Superintendent, as well as members of the school board have known about it and done nothing. I waited until the end of the school year because I did not want this to interfer with my students and their education. Read my story and see if you feel I am justified in my claims.

My name is Frankie J. Monroe. You can contact me at ███████████

Sincerely,

Frankie J. Monroe

I sent this letter along with a story about the school district that I work in to our local newspaper as well as the local

6/7/05

220

TV stations. Not one local news media contacted me. Did you know that black is the new invisible color in Corpus Christi, TX? Perhaps it is because I am a black upstanding citizen. If I were an uneducated black criminal type I would be all over the news. But because I am complaining about a serious issue I am ignored.

Maybe I can get you to write my story. It is a shame that I have to go to another city to see if I can get justice.

I have a strange feeling that If you write this story the locals will become interested in something that is occurring in their backyards.

If you are interested please e-mail me at ███████████. I will be happy to send the story to you.

This e-mail message is intended only for the personal use of the recipient(s) named above. If you are not an intended recipient, you may not review, copy or distribute this message.

If you have received this communication in error, please notify the Houston Chronicle Postmaster (postmaster@chron.com) immediately by e-mail and delete the original message.

Exhibit 42

My attorney requested my case be closed by EEOC because he felt my case hadn't been adequately investigated. The district felt because the case was closed nothing had been discovered. My attorney contacted Corpus Christi ISD and asked that a meeting be set up to discuss my claims with Dr. Chavez. It was originally scheduled for May 8, 2005. He was contacted and told Dr. Chavez wouldn't be available at that time and a June 15, 2005 meeting was scheduled. (Documentation of that meeting)

U.S. Department of Justice

Civil Rights Division

NOTICE OF RIGHT TO SUE
WITHIN 90 DAYS

CERTIFIED MAIL
5059 2486

950 Pennsylvania Avenue, N.W.
Karen Ferguson, EMP, PHB, Room 4239
Washington, DC 20530

Ms. Frankie J. Monroe
c/o Charles C. Smith, Esquire
615 N. Upper Broadway
Ste. 510
Corpus Christi, TX 78477

June 17, 2005

RECEIVED

JUL 1 1 2005

OFFICE OF SUPERINTENDENT
CORPUS CHRISTI ISD

Re: EEOC Charge Against Corpus Christi Independent School Dist.
     No. 360200500072

Dear Ms. Monroe:

Because you filed the above charge with the Equal Employment
Opportunity Commission, and more than 180 days have elapsed since
the date the Commission assumed jurisdiction over the charge, and no
suit based thereon has been filed by this Department, and because
you through your attorney have specifically requested this Notice,
you are hereby notified that you have the right to institute a civil
action under Title VII of the Civil Rights Act of 1964, as amended,
42 U.S.C. 2000e, et seq., against the above-named respondent.

If you choose to commence a civil action, such suit must be
filed in the appropriate Court within 90 days of your receipt of
this Notice.

This Notice should not be taken to mean that the Department of
Justice has made a judgment as to whether or not your case is
meritorious.

Sincerely,

Brad Schlozman
Acting Assistant Attorney General
Civil Rights Division

by *Karen L. Ferguson*

Karen L. Ferguson
Supervisory Civil Rights Analyst
Employment Litigation Section

cc: San Antonio District Office, EEOC
     Corpus Christi Independent School Dist.

RECEIVED

JUL 1 3 2005

CCISD OFFICE OF
LEGAL SERVICES

EEOC FORM 131 (5/01)   **U. S. Equal Employment Opportunity Commission**

	PERSON FILING CHARGE
Randall L. Meredith C.C.I.S.D. Staff Attorney Office of Legal Services **CORPUS CHRISTI I.S.D.** P.O. Box 110 Corpus Christi, TX 78403-0110 RECEIVED OCT 2 0 2004 CORPUS OFFICE OF LEGAL SERVICES	**Frankie J. Monroe**
	THIS PERSON *(check one or both)* [X] Claims To Be Aggrieved [ ] Is Filing on Behalf of Other(s)
	EEOC CHARGE NO. **360-2005-00072**

NOTICE OF CHARGE OF DISCRIMINATION
(See the enclosed for additional information)

This is notice that a charge of employment discrimination has been filed against your organization under:

[X] Title VII of the Civil Rights Act   [ ] The Americans with Disabilities Act

[X] The Age Discrimination in Employment Act   [ ] The Equal Pay Act

The boxes checked below apply to our handling of this charge:

1. [ ] No action is required by you at this time.

2. [ ] Please call the EEOC Representative listed below concerning the further handling of this charge.

3. [X] Please provide by **19-NOV-04** a statement of your position on the issues covered by this charge, with copies of any supporting documentation to the EEOC Representative listed below. Your response will be placed in the file and considered as we investigate the charge. A prompt response to this request will make it easier to conclude our investigation.

4. [ ] Please respond fully by   to the enclosed request for information and send your response to the EEOC Representative listed below. Your response will be placed in the file and considered as we investigate the charge. A prompt response to this request will make it easier to conclude our investigation.

5. [X] EEOC has a Mediation program that gives parties an opportunity to resolve the issues of a charge without extensive investigation or expenditure of resources. If you would like to participate, please say so on the enclosed form and respond by **02-NOV-04**
to **Katherine S. Perez, ADR Coordinator, at (210) 281-2506**
If you <u>DO NOT</u> wish to try Mediation, you must respond to any request(s) made above by the date(s) specified there.

For further inquiry on this matter, please use the charge number shown above. Your position statement, your response to our request for information, or any inquiry you may have should be directed to:

Rodney R. Klein, **Supervisory Investigator** *EEOC Representative* Telephone: **(210) 281-7621**	**San Antonio District Office** **5410 Fredericksburg Rd** **Suite 200** **San Antonio, TX 78229**

Enclosure(s): [X] Copy of Charge

CIRCUMSTANCES OF ALLEGED DISCRIMINATION

[X] RACE   [ ] COLOR   [ ] SEX   [ ] RELIGION   [ ] NATIONAL ORIGIN   [X] AGE   [ ] DISABILITY   [X] RETALIATION   [ ] OTHER

See enclosed copy of charge of discrimination.

Date	Name / Title of Authorized Official	Signature
Oct 18, 2004	**Pedro Esquivel,** **Director**	

224

EEOC Form 151-B (3/98)

U.S. EQUAL EMPLOYMENT OPPORTUNITY COMMISSION

NOTICE OF RIGHT TO SUE (ISSUED ON REQUEST)

To: Frankie J. Monroe
c/o Charles C. Smith
Attorney at Law
615 N. Upper Broadway, Suite 510
Ccorpus Christi, Texas 78477

From: EEOC
San Antonio District Office
5410 Fredericksburg Rd., Suite 200
San Antonio, Texas 78229

☐ On behalf of person(s) aggrieved whose identity is
CONFIDENTIAL (29 CFR § 1601.7(a))

Charge No.	EEOC Representative	Telephone No.
360-2005-00072	Guillermo Zamora, Supervisor	210-281-7644

(See also the additional information enclosed with this form.)

NOTICE TO THE PERSON AGGRIEVED:

Title VII of the Civil Rights Act of 1964 and/or the Americans with Disabilities Act (ADA): This is your Notice of Right to Sue, issued under Title VII and/or the ADA based on the above-numbered charge. It has been issued at your request. Your lawsuit under Title VII or the ADA must be filed in federal or state court WITHIN 90 DAYS of your receipt of this Notice or your right to sue based on this charge will be lost. (The time limit for filing suit based on a state claim may be different.)

☐ More than 180 days have passed since the filing of this charge.

☐ Less than 180 days have passed since the filing of this charge, but I have determined that it is unlikely that the EEOC will be able to complete its administrative processing within 180 days from the filing of the charge.

☐ The EEOC is terminating its processing of this charge.

☐ The EEOC will continue to process this charge.

Age Discrimination in Employment Act (ADEA): You may sue under the ADEA at any time from 60 days after the charge was filed until 90 days after you receive notice that we have completed action on the charge. In this regard, the paragraph marked below applies to your case:

☒ The EEOC is closing your case. Therefore, your lawsuit under the ADEA must be filed in federal or state court WITHIN 90 DAYS of your receipt of this Notice. Otherwise, your right to sue based on the above-numbered charge will be lost.

☐ The EEOC is continuing its handling of your ADEA case. However, if 60 days have passed since the filing of your charge, you may file suit in federal or state court under the ADEA at this time.

Equal Pay Act (EPA): You already have the right to sue under the EPA (filing an EEOC charge is not required.) EPA suits must be brought in federal or state court within 2 years (3 years for willful violations) of the alleged EPA underpayment. This means that backpay due for any violations that occurred more than 2 years (3 years) before you file suit may not be collectible.

If you file suit based on this charge, please send a copy of your court complaint to this office.

On behalf of the Commission

Pedro Esquivel, District Director

6/3/05
(Date Mailed)

Enclosure(s

cc: **Corpus Christi Independent School District**

June 15, 2005

Documentation of Meeting on 6/15/05 2:00pm

People in attendance
Dr. Jesus Chavez, Superintendent
Ms. Imelda Martinez, (School Attorney)
Frankie J. Monroe, (Complainant)
Mr. Charles Smith (Attorney for Complainant)

The meeting took place in meeting room next to the superintendent's office. Everyone took a seat. Mr. Smith stated that the reason we were meeting was to discuss the charges that I had filed and to see what resolution was being offered to bring closure to this matter.

Dr. Chavez immediately stated that he wanted it to go on record that nothing discussed in meeting in no way was an admission of guilt on his or the districts part. He stated approximately 4 times that he had attempted to meet with me for about five months to discuss the grievances that I had filed but that I had refused to meet. He stated that at the time that I had filed charges with EEOC I had also filed a grievance with the district. This meeting was to discuss the grievances.

Dr. Chavez started by saying that he was surprised that I did not know the hiring procedure. I told him I was well aware of what should be the procedure. He stated that the hiring process had several layers to it. First you had to go through a paper screening. This screening was based on points. These points were based on whether you had completed your application, were all of your credentials and reference completed? How much experience did you have etc.? If you made it through the paper screening then you were put on a list to be interviewed by the principal. For some reason my application was not making the cut to get put on the list. I was always just below or very far from the cut off.

Ms. Martinez asked me why did I continue to apply for an assistant principal position wasn't there any other positions that I was interested in. I proceeded to inform her that had indeed applied for several other positions offered by the district, Principal, Special Education Consultant, Assistant Superintendent, Special Education Director, Director of Human Resource and the list goes on. But of course I would not get those positions because I had not had the three to five years of administration experience that they claimed I needed to qualify. With my Certification in Mid-Management, Superintendency and course work in the doctoral program as well as twenty years of teaching experience did not qualify for any of these positions.

Dr. Chavez interjected by saying a lot of people feel the same way. They had much better credentials than I did and they didn't get hired either. He continued by stating "Frankie

226

think of it this way. I want to be the CEO of Exxon. I apply and don't get it. I apply again and I don't get. I keep applying. Of course I want get it because I don't have the experience."

I responded to Dr. Chavez by saying "And I will never get that position if I am not allowed in on the ground floor to obtain the necessary experience to advance in my career. I proceeded to tell Ms. Martinez this is why I have continuously applied for an assistant principal position to get my foot in the door. This position only requires that you be a teacher in a classroom for at least three years with the necessary credentials. But as you can see for the last 4 years it has not happened." I went on to say that people from other districts had been interviewed and hired as assistant principals. I had worked for the district for nearly 15 years.

Dr. Chavez continued by saying that as a head administrator he had to hire the best qualified for the position and that even if he had to go outside of the district that is what he was obligated to do. I responded by asking the question "Can you explain to me how a 26 year old with 2 1/2 years of teaching experience was hired for an assistant principal position more experienced and better qualified than I was? I got no response from either Dr. Chavez or Mrs. Martinez.

I informed Dr. Chavez and Mrs. Martinez that I had not once gone through the personnel office to get any position after initially being hired. It had always been someone that was familiar with my work ethic that would pull my application from the main office and request that I be assigned to his or her campus.

Dr. Chavez proceeded to tell me what he was willing to do to make this all go away since I had continuously said I wanted to be allowed to at least get an interview. He offered to not require me to go through the paper screening. He would put my name on the list and I could be sent out to the principals to get interviewed.

Mrs. Martinez reiterated what Dr. Chavez said. " Ms Monroe, what Dr. Chavez is saying is that since you have been able to sell yourself to the principals before you could go ahead and do that this time. Now that the paper screening process had been eliminated.

I asked Dr. Chavez why did I have to be boosted up past everyone else. Why couldn't I get an equal shot at being placed on the list based on my own qualifications and merits?

Mr. Smith asked them what if I went through the interviewing process and I still did not get hired then what.

I stated " I will do like I have done for the past 4 years that I have tried for administrative positions, I will return to the classroom and teach."

Ms. Martinez stated that EEOC had come to the district and gone through their hiring process very thoroughly. They had closed the case. She offered to give us a copy of the letter.

Mr. Smith informed her that he had requested that the case be closed he did not need a copy of the letter.

Dr. Chavez stated that he would be happy to show us the interviewing process. Mr. Smith stated that he would like to be shown that process. Dr. Chavez told Mr. Smith that he would inform Mr. Briones and a time next week would be set up to meet.

Everyone shook hands and left the meeting. The time was approximately 2:35.

Exhibit 43

On July 1, 2005 I received a phone message from Ms. Delia McClerran, principal of Wynn Seal middle school. I found the phone call strange because I hadn't applied for this particular position. I told Dr. Chavez in the meeting on June 15, 2005 I didn't want to be given an interview without going through proper procedures because what he was implying to me was I wasn't capable of getting an interview on my own merits and qualifications. He implied I needed special considerations and exceptions had to be made for me. I discussed this position with my attorney and he told me to go for it. For documentation purposes I e-mailed my response to the phone message.

Mail Message

N

Close   Next   Forward   Reply to Sender   Reply All   Move   Delete   Read Later   Properties

Print View

From: Delia McLerran
To: Frankie Monroe
Date: Friday - July 1, 2005 5:15 PM
Subject: Re: Assistant Principal Position

Frankie,

Thank you for the email. If possible, we would like to interview you on Tuesday, July 5th, 2005. The Roy Miller High School committee and the Wynn Seale Academy committee will be interviewing applicants on that day. You will sit with both committees simultaneously (not one first and then the other). The interviews are being held at the Corpus Christi Library in the Board Room on the 2nd floor. If you are able to attend on Tuesday at 2 p.m., please respond via email. Thank you for your interest.

Delia M. McLerran
Principal, Wynn Seale Academy of Fine Arts
Success through body, mind, and spirit
361-886-9359, ext. 105
361-886-9892, fax

email: demclerran@ccisd.us

>>> Frankie Monroe 07/01/05 4:31 PM >>>
Hello Mrs. Mclerran:

My name is Frankie J. Monroe. I decided to e-mail you on the off chance that you might be reading your school e-mail this summer.

I am e-mailing you in reference to a message that was left on my answering machine on 6/29/05 at approximately 4:45 p.m. I attempted to contact you by phone on 6/30/05 at approximately 1:30 pm and also at 5:30 pm when I discovered the message.

When you did not return my call I thought that you may have gotten an early start on your 4th of July break. I just wanted to inform you that I am interested the assistant principal position. I would like to be considered for an interview at your earliest convenience.

Thank you in advance for your consideration.

http://webmail.ccisd.us/servlet/webacc?action=Item.Read&User.context=kt7rs2XpenrfiqcCm5...   7/3/05

Exhibit 44

July 5, 2005 I wrote a letter to Dr. Chavez laying out my demands, which would answer the question he posed in the meeting, "How can we make this all go away?" I used the U.S postal system to mail this letter as well as e-mailed these demands.

July 7, 2005 my attorney sent a letter to Dr. Chavez attempting to resolve my issue of discrimination as well.

FRANKIE MONROE

July 5, 2005

Dr. Jesus Chavez, Superintendent
Corpus Christi Independent School District
801 Leopard Street
Corpus Christi, Texas 78401

    Re: Discrimination Charge

Dear Dr. Chavez:

    As you know, on June 15, 2005, a meeting was held at your office to discuss employment related concerns that I earlier raised in regards to employment opportunities. I indicated, among other things, that I believe that I had been discriminated against as it relates to screening procedures used by the school district. What's more, despite my qualifications, I believe lesser qualified individuals have been selected and I have not received due consideration.

    Previously, I filed a discrimination charge through the Equal Employment Opportunity Commission. Recently, on June 23, 2005, I received a Notice of Right to Sue from the U.S. Department of Justice. Consequently, if the district, through you, is interested in resolving my claim at this level, it is important that an agreement include two components that I will outline below.

    For some time, I have been denied administrative positions for which I believe I was qualified. For example, there have been a number of assistant principal positions that have been available over the past several years. Therefore, a resolution of my discrimination claim would have to include an appointment in an administrative capacity in the main office or the district campuses.

Mail Message

N

Close   Next   Forward   Reply to Sender   Reply All   Move   Delete   Read Later   Properties
    Print View

From: Delia McLerran
To: Frankie Monroe
Date: Friday - July 1, 2005 5:15 PM
Subject: Re: Assistant Principal Position

Frankie,

Thank you for the email. If possible, we would like to interview you on Tuesday, July 5th, 2005. The Roy Miller High School committee and the Wynn Seale Academy committee will be interviewing applicants on that day. You will sit with both committees simultaneously (not one first and then the other). The interviews are being held at the Corpus Christi Library in the Board Room on the 2nd floor. If you are able to attend on Tuesday at 2 p.m., please respond via email. Thank you for your interest.

Delia M. McLerran
Principal, Wynn Seale Academy of Fine Arts
Success through body, mind, and spirit
361-886-9359, ext. 105
361-886-9892, fax

email: demclerran@ccisd.us

>>> Frankie Monroe 07/01/05 4:31 PM >>>
Hello Mrs. Mclerran:

My name is Frankie J. Monroe. I decided to e-mail you on the off chance that you might be reading your school e-mail this summer.

I am e-mailing you in reference to a message that was left on my answering machine on 6/29/05 at approximately 4:45 p.m. I attempted to contact you by phone on 6/30/05 at approximately 1:30 pm and also at 5:30 pm when I discovered the message.

When you did not return my call I thought that you may have gotten an early start on your 4th of July break. I just wanted to inform you that I am interested the assistant principal position. I would like to be considered for an interview at your earliest convenience.

Thank you in advance for your consideration.

http://webmail.ccisd.us/servlet/webacc?action=Item.Read&User.context=kt7rs2XpenrfiqcCm5... 7/3/05

| TELEPHONE NO. | | TELECOPIER NO. |
| (361) 883-1055 | | (361) 883-4041 |

Charles C. Smith
ATTORNEY AT LAW

615 N. UPPER BROADWAY, STE. 510
CORPUS CHRISTI, TEXAS 78477

July 7, 2005

CMRRR# 7004-1160-0005-8886-1898

Dr. Jesus Chavez, Superintendent
Corpus Christi Independent School District
801 Leopard Street
Corpus Christi, Texas 78401

    Re: Discrimination Charge

Dear Dr. Chavez:

    Following the June 15, 2005, meeting held at your office, my client prepared a statement that was e-mailed to you on July 5, 2005. On account of the school district's two-week shut down, I am not certain whether or not you have received or reviewed this e-mail. Nonetheless, I am enclosing another copy of this e-mail for your review and records.

    At the June 15, 2005 meeting, we did not discuss all of the related concerns that Ms. Monroe has regarding her race discrimination charge. However, the e-mail outlines those related issues that are outstanding. Accordingly, after you have had an opportunity to review this information, please contact me should you wish to finalize this matter.

                        Sincerely,

                        Charles C. Smith

CCS/mg
enclosure

cc: Ms. Imelda Martinez

       Ms. Frankie Monroe

Mail Message

N

Close   Next   Forward   Reply to Sender   Reply All   Move   Delete   Read Later   Properties

Print View

From: Delia McLerran
To: Frankie Monroe
Date: Friday - July 1, 2005 5:15 PM
Subject: Re: Assistant Principal Position

Frankie,

Thank you for the email. If possible, we would like to interview you on Tuesday, July 5th, 2005. The Roy Miller High School committee and the Wynn Seale Academy committee will be interviewing applicants on that day. You will sit with both committees simultaneously (not one first and then the other). The interviews are being held at the Corpus Christi Library in the Board Room on the 2nd floor. If you are able to attend on Tuesday at 2 p.m., please respond via email. Thank you for your interest.

Delia M. McLerran
Principal, Wynn Seale Academy of Fine Arts
Success through body, mind, and spirit
361-886-9359, ext. 105
361-886-9892, fax

email: demclerran@ccisd.us

>>> Frankie Monroe 07/01/05 4:31 PM >>>
Hello Mrs. Mclerran:

My name is Frankie J. Monroe. I decided to e-mail you on the off chance that you might be reading your school e-mail this summer.

I am e-mailing you in reference to a message that was left on my answering machine on 6/29/05 at approximately 4:45 p.m. I attempted to contact you by phone on 6/30/05 at approximately 1:30 pm and also at 5:30 pm when I discovered the message.

When you did not return my call I thought that you may have gotten an early start on your 4th of July break. I just wanted to inform you that I am interested the assistant principal position. I would like to be considered for an interview at your earliest convenience.

Thank you in advance for your consideration.

United States Courts
Southern District of Texas
FILED

AUG 1 2 2005

Michael N. Milby, Clerk of Court

IN THE UNITED STATES DISTRICT COURT
FOR THE SOUTHERN DISTRICT OF TEXAS
CORPUS CHRISTI DIVISION

FRANKIE J. MONROE,	*	CIVIL ACTION NO. _____
PLAINTIFF	*	
	*	
V.	*	
	*	
CORPUS CHRISTI INDEPENDENT	*	
SCHOOL DISTRICT,	*	
DEFENDANT	*	JURY DEMAND

ORIGINAL COMPLAINT

I.

JURISDICTION AND VENUE

1.   This is a civil action seeking redress for violation of rights guaranteed to the

Plaintiff under 42 U.S.C. §2000(e), et seq., commonly referred to as Title VII, of the Civil

Rights Act of 1964, as amended, by the Civil Rights Act of 1991, in accordance with its

provisions against race and age discrimination. More specifically, this action seeks

monetary damages, including mental anguish, and all other appropriate relief to which

Plaintiff is entitled to under the law on account of discrimination on the basis of race

(Black) and age (D.O.B. March 29, 1952), pursuant to 29 U.S.C. §621 et, seq.

2.   This is a civil action seeking redress for violation of rights guaranteed to the

Plaintiff under Title VII, §704(a) of the Civil Rights Act of 1964, as amended, by the

Civil Rights Act of 1991, in accordance with its provisions prohibiting retaliation

involving a discriminatory and hostile work environment. This cause of action seeks to

compensate Plaintiff for appropriate relief to which she is entitled under the law.

Page -1-

236

3.   This is also a civil action under the provisions of 42 U.S.C. § 1981, (a), as amended, in accordance with its provisions against racial discrimination involving the right to enter into contracts and other aspects of employment as enjoyed by other citizens of the United States. More specifically, this action seek to compensate Plaintiff for the appropriate relief to which she is entitled under the law, including compensatory.

4.   The jurisdiction of this Court is invoked pursuant to 28 U.S.C. § 1343(a), 28 U.S.C. § 1331, 42 U.S.C. § 2000(e) et seq., as amended, §704(a) and 42 U.S.C. § 1981(a), as amended.

II.

PARTIES

5.   Plaintiff, Frankie J. Monroe, is a 53-year-old Black female who is employed by the Corpus Christi Independent School District as a Teacher. Plaintiff is a citizen of the United States and is a person as contemplated under 42 U.S.C. § 1981(a), as amended, and at all times relevant to this complaint was a resident of the district residing in the County of Nueces, State of Texas.

6.   Defendant, Corpus Christi Independent School District is a governmental agency in the State of Texas, and is an employer as contemplated under 42 U.S.C. § 2000(e) et. seq and a person as contemplated under 42 U.S.C. § 1981(a), as amended. Pursuant to Rule 4(j)(2) of the Federal Rules of Civil Procedure, service of process may be served upon the School Superintendent, Dr. Jesus Chavez, Corpus Christi Independent School District, 801 Leopard Street, Corpus Christi, Texas 78401.

7.   All relevant events and transactions alleged herein in connection with Plaintiff's charge of race and age discrimination, including retaliation, unfair employment practices and other misconduct related to her employment occurred within this division.

Page -2-

8. Whenever in this complaint it is alleged that Defendant did any act or thing, it is meant that Defendant, Corpus Christi Independent School District, its officers, agents, servants, employees or representatives, did such an act or thing, and that at the time such act or thing was done, it was done with the full authority or ratification of Defendant, or was done in the normal and routine course and scope of employment of Defendant, Corpus Christi Independent School District, its officers, agents servants, employees or representatives; or was done in accordance with the policies and/or procedures of the Defendant.

III.

JURY DEMAND

9. Plaintiff hereby requests and demands a jury trial and has otherwise timely and properly made her demand for a jury trial pursuant to Federal Rules of Civil Procedures.

IV.

ADMINISTRATIVE PROCEEDINGS

10. On or about October 7, 2004, Plaintiff filed her written Charge of Discrimination with the Equal Employment Opportunity Commission through the Corpus Christi Human Relations Commission.

11. On or about June 3, 2005, the U.S. Equal Employment Opportunity Commission issued a Notice of Right to Sue on Plaintiff's claims of race discrimination and retaliation, which Plaintiff subsequently received.

12. On or about June 17, 2005, the U.S. Department of Justice issued a Notice of Right to Sue on Plaintiff's claim of age discrimination, which Plaintiff also subsequently received.

Page -3-

13.   Plaintiff has exhausted her administrative remedies with EEOC and has timely filed this action.

V.

FACTUAL BACKGROUND

14.   In approximately 1986 and continuing until approximately 1989, Plaintiff worked for the Defendant, Corpus Christi Independent School District (hereinafter CCISD) as a school teacher. Following a brief separation from CCISD, Plaintiff resumed her employment with CCISD in approximately 1996 where she remains employed as a school teacher.

15.   Since approximately 2000, Plaintiff has applied for several different administrative positions available at CCISD. In September, 2004, Plaintiff has been denied and otherwise rejected from various positions and the same practice of discrimination against Plaintiff has continued to the present. For each position applied for by Plaintiff, CCISD has provided Plaintiff with a rejection notice. To address her concerns regarding her non-selection to these various job opportunities, Plaintiff contacted the school superintendent, Jesus Chavez and Michael Briones and addressed her concerns of not being given an opportunity for an interview for the positions applied for.

16.   Several times throughout Plaintiff's employment with CCISD, Plaintiff has filed repeated grievances with CCISD alleging, among other things, discrimination and violation of civil rights on account of her race, age and retaliation following CCISD's decision not to select her for various available positions. For example, on January 13, 2005, Plaintiff filed an internal grievance with Defendant, CCISD, regarding unlawful employment practices based upon race and age. Notwithstanding, following this

Page -4-

239

assertion, Plaintiff has been targeted for retaliation for her contention and has been victimized because of this stance in retaliation for her protestation of discriminatory practices.

17.   Although Plaintiff meets the standards and requirements for the positions she applied for, the Defendant, CCISD, through its discriminatory selection process, continues to deny Plaintiff the opportunity for advancement. What's more, the Defendant has discriminated against Plaintiff when it made the decision not to select Plaintiff for the positions she applied for. Other employees outside of Plaintiff's protected area with less relevant and useful experience, have been selected for positions that Plaintiff has been duly qualified for.

18.   Despite Plaintiff's experience as an educator, Plaintiff has not been selected, hired or promoted on account of a discriminatory selection process used by CCISD to discriminate against Plaintiff on account of her race and age. What's more, similarly situated individuals who did not have the requisite or necessary qualifications were hired by CCISD.

VI.

FIRST CAUSE OF ACTION

19.   Plaintiff repeats, realleges and incorporates herein as part of her First Cause of Action paragraphs 1 through 18 of this Complaint, inclusive and in their entirety, and further alleges:

20.   Defendant's conduct and treatment of Plaintiff was in violation of Title VII of the Civil Rights Act of 1964, 42 U.S.C. §2000(e) et seq., as amended by the Civil Rights Act of 1991, and Equal Employment Opportunity Commission's guidelines promulgated thereunder with respect to race discrimination.

Page -5-

21.   Plaintiff is a member of a protected class as a Black employee.

22.   Plaintiff was qualified and performed her duties satisfactorily.

23.   Despite Plaintiff's qualifications and her satisfactory performance of her duties, she was singled out and treated differently because of her race when compared against non-black employees similarly situated who were treated differently.

VII.

SECOND CAUSE OF ACTION

24.   Plaintiff repeats, realleges and incorporates herein as part of her Second Cause of Action paragraphs 1 through 18 of this Complaint, inclusive and in their entirety, and further alleges:

25.   Plaintiff's treatment by the Defendant was in violation of the law with respect to age discrimination.

26.   Plaintiff is a 53-year-old individual who is a member of a protected group.

27.   Plaintiff was qualified to perform the duties for which she was hired, and performed her duties satisfactorily. Even so, Plaintiff was treated differently on account of her age.

VIII.

THIRD CAUSE OF ACTION

28.   Plaintiff repeats, realleges and incorporates herein as part of her Third Cause of Action paragraphs 1 through 18 of this Complaint, inclusive and in their entirety, and further alleges:

29.   Plaintiff's treatment by the Defendant was in violation of the law with respect to retaliation. The violation, as noted above, against Plaintiff can be shown in the following manner:

Page -6-

30.   She was an employee who engaged in protected activity or conduct involving a discriminatory practice as it relates to conduct covered under this statute, or participating in any manner in an investigation or protestation of proscribed conduct.

31.   The Defendant took an adverse employment action against Plaintiff.

32.   There is a causal connection between the protected activity and the adverse employment action.

VIIII.

FOURTH CAUSE OF ACTION

33.   Plaintiff repeats, realleges and incorporates herein as part of her Fourth Cause of Action paragraphs 1 through 18 of this Complaint, inclusive and in their entirety, and further alleges:

34.   Plaintiff's treatment by the Defendant was in violation of 42 U.S.C. § 1981(a), as amended, with respect to race discrimination.

35.   Plaintiff alleges that in doing the acts and things complained of, the Defendant engaged in an activity that denied her the full benefit of securing and pursuing employment opportunities enjoyed by non-black employees as provided under 42 U.S.C. § 1981(a), as amended.

36.   In doing the acts and things complained of, Defendant intentionally discriminated against Plaintiff on account of her race, Black.

WHEREFORE, PREMISES CONSIDERED, Plaintiff requests that Plaintiff have:

1.   Judgment be entered for the Plaintiff against Defendant for damages.

2.   Award Plaintiff equitable relief, including back pay and benefits pursuant to Title VII of the Civil Rights Act of 1964, as amended, and 29 U.S.C. §621 et, seq., and 42 U.S.C. §1981a.

Page -7-

3. Award Plaintiff front pay pursuant to Title VII of the Civil Rights Act of 1964, as amended, and liquidated damages pursuant to 29 U.S.C. §621 et, seq.

4. Award Plaintiff damages for physical and mental pain and suffering, including compensatory in connection with those claims made herein, pursuant to 42 U.S.C. §1981a(b)(3).

5. Costs of suit incurred herein.

6. Pre-judgment interest where permitted by law.

7. Interest at the legal rate on the foregoing sums from the date of judgment until paid.

8. Attorney's fees and costs as provided by 42 U.S.C. §§2000e-5(k), 5(g), 42 U.S.C. §1988.

9. Such other and further relief to which Plaintiff may be justly entitled.

Respectfully submitted,

Charles C. Smith
Attorney for Plaintiff
615 N. Upper Broadway
Wells Fargo Tower, Suite 510
Corpus Christi, Texas 78477
Telephone Number: (361) 883-1055
Facsimile Number: (361) 883-4041
Texas State Bar No. 18550210
Admission No. 4312

Page -8-

243

Exhibit 46

Documentation of Mediation day

April 28, 2006

On mediation day I got up early, took a bath and got dressed. All kinds of thoughts were running through my mind. I wasn't sure what to think because I hadn't been through anything like this. The evening before the scheduled meeting I had spent time in my attorney's office sifting through documents that Corpus Christi ISD sent as well as what I had. The previous month I had gone through every shred of paperwork that had been provided to him by Corpus Christi ISD and wrote down every discrepancy I found. I think I was more familiar with the documents than my attorney. But why wouldn't I be; after all I knew what had happened I just didn't have proof. Now I had many of the pieces of the puzzle I needed. After we finished discussing our game plan and what to expect the next day I left his office and headed down Water Street to locate where the mediation meeting was going to be held. It was on Third and Santa Fe. I didn't want to be late looking for the location the day of the meeting since I was not sure where it was. I found it and headed home.

It was a clear morning when I cranked up my car and headed for the meeting. I arrived at Anderson & Lerman's office at about 8:10 the meeting was to take place at 8:30. I was in a melancholy mood. Why did I have to be put in this predicament once again fighting for what I had earned? I never asked anyone to give me anything. I worked hard to prepare myself. It had taken me 20 years. Here I stand going against the district that I had dedicated most of my career too. I knew that once I did this I was marked but I had to do what was right no matter what the consequences were. My grandchildren's futures depended on it. I didn't want them to have to continue to fight for what was supposed to be gone from our society which was discrimination because of the color of your skin. Forget the content of your character. Did I have righteous indignation? You bet your booty I did.

I walked in the office and gave my name to the receptionist. "Good morning my name is Frankie Monroe. I have an appointment at 8:30 today." She confirmed my appointment and informed me that no one had arrived yet and to please have a seat. A few minutes later the mediator arrived and escorted me to a room that had a long mahogany table and several leather chairs perched around it. He offered me some coffee which I promptly declined. He then asked if I wanted anything else. I thanked him and told him I didn't want anything at that time. In actuality I had been having stomach problems. Anything I ate or drank ran straight through. I had been having these problems for about six months and I had forgotten to take the medication I needed to retain my food or water for any length of time. I had lost about 20 lbs. I wanted to loose weight but not like this.

244

Mr. Smith arrived and joined me in the room. He told me he had been sitting out in the parking lot watching to see who entered. A few minutes later we were joined by the mediator. He stated that he had been performing mediation for seven years and was familiar with school law. His position in this matter was neutral. He had no vested interest in the outcome. His job was to help the warring parties reach a happy medium. It had been his experience that many times neither party would be totally happy with the decision that would be reached. Sometimes this process could go well into the night and into the next day. He went on to tell me that I would probably hear some very negative things about myself from the other party. I told him I expected nothing less given that I had charged them with discrimination. He said there are times when you are only offered $500.00 as a nuisance payment. He explained that if a settlement was not reached my jury pool would probably be pulled from Aransas pass. Juries were kind of funny. Based on who was there I could win a large judgment or I could get nothing. Even if I won the case it could be tied up in court for years because the district would demand a retrial.

The mediator asked me how it had come to this. I proceeded to explain different events that lead up to this moment. I told him about the meeting with Dr. Chavez and Imelda Martinez. Dr. Chavez had belittled me and insulted my intelligence by telling me what he was prepared to do to make this go away. He implied that I was too dumb to understand that I could not get a job because I lacked the experience. He proceeded to give me an example "Frankie I want to be the CEO of Exxon. I keep applying, and I keep applying, and I keep applying but I never get the job. Do you know why I don't get the job? I lack the experience." I responded to Dr. Chavez by saying "Dr. Chavez I understand that concept but can you explain to me how a young Hispanic female in her mid to late 20s with 2 ½ to 3 years of experience verses 17 years of experience not only gets several interviews but is also hired for an assistant principal position?" The mediator asked me what he said and I told him Dr. Chavez ended that particular conversation. I went on to tell him that Dr. Chavez informed me because I just didn't have the ability to get past the paper screening process he was going to remove that obstacle and let me get an interview. I asked him why he felt I needed this. Why couldn't I be provided the same opportunity as all the other applicants who applied? I told him I was not interested and we ended the meeting.

About three weeks later I got a call out of the blue from Mrs. McCleran she stated that she was the principal from Wynn Seal and I had been placed on the list. She asked me if I was interested in an interview at Wynn Seal.

I told the mediator I found myself in a catch 22. He asked me, "What do you mean?" I told him, "Whether I accepted this interview or not it would be used against me by the district." I was also leery about the call because I hadn't applied for this particular position. I contacted my attorney and he told me to go ahead and go for it. I felt the entire interview was a set-up. There was no intention of hiring me. This was merely a smoke screen to give the appearance of an equal opportunity but I just did not cut it. So when I saw the low scores that I got I wasn't surprised.

After talking to me the mediator informed me that three representatives from the school district were suppose to be there to represent the district. Mr. Michael Briones, the certified personnel director, Mrs. Imelda Martinez, the school districts in-house-attorney and the attorney that had been hired out of Houston, Texas. Imelda declined to attend the meeting but he had been assured that the people in attendance had been given legal authority by the district to act on their behalf. He then left the room to bring them in.

Mr. Smith, my attorney, began telling me how this procedure worked. First everyone would meet, lay everything out on the table and then both parties would be put in different rooms. The mediator would go from room-to-room sharing what was being discussed and tell what was going to be offered by each party.

A few minutes later the mediator returned with Mr. Briones and the attorney representing Corpus Christi ISD. My attorney began the meeting by stating my position and why I felt I had been discriminated against. The attorney representing Corpus Christi ISD then spoke. He stated that the district had tried to work with me but I had refused. I had constantly refused to re-submit my application. They had tried numerous times to sit with me and discuss the matter but I had refused. I had been given an interview but I had scored next to the lowest of the applicants after the interview. I interjected by saying, "No! I didn't score next to the lowest; I scored the lowest." I had seen the paperwork.

He went on to say that there had been a Black interviewer that participated in the interviewing process. The attorney stated that he had expected this particular interviewer to score me very high but was surprised that he scored me the lowest. It appeared that I had felt entitled to a position just because I had gotten an education. Just because I had continued my education did not mean that the district was obligated to advance me into a higher position.

My attorney had instructed me not to make any comments because we didn't want to sit around debating. I was to let him speak for me and let them speak and then they would be taken to another room. What was being said was merely a formality.

It was hard sitting there listening to what I felt was them adding insult to injury. I wanted to scream at him and say "No, I am not entitled to a job because of my education. I earned a position!" But I grinned and barred it. When the mediator asked did I want to respond at that time I looked at my attorney and told them, "No."

Then the negotiations began. The mediator asked me how was I feeling about what had been said. He stated that he could see I was angry. I told him I was not angry I was curious about how they had come up with all their claims. The mediator left and came back explaining why they felt that I wasn't selected as a candidate. Mr. Briones had stated that I hadn't addressed the nine criteria that were required to be considered. My attorney and I were confused. We didn't know what he was talking about. We started sifting through the papers that we had and found one of my applications that the district had provided. We asked if it would be possible for Mr. Briones to come and explain what he meant by the nine criteria that was not addressed in my application. I had addressed what I had been told were the criteria.

The mediator returned with Mr. Briones. He began to explain that I hadn't filled out the nine criteria sufficiently when I submitted my application. I handed the copy of my resume and the criteria that I had addressed to Mr. Briones. I asked him did he even look at my resume. Then I showed him what I had addressed. He seemed a bit stunned because he could see that I had indeed addressed what he stated I hadn't. Then he proceeded to point out the inadequacies of my answers. He stated that when I addressed the issue of budget I didn't explain it in enough detail. Others that were selected did a much better job. He went on to explain that other applicants that had been interviewed did their homework on the district during the interview and did much better than I did. I asked him how I was going to be able to demonstrate my knowledge because I had not been allowed to interview that much.

I then asked the mediator could I ask Mr. Briones an additional question. He told me I could. I asked Mr. Briones, "If I was so inadequate in my responses on the application how did I get an interview that I didn't apply for in July of 2005." He stopped right in the middle of tearing my application apart and stated that Dr. Chavez had told him to put me on the list. I felt this was done to pretty much shut me up. I looked up at the mediator. This confirmed what I had told him before the meeting began. So he could see why I didn't trust the interviewing process.

The meeting went on back and forth. Then the mediator came back and informed us that the attorney and Mr. Briones, was on the phone with Mrs. Kelley, the acting superintendent. They wanted to make sure that it was okay to make the final offer that was decided upon. There had been an incident with another case where someone had made a settlement agreement without permission and the board had to approve the settlement and pay.

I was torn apart with the decision I had been convinced to make. I felt I was selling out. What I had been offered didn't begin to compensate for what I had suffered through. I wanted the world to know how the district had treated me but by agreeing to this settlement I had pretty much squashed that dream. After I signed the agreement, I told the mediator that I wasn't happy with what I had signed but I remembered what he said that neither party would be expected to be totally happy.

Exhibit 47

Settlement agreement that wasn't honored
Breach of Contract rendered Null and Void

CAUSE NO. 05-412

Monroe
_____
Plaintiff(s)/~~Claimant(s)~~

CCISD
_____
Defendant(s)/~~Respondent(s)~~

§
§
§
§
§

IN THE U.S DISTRICT/
~~COUNTY COURT #~~ ____ /
SOUTHERN DISTRICT

_____ ~~COUNTY~~, TEXAS

SETTLEMENT AGREEMENT PURSUANT TO RULE 11 T.R.C.P. AND § 154.071 TX. CIV. PRAC. & REM. CODE

All parties hereto agree that this lawsuit and/or all claims and controversies between them are hereby settled in accordance with the following terms of this Settlement Agreement.

1. All parties acknowledge that bona fide disputes and controversies exist between them, both as to liability and damages, if any, and by reason of such disputes and controversies they desire to compromise and settle all claims and causes of action of any kind whatsoever which the parties have or may have arising out of the transaction or occurrence which is the subject to this litigation. It is further understood and agreed that this is a compromise of a disputed claim, and nothing contained herein shall be construed as an admission of liability by any party, all such liability being expressly denied.

2. Each signatory to this **Settlement Agreement** hereby warrants and represents that:

   a. such person has full authority to bind the party or parties for whom such person acts.
   b. the claims, suits, rights, and/or interests which are the subject matter hereto are owned by the party asserting same, have not been assigned, transferred or sold, and are free of any encumbrance.

3. The consideration to be given for this settlement is as follows:

   Plaintiff, shall receive the sum of $ 25,000.00 /XY _____, on or before
   14 days after Board of Trustees for CCISD approval _____, paid by
   Defendant(s) to Plaintiff(s) as follows: _____

   _____

   The above-styled and numbered case/claim shall be resolved by:

   ✓ a. Order of Dismissal with **PREJUDICE** with taxable court costs taxed against party incurring the ~~same~~/Defendant(s) — mediation fee / filing fees / service fees only

   ___ b. Agreed Judgment/Take Nothing Judgment:

   ✓ c. Agreed Full Release and Hold Harmless Agreement

Plaintiff(s) hereby agrees to completely release, discharge, and forever hold Defendant(s) their insurers, representatives, employees, ~~agents and attorneys~~ harmless from any and all claims, demand, or suits, known or unknown, fixed or contingent, liquidated or unliquidated, whether or not asserted in the above case, as of this date, arising from or related to the events and transactions which are the subject matter of this case.

Plaintiffs agree to completely indemnify and hold Defendant(s), their insurers and employees harmless from any and all outstanding liens of any kind including, but not limited to, any ~~healthcare/provider liens, medical liens, Medicare,~~ Medicaid, hospital, ~~Worker's Compensation,~~ subrogation and attorney's fees liens, and referral fee liens of any kind, arising from or related to the events and transactions which are the subject matter of this case.

All parties and their representatives agree that the terms and conditions of this **Settlement Agreement** are **CONFIDENTIAL** and shall not be disclosed to any third party. In exchange for **Releasor's** foregoing agreement, **Releasee(s)** and their **Attorney(s)** agree that, except as otherwise required by specific court order, statute or other binding requirement of law, they will keep any and all information obtained in this litigation confidential, including all investigations, mediations and settlement negotiations relating to **Releasor(s)** and their claims while **Releasee(s)**

249

and **Releasor(s)** represent that this agreement would not have been consummated absent of any foregoing confidentiality covenants. **Releasee(s)**, **Releasor(s)** acknowledge that no portion of the settlement amount represents consideration for the mutual promise to maintain strict confidentiality of all the terms of this agreement. Rather, the **Releasee(s)** and **Releasor(s)** have expressly agreed that each others' reciprocal confidentiality covenant is a sole consideration given in exchange for that of the other.

8. Additional terms of this **Settlement Agreement** agreed to by all parties are as follows:
- *See attached Exhibit "A" setting out additional terms incorporated herein*
- *This settlement is subject to CCISD Board Approval*

9. Counsel for _____**Def.**_____ shall deliver all settlement documents required to be executed in connection with this settlement to opposing counsel within __14__ days from the date hereof. All parties and their counsel agree to cooperate with each other in the drafting and execution of such additional documents as are reasonably requested or required to implement the provisions and spirit of this **Settlement Agreement**, but notwithstanding such additional documents, *the parties confirm that this is a written Settlement Agreement as contemplated by Section 154.071 of the Texas Civil Practice and Remedies Code.*

10. This **Settlement Agreement** is made and performable in _**Nueces**_ **County, Texas,** and shall be construed in accordance with the laws of the State of Texas.

11. If one or more disputes arise with regard to the interpretation and/or performance of this **Settlement Agreement** or any of its provisions, the parties agree to attempt to resolve same with *Andrew J. Lehrman*, "the Mediator" who facilitated. If the parties cannot resolve their differences by telephone conference, then the parties agree to schedule a mediation with him as soon as possible to resolve the disputes. If litigation is brought to construe or enforce this **Settlement Agreement**, the prevailing party shall be entitled to recover attorney's fees as well as costs and expenses, including the cost of the mediation.

12. Although the Mediator has provided a basic outline of this **Settlement Agreement** to the parties' counsel as a courtesy to facilitate the final resolution of this dispute, the parties and their counsel have thoroughly reviewed such outline and have, where necessary, modified it to conform to the requirements of their agreement. All signatories to this **Settlement Agreement** hereby completely release the Mediator from any and all liability arising from the drafting of this **Settlement Agreement**.

13. Each party acknowledges that they have conferred with their counsel or, if not represented by counsel, have been advised to have this **Settlement Agreement** independently reviewed by their own counsel before executing this **Settlement Agreement**. Each signatory to this **Settlement Agreement** has entered into same freely and without duress after having consulted with professionals of his or her choice.

14. **THIS SETTLEMENT AGREEMENT IS NOT SUBJECT TO REVOCATION**

AGREED TO THIS ___*25th*___ DAY OF ___*April*___, 200 *6*.

Plaintiff(s)/Claimant(s)

_____

Attorney for Plaintiff(s) / Claimant(s)

_____

Defendant(s)/Responding Party

_____

Attorney for Defendant(s) / Responding Party

_____

Other Parties/Intervenors/Insurers

_____

Attorney for the Other Parties/Intervenors/Insurers

_____

Page 7

250

Exhibit "A"

(1) CCISD agrees to provide Plaintiff with information and advice on filling out applications with CCISD

(2) CCISD agrees to provide Plaintiff with other applications/ evaluations that have been considered and ranked in the top (3) applicants for Asst Principal or Principal with personal information redacted

(3) CCISD will provide Plaintiff with advice and suggestion on enhancing her opportunity for consideration as Asst Principal or Principal

(4) CCISD will arrange for Plaintiff to speak with HR / and a principal to discuss improving Plaintiff's interviewing techniques

(5) CCISD agrees that Plaintiff will be allowed to interview for the next Asst Principal opening –

(6) CCISD is NOT agreeing or guaranteeing Plaintiff will receive a new position after applying, but agrees they will not discriminate against her in any way.

Exhibit 48

I couldn't sleep for feeling the district was laughing and congratulating each other on having dodged a bullet. I wrote an e-mail to Mrs. Mary Kelly expressing my feelings and requested she get a message to the school board.

Fwd: For the Kids

Tuesday, May 30, 2006 10:19 AM

From: "Frankie Monroe" <FJMonroe@ccisd.us>

To: fjmonroe.████████████

2 Files (1KB)

For the Ki...   Frankie M...

Forwarded Message: For the Kids

For the Kids

Wednesday, April 26, 2006 8:57 AM

From: "Frankie Monroe" <FJMonroe@ccisd.us>

To: "Mary Kelley" <MAKelley@ccisd.us>

1 File (202b)

Frankie M...

Good Morning Mrs Kelley,

I met you when I was doing my superintendent practicum. I realize that
you had nothing to do with this fiasco that has taken place in the last
4 years. I would like you to pass this message on to the board.

I settled not because I wasn't discriminated against but because of the
love I have for the kids in the district. I didn't want to create a
media circus.

253

Exhibit 49

We had been told that after the board met on May 8th 2006 we would receive the settlement. As the days passed I finally stopped beating up on myself. Then on May 16, 2006 around 6:30 p.m., I turned on my cell phone and had an urgent message from Mr. Smith. I thought he was calling to tell me the check had come in and I needed to come in and sign off.

I called him the next day to let him know I would be coming after school. When I got there, to my surprise, he hadn't received a check but an injunction that had been filed by the Corpus Christi ISD attorney to have my case thrown out. Apparently it had been filed on May 15, 2006.

My attorney confided in me, he hadn't experienced this type of breach of good faith in his career. Evidently the school district had no intention of honoring the agreement. They were merely going through the formalities to appease the federal judge's court order to mediate. They realized the trial date had been scheduled for August 2006 which was fast approaching, and they were attempting to stop the process before that date.

I couldn't believe it. Here I was acting in good faith and they were playing games. I had e-mailed Mrs. Kelley after the mediation meeting and asked her to give a message to the board that I *settled* not because I hadn't been discriminated against but because I truly did care for the kids and didn't want a media circus. My question was and still is, "If you knew you weren't going to honor the agreement why sign off on it in the first place?" I think they felt if I wasn't willing to cause a ruckus they could do what they wanted without any consequences. They took my kindness for weakness.

Mr. Smith sent me a copy of the papers that had been filed in federal court and asked me to go through it. I couldn't believe what I was reading. I will only give you a portion of the Motion for Summary Judgment just to demonstrate what the district attempted to do to have my case thrown out.

Over the next few months of preparation for trial several statements sworn under oath by Mr. Briones in the Motion for Summary Judgment proved not to be true. I don't know what you would call it but I think they say it's called perjury. That alone should have allowed me to go to trial. It was stated repeatedly that I didn't qualify for most of the positions I applied for because the people hired were more experienced and more qualified than I was. I've already provided you with one young ladies application that dispels that statement. It was also later discovered that I had been denied the right to compete because of my temporary mid-management certification but others with the same credentials, had been allowed to work in the district, in administrative positions for at least five years.

As I reflected back on the day I was denied my day in court all sorts of thoughts ran through my head. On July 26, 2006 Judge Brian L. Owsley, The United States Magistrate Judge, Granted Corpus Christi ISD a Motion for Summary Judgment.

I believe the Judge had determined he was not going to let my case move forward long before he rendered his judgment but needed to make sure he could justify his decision. It appears from reading his decision he based it solely on what he read in Corpus Christi ISDs initial Motion for Summary Judgment and Brief rather than reading our response to that Motion for Summary and Brief. Perhaps his motivation was the fact that he didn't want the media attention this type of case could generate.

On page # 6, in The Summary Judgment Standard, Judge Owsley states "In making this determination, the court must consider the record as a whole by reviewing all pleadings, depositions, affidavits and admissions on file, and drawing all justifiable inferences in favor of the party opposing the motion. Caboni v. Gen. Motors Corp., 278 F.3d 448,451 (5th cir. 2002). The court may not weigh the evidence, or evaluate the credibility of witnesses. Id. Furthermore, "affidavits shall be made on personal knowledge, shall set forth such facts as would be admissible in evidence, and shall show affirmatively that the affiant is competent to testify to the matters stated therein.

I feel *had* Judge Owsley fully examined the initial Motion of Summary, affidavit and deposition Mr. Michael Briones submitted to the Courts on May 15, 2006 and May 26, 2006 from Corpus Christi ISD, as well as my response as the plaintiff to those claims submitted on June 5, 2006 he would have observed, the following claims:

Under Defendant's Motion for Summary the following claims were made.

a) Page # 2   "Defendant CCISD employs a neutral selection process and has always hired individuals whose credentials, work experiences, and knowledge of both state and federal laws place them at the top of the applicant pool."

b) Page # 3   "There is an absence of evidence to support the non-moving party's case." Id. at 325. The burden is on the non-moving party to "set forth facts showing that there is a genuine issue for trial." Id. at 325."

c) Page #5   "The only exception to this is if Plaintiff can show there were "continuing violations." A continuing violation may be found where there is proof of specific ongoing discriminatory policies or practices, or where specific and related instances of discrimination are permitted by the employer to continue unremedied for so long as to amount to a discriminatory policy or practice. Robinson V. Time Warner Inc., 92 F. Supp.2d 318"

It has now been six years since I initially filed charges of discrimination in 2004 with EEOC against CCISD. For five of those years I continued to apply for different administrative positions. After all decisions had been rendered in my

court cases in 2007, in the school districts favor, I was never sent on another interview. Could this be considered "continuing violations?"

d) Page # 11   "Although Plaintiff may have applied and qualified for the remaining positions for which she applied, plaintiff is still unable to prove racial discrimination under Title VII. The evidence, as detailed in Mr. Briones' affidavit, based upon CCISD's neutral selection process, more qualified candidates with more administrative experience were selected for the following job openings, regardless of race or age."

e) Page #12   "To overcome Plaintiffs *prima facie case,* Defendant CCISD has demonstrated a legitimate nondiscriminatory reason for its employment action. As Michael Briones has explained in has affidavit, attached as Exhibit 1, <u>candidates were evaluated and selected solely on the basis of their qualifications.</u>"

f) Page #12   "Plaintiff is not able to show that the differences between her qualifications and those of the other candidates are so favorable to her that there can be no dispute among reasonable persons of impartial judgment that Plaintiff was clearly better qualified for the position at issue. *Deines v. Tex. Dept of Protective and Regulatory Servs.* 164 F .3d w77,280 (5th Cir. 1999)."

g) Page # 15   "Plaintiff Monroe has failed to provide evidence to support an essential element of her *prima facie* claim, namely, that she was qualified for many of the jobs for which she applied as explained above in Section c. Furthermore, in regard to the positions for which Monroe applied and was qualified, the candidates ultimately selected for those positions <u>were all more qualified than Monroe.</u>"

Affidavit of Michael Briones under oath stated:

a) Page # 19 "Although Ms. Monroe did qualify for the remaining 7 positions for which she applied, Ms. Monroe was not the most qualified candidate for these positions. <u>Other more qualified applicants</u> were recommended for the positions without regard to Ms. Monroe's race, color, sex, religion, national origin, age, disability complaints regarding retaliation, or complaints with the EEOC"

b) Page # 19 "In regard to the selection, hiring or promotion of individuals, Defendant CCISD employs a nondiscriminatory selection process and <u>has always</u> hired individuals whose <u>credentials, work experiences,</u> and <u>knowledge of both state and federal laws</u> place them at the top of the applicant pool."

c) Page #19 "The screening committee reviews all qualified job applicants. Principal and assistant principal applicants are then scored by a committee according to <u>the years of experience</u>, <u>training</u>, <u>performance</u>, <u>certifications</u>, etc."

d) Page #20 "Although Ms. Monroe applied for and qualified for certain job openings, <u>more qualified candidates with more administrative experience</u> were selected for these openings."

Oral Deposition of Michael Briones May 25, 2006

In January 6, 2005 meeting I had with Mrs. Imelda Martinez, CCISD's in-house attorney I complained about Mr. Michael Briones. She stated Mr. Michael Briones had nothing to do with the hiring process he merely collected the initial information and disseminated it. In his deposition, Mr. Briones states something entirely different.

Page #6

A. Q. As the Director for Certified Personnel for CCISD, did you have any direct involvement in the interview process of the potential applicant?

B. A. Yes

C. Q. As part of your duties or responsibilities, could you explain to what extent you were involved in the interviews of potential applicants?

D. A. For any principalship position, my involvement was to function as the Interview Committee Facilitator. I was the person that coordinated the entire interview process and I was also a member of the Committee, Where I got to respond to how I felt that person did in the Interview.

Page # 7

A. Q. As the Director for the Certified Personnel for CCISD, did you get involved in the selection process in any way before the interviews took place?

B. A. Yes

C. Q. And if you could explain how you got involved in the selection process prior to any interviews being conducted for an applicant for a position.

D. A. The second part of the process was to have a Paper-Screening Committee of three, **which I was a part of**, that would determine of those applicants that went through the first filter, let's say 20, for instance---we may have 50 that applied, but only 20 met the minimum requirements – of those 20, we would paper-screen those 20 applicants to determine in descending order which ones were the best qualified.

Page # 38

A. Q. Mr. Briones. Do you have any personal knowledge regarding anything that you have seen, read or reviewed that would suggest

to you **other more qualified individuals** were selected for those
positions for which Ms. Monroe applied for and was deemed
qualified for as reflected in "Briones Exhibit Number 1 ?

B. A. Would you just rephrase the first part of the question?

C. Q. Can you tell me whether or not you have any personal knowledge
of anything that you have looked at or reviewed that would lead
you to believe that **other more qualified applicants** were selected
instead of Ms. Monroe for the positions that she sought that the
District deemed that she was qualified for?

D. A. No, sir.

Page # 40

A. Q. As a part of that process and in particular with regard to Ms.
Monroe's application, did you personally review her application
for those particular positions?

B. A. No.

C. Q. Did you participate as a member of the Screening Committee that
reviewed her application for those positions?

D. A. No

**In the meeting it was stated that there was no way The Screening Committee
Members could have known who I was. But when I was provided the screening
information I knew nearly every person on the Screening Committee and they knew
me personally so they were well aware of my race.**

Page # 43-44

A. Q. The Screening Committee Members who make up the Paper-
Screening Committee, at the time they perform their duties are
they provided the names of the applicants?

B. A. Yes

C. Q. Do you know, Mr. Briones, whether or not the Paper-Screening
Committee Members are prohibited from talking with other
individuals not on the Committee while they perform their
screening responsibilities of an applicant's paperwork?

D. A. The first part, if you could just say that again.

E. Q. Certainly, sir. You are not aware, are you, Mr. Briones, of any
prohibitions of or against any Paper-Screening Committee
Members talking with individuals about their screening of an
applicant's paperwork, are you?

F. A. No. no.

G. Q. Now, on the second page of your affidavit, Mr. Briones, last
paragraph, you indicate that "CCISD has never engaged in any
discriminatory actions" against Ms. Monroe. Do you see that
sentence?

H. A. Yes, Sir.

I. Q. If you would, tell us what personal knowledge you have to support that assertion sir.

J. A. I believe that CCISD has not discriminated against Ms. Monroe, to my knowledge, and that is why I put that statement there.

K. Q. But you are only speaking for yourself, are you not?

L. A. Yes.

M. Q. You are not attempting to speak for anyone else, are you?

N. A. I'm speaking for myself as the Executive Director for H.R.

O. Q. And as the District is comprised of both administrators and other individuals who may be involved in the selection process, you are not speaking for those persons, are you?

P. A. No.

Page # 45-46

A. Q. On the first sentence of the second page, you indicate or assert that "Ms. Monroe did not qualify for eight of the positions for which she applied." Do you see that first sentence?

B. A. First paragraph?

C. Q. Yes.

D. A. Yes, sir.

E. Q. What facts are you relying on in support of that statement, sir?

F. A. I believe that was from "Exhibit Number 2" that we provided where it indicated why Ms. Monroe did not meet the qualifications of those positions.

G. Q. Did you personally review Ms. Monroe's file to verify the explanation that was provided in the "Exhibit 2"?

H. A. No. sir.

I. Q. I mean, for example, if there was an assertion that Ms. Monroe did not have a certification or something at the time she applied for a position, did you have any personal knowledge if that was true or not?

J. A. No, other than being informed by my analyst that does that.

One of his analysts was Mrs. Maria Villarreal, Human Resource Specialist, the person that I repeatedly questioned over the span of 10 years to several administrators including superintendents, Dr. Jesus Chavez and Mr. Scott Elliff concerning her motives for not submitting my information to the Screening Committee in a timely fashion or not at all.

Page # 48-50

A. Q. Mr. Briones in Ms. Monroe's deposition she stated that there were other people in CCISD that were allowed to work in administrative positions such as assistant principal with the same Temporary Mid-

259

Management certification she held, for at least five years but she was denied the same opportunity. She named Mr. ██████████ as one such person that had been allowed to work in an assistant principal position with a Temporary Mid-Management position for at least five years. Is this true?

B. A. Yes. And we have others.

C. Q. Can you tell me what position Mr. ██████████ holds now and where he is assigned?

D. A. He is an administrator in the main office.

After assessing this situation in one sense I was upset but on the other hand I was relieved because I had prayed and asked God to guide me in the way he wanted me to go.

I told my husband I didn't care if I didn't get a dime I was going to tell it. By the district rejecting the settlement I felt the agreement was null and void and I was free to tell whatever I wanted to whomever I wanted. So here we are today. I'm telling.

As I prepared for my lawsuit I started going through my e-mails at school to double check and make sure I had forwarded everything I needed to my own personal e-mail address at home and discovered that in the archived e-mails everything that had been communicated between Dr. Chavez and me concerning the discrimination charges had been deleted. My lawyer had asked that these e-mails be sent but they were not. The districts response to his request was those e-mails that he referenced never existed or they no longer existed. They were not aware that I had already printed, saved, or forwarded them to my home e-mail address.

IN THE UNITED STATES DISTRICT COURT
FOR THE SOUTHERN DISTRICT OF TEXAS
CORPUS CHRISTI DIVISION

FRANKIE J. MONROE   §
Plaintiff   §
                                   §
                                   §
VS.   §   CIVIL ACTION NO. C-05-412
                                   §
CORPUS CHRISTI INDEPENDENT   §
SCHOOL DISTRICT   §
Defendant   §

AFFIDAVIT OF MICHAEL BRIONES

STATE OF TEXAS   §
                     §
COUNTY OF NUECES   §

BEFORE ME, the undersigned authority, personally appeared Michael Briones, who being duly sworn upon his oath deposed and said:

"My name is Michael Briones. I am qualified, competent and capable of making this affidavit. The facts stated in this affidavit are within my personal knowledge and are true and correct.

I am over twenty-one (21) years of age and have never been convicted of a felony or a crime of moral turpitude.

I am the Executive Director for Human Resources at Corpus Christi Independent School District ("CCISD"). In my position as Executive Director, my duties involve the handling of human resources matters, including overseeing the hiring, firing and promoting of employees. In my position as Director for Certified Personnel, I have become familiar with Frankie J. Monroe ("Ms. Monroe").

Ms. Monroe has served as a schoolteacher with CCISD from 1986 to 1989 and from 1996 to the present. During the period between January 1, 2000, and September 7, 2004, Ms. Monroe applied for 16 different positions within CCISD. The positions for which Ms. Monroe applied and the dates she applied for same have been compiled into a chart, by members of the Human Resources department, for the purpose of responding to Ms. Monroe's EEOC Charge of Discrimination and is attached as Exhibit A.

Ms. Monroe did not qualify for 8 of the positions for which she applied. Of the remaining positions for which Ms. Monroe did apply and for which she was qualified, one of the job openings for Assistant Principal - all levels, was never filled. Specifically, the deadline for the April 8, 2004 job opening was extended until June 4, 2004, at which time Ms. Monroe did resubmit her application for the position. A separate chart, attached as Exhibit B and entitled "Chart of Candidates Selected for the Seven Job Openings Which Party Met Requirements" was also compiled for the purpose of responding to Ms. Monroe's EEOC Charge of Discrimination. Exhibit 2 was also created by members of the Human Resources department in order to show, among other things, the candidates who were ultimately selected for the job openings for which Ms. Monroe applied and for which she qualified. *See Exhibit 2.*

Although Ms. Monroe did qualify for the remaining 7 positions for which she applied, Ms. Monroe was not the most qualified candidate for these positions. Other more qualified applicants were recommended for the positions without regard to Ms. Monroe's race, color, sex, religion, national origin, age, disability, complaints regarding retaliation, or complaints with the EEOC. *See Chart of Candidates Selected for the Seven Job Openings which Party Met Requirements, attached as Exhibit 2.*

In regard to the selection, hiring or promotion of individuals, Defendant CCISD employs a nondiscriminatory selection process and has always hired individuals whose credentials, work experiences, and knowledge of both state and federal laws place them at the top of the applicant pool.

The selection for professional staff in CCISD requires that the Office of Secondary Certified Personnel review and screen all timely submitted applications for compliance with the minimal requirements established by the job position. The screening committee reviews all qualified job applicants. Principal and assistant principal applicants are then scored by a committee according to the years of experience, training, performance, certifications, etc. The score sheets are then presented to the Office of Certified Personnel for their review and ultimate selection of candidates for interviews. Once the interviews have been conducted, the supervisor submits the name of the applicant selected for the position to the personnel department for further background checks.

Guidelines for Selection of Assistant Principals and the accompanying forms are attached to this Affidavit as Exhibit C. These forms are used by supervisors, scoring committees, interviewing committees, and the personnel department during the process of selecting applicants for professional staff in CCISD.

At no time during the selection process is the applicant's race, color, sex, religion, national origin, age, disability, or status of an EEOC complaint reflected or available to the screening and interview committees.

CCISD has never engaged in any discriminatory actions or decisions regarding Ms. Monroe and her pursuit of an administrative position with the District.

262

Ms. Monroe first attempted to file a grievance with the District on or about November 5, 2004, in regard to a letter she had received on October 28, 2004, notifying her that a position for which she had applied had been filled. Ms. Monroe had not filed any sort of grievance with CCISD prior to November 5, 2004.

Ms. Monroe applied for several job openings posted by CCISD. At the time she applied, however, she failed to meet specific job requirements called for by the following positions:

- **6/7/01 - Administrative Officer for Special Education**
  Ms. Monroe did not have a Texas Mid-Management/Principal certificate, as was required by the position.

- **6/7/01 - Assistant Principal 2001-2002 School Year**
  Ms. Monroe did not have a Texas Mid-Management/Principal certificate, as was required by the position.

- **12/10/01 - Consultant Special Education School Services**
  Ms. Monroe did not have a Texas Mid-Management/Principal certificate, as was required by the position.

- **8/13/02 - Assistant Superintendent for School Services**
  Ms. Monroe lacked a minimum of 3 years experience in an administrative and/or instructional role.

- **6/30/03 - Executive Director for Human Resources**
  Ms. Monroe lacked a minimum of 5 years experience in an administrative and/or instructional role.

- **6/30/03 - Elementary Principal - Barnes, Coles SES, Crockett**
  Ms. Monroe lacked a minimum of 3 years experience in an administrative and/or instructional role.

- **6/30/03 - Middle School Principal - South Park**
  Ms. Monroe lacked a minimum of 3 years experience in an administrative and/or instructional role.

- **11/18/03 - Special Education Director**
  Ms. Monroe lacked a minimum of 3 years experience in an administrative and/or instructional role.

See Exhibit A - Chart of Positions Applied for by Frankie J. Monroe.

Ms. Monroe also applied for several positions for which she was qualified; however, she was not the most qualified candidate for these positions. Although Ms. Monroe applied for and qualified for certain job openings, more qualified candidates with more administrative experience were selected for these openings, utilizing CCISD's nondiscriminatory selection process, described above. In fact, two of the candidates selected were African Americans, and at least eight of the candidates were over 40 years old and in the same protected age class as Plaintiff. *See Exhibit A - Chart of Positions Applied for by Frankie J. Monroe and Exhibit B - Chart of Candidates Selected for the Seven Job Openings which Party Met Requirements."*

I am not aware of any incidents of discrimination based on age or race by CCISD. Furthermore, CCISD has never retaliated against Ms. Monroe.

I am a custodian of records for CCISD's Human Resources Department. Attached hereto are 27 pages of records from various documents contained within CCISD's Human Resources Department. These said 27 pages of records are kept by the CCISD Human Resources Department in the regular course of business, and it was the regular course of business for an employee or representative of CCISD, with knowledge of the act, event, condition, opinion, or diagnosis, recorded to make the record or to transmit information thereof to be included in such record; and the record was made at or near the time or reasonably soon thereafter. The records attached hereto are the original or exact duplicates of the original.

I attach the following documents, which are true and correct copies of the originals:

A. Chart of Positions Applied for by Frankie J. Monroe
B. Chart of Candidates Selected for the Seven Job Openings Which Party Met Requirements
C. Guidelines for Selection of Assistant Principals and Accompanying Forms
D. EEOC Charge of Discrimination dated October 7, 2004
E. EEOC Notice of Charge of Discrimination dated October 18, 2004
F. EEOC Notice of Right to Sue under ADEA dated June 3, 2005
G. EEOC Notice of Right to Sue under Title VII dated June 17, 2005
H. CCISD's Board Policy DGBA (Local)
I. Frankie J. Monroe's Texas Educator Certificate

Further affiant sayeth not."

SWORN AND SUBSCRIBED before me this 10th day of May, 2006.

JANET LONGWELL REAGAN
Notary Public
STATE OF TEXAS
My Comm. Exp. 02-20-2009

Janet Longwell Reagan
Notary Public
In and For The State of Texas

264

Exhibit 50

Documentation: Day before and Day of Deposition

After the injunction had been filed we had no choice but to proceed with the lawsuit. The first step was to set up a time for depositions to be taken.

May 24, 2006

I had been contacted by my attorney's assistant, Belinda. She reminded me I had to give my deposition to the school district. I asked; when was this scheduled to take place. She said it had been set for May 25, 2006 at 9:00 a.m. in Mr. Smith's office. My deposition was scheduled for the morning and Mr. Michael Briones, the district's *new* Executive Director of Human Resources, was to give his that afternoon.

It was the last week of school and I needed to do so many things to close down for the summer. In fact the day the depositions had been scheduled was going to be the last day for the students to attend class. I contacted my principal, Mr. Vargas, and asked him would there be anyone available to cover my class for the morning of May 25, 2006 because I had to go and give my deposition. I thought since my deposition was to take place that morning as soon as it was over I could return and continue working. I knew several teachers that had their classes covered so they could take care of personal business. This was not the case for me. I was instructed to go ahead and get a substitute teacher.

I had to meet with Mr. Smith right after school to discuss what to expect during the deposition. I got in my car and headed for his office. As I drove I thought about some information I had come across. I had been very involved in my case. Mr. Smith had given me access to all the data he had collected from EEOC and Corpus Christi ISD. He asked me to go through it and respond. It was a massive amount of paperwork. I skimmed through all the documents and wrote responses to things I felt would be of importance. EEOC had supplied a chart of all the principal and assistant principal positions of people hired from 2003-2004 that had been supplied to them from Corpus Christi ISD. It was a total of 44 positions of which only 6 (Blacks) had been hired. I also came across a letter from EEOC. I don't know why I hadn't seen it before. Perhaps it was because I had had so much material at first to decipher through. I guess you could say it was something like not being able to see the forest for the trees.

To prepare for my case I had decided to scan all the letters and e-mails I had into my computer by the dates that the incidents occurred. As I scanned the material into my computer the story started to unfold. It was as if the puzzle pieces had started falling into place right before my eyes to reveal the complete picture.

About 4:00 a.m. I came across the letter from EEOC and stopped to read it. When I finished reading it I was overcome with emotions, and tears filled my eyes. I got up from my computer and walked to the kitchen. I looked to the ceiling and started talking to God. I hadn't known why I couldn't get my story out but now I understood. It wasn't time. This all had been very traumatic for me. As the years had gone on and I had experienced one discriminatory act against me after another, I finally reached a boiling point and decided that enough was enough and then I wept intensely.

My deposition was to take place at 9:00 a.m. Thursday morning in Mr. Smith's office. This was the last day I would be able to see my students. It was at the end of the school year. I had wanted to talk to them because I knew after this summer there was a great possibility I wouldn't see them again, at least not as their teacher. After all I was suing the school district for discrimination.

I was in a bittersweet mood. I felt I had been given no way out of this situation and had pretty much been backed into a corner. I didn't want to do this. I had given the district two chances to resolve this issue and both times they had pretty much thrown it back in my face.

As the time approached for me to go to meet with my attorney I felt the weight of world was on my shoulders. This had taken an emotional and physical toll on me. I had gone to the doctor because I wasn't sleeping and then I noticed chunks of my hair had fallen out. I also knew the ramifications of my lawsuit. If it was proven that any portion of my lawsuit against the district was true the district stood the chance of having millions of federal dollars taken away. Not only would this affect the students that I had championed, but it would also affect my coworkers. After all, many of them were just like me, a paycheck or two away from being homeless.

I don't know if it was my imagination or if it was real, but I had noticed a sadness in Mr. Vargas's eyes. He had worked on Ray campus for at least 15 years, first as a coach and language arts teacher then as an assistant principal. When Dr. Dorsey resigned he became the third principal I had had since starting work on the Ray High School campus, four years earlier. He was very aware of what I was going through and what affect my case would have, not just on the district but him as well.

Before Mr. Vargas became the head principal he had had such a jovial attitude. Now he had become stern towards not just me but the entire campus. One of the people I wanted to have deposed was his immediate boss and good friend, Mr. Jaime Arredondo. He was one of the people that signed off on my paper screenings for the positions in administration. Earlier in the day I was taking some papers to the office and I passed Mr. Vargas and Mr. Arredondo heading for one of the exits when I looked towards Mr. Vargas to speak he looked at me and then looked away. It was at that point I knew the respect we had held for each other no longer existed.

I left campus that day and headed for Mr. Smith's office. Traveling down the freeway and exiting Leopard Street I had to pass Corpus Christi ISD's administrative building. I didn't have the animosity I once had when I had to pass that building because I knew that the man I felt had caused me to go down this path was no longer there. He had managed to get out of town and secure another $200,000 position in Round Rock ISD. I know he felt he had escaped the problems that he had created.

When I arrived I had to wait until Mr. Smith finished seeing another client. I entered his office prepared to discuss my case. We talked for about ten minutes when he got a call from home. He told me he was going to have to leave. He took my home and cell phone numbers and told me he would call me later. About nine-thirty that evening I got a call. We started discussing things I could expect during the deposition that was scheduled for Thursday. We talked about 30 minutes. He was shooting so many things at me. I was writing as fast as I could to take down notes. When we finished our conversation I had planned to re-write the notes so I could go over them but I was exhausted. Instead of re-writing the notes I crashed. I fell into such a deep sleep. I usually wake up at least 2 or 3 times a night especially when I have something pressing that I can't get off my mind. This time it was as if I had taken a sleeping pill.

I had sat up for three nights straight until 4:00 in the morning trying to organize my e-mails and letters. I had been scanning them into my computer and putting notations just above them so Mr. Smith would know what had been taking place over the years. After all I hadn't secured him until about April of 2005 much of this had occurred about three years earlier.

May 25, 2006

On Thursday morning I got dressed. I was trying to review the notes I had taken the night before but they were all jumbled and made no sense so I had to try to rely on my memory which was also jumbled because of the order that we had discussed different topics in our conversation the night before.

I decided to wear this black and yellow flowered outfit. The dress was basically black with yellow flowers. It came with a yellow jacket. I had once been told that colors affected the mood of people. I had also been told that pastel colors were my color especially pinks and yellows.

When I arrived there was no one in the office but Mr. Smith. I took a seat in the outer-office and waited. About 5 minutes later the secretary arrived. She told me Mr. Smith would be ready for me to come into his office in a few minutes. I entered his office and took a seat. He went over what I could expect. He told me that 80 percent of the responses to the questions would be, yes or no. If I had to respond it should be no more than 3 or 4 sentences. He told me they were probably going to take one charge at a time. After all I had charged racial, age, and retaliation discrimination. We discussed some other things and then it was time.

The stenographer was there along with the districts attorney and Mr. Briones the districts Executive Director of Human Resources. The room they were in had been decorated beautifully. In the middle of the room was a long mahogany table with six plush chairs placed strategically around it. I guess this was the standard furniture all attorneys subscribed to, because this décor was very similar to what I saw during the mediation meeting. The walls were covered with beautiful paintings. There was a Shrunk with beautiful flowers placed on it. When I entered the room they were sitting and discussing the decorations and the colors of the office. I knew this tactic, talk about the weather to get your mind off of the task at hand. If they can get you to relax they can get you to admit things. I didn't want to respond to anything. Mr. Smith finally joined me. I had taken a seat to the far right and was asked to move next to the stenographer. Mr. Smith sat to my right. The districts attorney sat right across from me and Mr. Briones took a seat across from Mr. Smith. Then the questioning began.

It started off slow. I was asked to give my name. I was then asked if I had ever been deposed. I responded by saying yes. So far so good and from this point on I didn't follow the script at all that Mr. Smith had laid out. I was then asked what caused me to be deposed. I told them I had been in a car accident and I had also filed a discrimination lawsuit against the Texas Welfare department. Of course this was a sore spot for me and I was off to the races. When I finished I was asked what was my credentials I told them I had a bachelors degree in business administration, masters in education administration, superintendent certification, mid-management certification, I then asked did they want my PDAS and Instructional Leadership certification and was told no. I finished with special education certification and vision impairment certification.

And then we got to the meat of the problem. How had I been discriminated against? We first tackled *age.* I told him about the two young ladies that had been hired who were in their mid to late twenties and had taught school no more then three years. I then told him how long I had taught school. We went around and around. Then we moved on to *race.* He stated that during the period that I could use for my discrimination claims two Blacks had been hired, so my claim of discrimination based on race and retaliation could not be used. I explained to him that I knew the Blacks that had been hired. Mrs. Valarie Pearse had held her Mid-Management Certification for at least 11 years and not been afforded an opportunity to advance in her career until after I brought charges against the district. I also knew Mr. Edward Jennings. I knew for at least 7 years he had held the position of part-time assistant principals because I worked on the same campus with him. It wasn't until I filed the complaint that he was hired. What that was saying to me was we do need to hire some Blacks but we won't hire you. I felt this was *retaliation.*

My attorney asked if we could take a break. I went into his office and he looked disappointed. He proceeded to scold me. He told me I did the exact opposite of what he had told me to do. I knew just what he was talking about. I told him he was use to following certain guidelines this was what he did. I needed more than one night to absorb everything he had instructed me to do. I apologized and told him well what's done is done. I then asked him did we still have a chance. He kind of shook his head as if to say I don't know. I told him about the forms that had been submitted by the district. They had only submitted one form to the court as far as people being hired. There had actually been three. I also asked him to ask the credentials of Mr. Briones. I had heard something but I wasn't sure. We finished our conversation and as I rose to leave I felt quite defeated. I told him, "Well let's go ahead and finish nailing my coffin shut."

The deposition continued. Then the districts attorney asked me a question that I think was the turning point in the way my case was going. He said to me "Ms. Monroe you keep saying you know someone that was allowed to hold a temporary mid-management certification and held an assistant principal position." I told him, "Yes I do know someone." He then proceeded to ask me to tell them who it was. I took a deep breathe, I really didn't want to use this mans name because I liked him. I felt like a Judas. But then I blurted his name out, Julius Garza. I noticed Mr. Briones expression. He seemed somewhat shocked. He shouldn't have been. After all I had told him I knew about exceptions being made for others but not me for at least three years. I was then asked did I think people that were not qualified should be hired for positions. I told him of course not but I did feel that if you did things for others to advance in their careers those same allowances should be made for others. It was a matter of being ethical. A few more questions were asked of me and my deposition was over.

I thought after I was done with my deposition I could go back to school. I had forgotten to bring all the e-mails and other information I had scanned into my computer. I had do go home, get this information and return before 12:30. It was now 11:30 and I lived across town. I rushed home, got the information and told my husband I had blown it. I had given too much information. He sympathized with me and told me what's done is done. I left and rushed back across town to my attorney's office. I handed Belinda the folder and told her I was leaving. She told me I needed to stay so I could in sit on the other deposition. I hadn't eaten anything all day but I agreed to stay. Mr. Smith entered the room and we started going through the folder. I was a little nervous because I couldn't put my hands on the papers I had told him about. Everyone had returned from lunch and was waiting in the meeting room.

Mr. Smith went slowly through the materials and found what I had been so frantically searching for. He told me he would try to salvage the fiasco I had created by sticking to technicalities. He told me before I had gotten to the point that I felt I needed to file charges of discrimination something had happened to me and it had happened to me during the selection process. This was going to be his focal point.

I had switched places with Mr. Smith and Mr. Briones had switched places with his attorney. It was now Mr. Briones turn to be put on the hot seat. I was sitting there feeling so dejected because I had talked too much. Everything I had said could be used against me now in the courts especially if I couldn't remember what I had said. Less would have been better but it was too late now.

Mr. Smith began by asking Mr. Briones what position he held in the district. He explained his position and the previous position as well. He then asked for Mr. Briones credentials. As I listened to this I realized Mr. Briones didn't have anything near the credentials I had. He held a business degree and so did I. He only held one certification but I don't think it had anything to do with education. But he had been allowed an executive position in the district. Then the tough questions started.

Mr. Smith asked Mr. Briones to look at the affidavit he had sworn to and submitted to the courts to get my case thrown out. He asked if Mr. Briones wanted to change any part of what he had stated in that affidavit. Mr. Briones stated that he did not want to change any thing. Then Mr. Smith had him to look at the section of the affidavit where he had stated that the people that were hired were more qualified than I was. He then asked had he ever looked at my application and Mr. Briones stated he had not. He then asked, "If you never even looked at Ms. Monroe's application, how could you swear under oath that she was less qualified than the ones that were selected?"

He then proceeded to discuss the paper screening forms that had been submitted to the courts. It was found that one form had been created in April of 2004 the other had been submitted in 2/06. How was it possible for me to be assessed on two different assessment tools that were two years apart? Then he asked the question that I felt nailed the coffin shut for Corpus Christi ISD. He asked Mr. Briones did he know the gentleman I had spoke of. Mrs. Briones broke into a sweat. I think he and his attorney had discussed this response at lunch. He was probably told he had to answer and tell the truth this time. He looked at Mr. Smith and said "Yes." Mr. Smith then asked him had the gentleman I mentioned been allowed to work as an assistant principal with a temporary-mid management certification. Mr. Briones stated **"Yes"** and added that **several others had also been allowed to work with temporary-mid-management certification.** Mr. Smith asked him what position this gentleman held now. Mr. Briones said. "He now is in the main office holding an administrative position."

Julius had been allowed to advance in his career but I was still in the classroom. I felt vindicated. I had been saying this all along. Now I felt Mr. Briones, through his testimony, had perjured himself. All of the positions they claimed I didn't qualify for because I didn't have my permanent mid-management certification but held a temporary mid-management certification were now in questions.

We took a break. I went to Mr. Smith's office and he asked was there anything else we needed to ask. I told him I couldn't think of anything. We went back to the meeting room and ended the deposition. The districts attorney told Mr. Smith, "I guess I will see you in court." It seemed he now knew he wouldn't be able to throw my case out of court because of what had just been disclosed.

I felt like pretty woman and Judas. Do you remember the scene where Julia Robert's character goes into this exclusive store on Rodeo Drive asking for one of the attendants to help her find a dress? The attendant turns up her nose at Julia and tells her to go down the street, because she couldn't afford anything in that store. She leaves and tells the man that wanted her to buy the dress what happened. He takes her shopping. She then returns to the store where they told her she couldn't afford to shop at and says, "I was in here yesterday. Don't you get commissions for how much you sell?" Dressed to the hilts and loaded down with expensive clothes she smiles, turns to model for them and then says,

"Big Mistake! Big Mistake!" then turns and walks out. That's what I felt like in that moment. Big Mistake!

They had signed a settlement agreement. I wasn't happy with it but I was doing it for the greater good. I didn't want to hurt the people that I cared about. This was the second time the district had pretty much thumbed their noses at me. Now it was all coming out in the wash. The dirty laundry was now being aired in public. The next morning I heard the mayor of New Orleans say something to this affect. He was quoting something from Gandhi. "First they ignore you, then they laugh at you, then they fight you, then you win." How apropos to be hearing that at that time?

When I woke up the next morning I was watching the news. I discovered that our school had been involved in a bomb threat and the kids had been forced to remain outside from about 7:40 a.m. to 11:30 a.m. Tempers were flaring and it had been total chaos. So even if I had been able to return to school I would have been caught up in the chaos.

When I wrote this documentation I was feeling P-R-E-T-T-Y good.

Chapter X

Are We Having Fun Yet! (NOT)

In their rush to try and get my case thrown out of court, I felt the school board and its representatives gave the air of a conspiracy. Were they trying to hide the truth? Could they actually have been found guilty of discrimination if they went to trial?

On Tuesday, July 19, 2006 I received a call from Corpus Christi ISD. I wasn't at home but a message was left on my answering machine. The message stated that they were conducting interviews for the next day and wanted me to come in for it. I didn't want to go initially because for several years I had wanted to be considered and now 11 days before we were to go to trial they had decided to call me.

They also called my husband who had dialysis that day. During his treatment he got a call. He thought it was me calling him but at the other end of the phone was someone from Corpus Christi ISD asking him could I be reached at that number. He told them no and hung up. When he got home he told me what had happened and suggested that I go ahead and call them to set up an interview. He felt what they were doing by calling all around town was to try to show the courts I had not been responsive to their attempts to offer me a job.

I returned their call and found out they wanted to schedule the interview for the next day in room 114 at 1:30-1:55. I then went to Mr. Smith's office. Belinda told me she had also received a strange call from Corpus Christi ISD. They told her they were trying to contact me as well. I told her they were merely trying to establish contact for court purposes.

The next day I got dressed. My husband told me he was going to take me and wait until the interview was over. I was a bit nervous about this interview. My brother told me they should have given me a letter and at least a week to prepare for the interview but instead I had been given less than twenty-four hours.

When I arrived at the interview I went to the receptionist and asked her were room 114 was because I had been scheduled for an interview at 1:30 p.m. She pulled out this paper and instructed me to go up the escalator and have a seat in one of the blue chairs in the center of the office. As I stepped off the escalator Mr. Briones, the Executive Director of Human resource was standing behind the counter. It was as if he was waiting to see if I was going to show up. When he saw me he looked a little disappointed but he motioned for me to approach the counter. I told him I was there for the interview and I thought the meeting was to take place in room 114. He told me the school board members kicked them out and they had to move the interview to the superintendent's conference room.

I immediately felt a red flag go up. I thought to myself, "What if this is an ambush and they start trying to talk about the case?" Well, they finally came to get me at about 1:45. When I entered the room I was greeted by about six people; the majority of them were elementary principals. They told me they were familiar with me and I didn't need to discuss the first question about my family or experience. They were going to omit that part of the interview. Each person asked a question and then asked me if I had any questions. I told them I didn't have any questions but hoped I would be selected. This meeting lasted about 12 min. This was the shortest interview I had ever experienced. I thanked them for their time and left. When I walked out I saw another constantly rejected friend of mine, who happened to be white. During this time, whites in the district had also become minorities. The districts employment make-up consisted mainly of Hispanics. I greeted her and she asked had I been interviewing for the AP position. I told her I had been trying for years. She said she had too. I already knew because I had seen her name in the paperwork that the district had supplied for my court case but I didn't say anything.

The next day I went to my lawyer's office to work on my case. I told Belinda I might as well buy a cot and move in the office since I was here more than I was at home. She smiled and agreed with me. Then the adventure continued. Belinda said she had gotten several other weird calls. Monica Salinas, Corpus Christi ISD's legal secretary, called and asked if Mr. Smith was still looking to hire a secretary because her sister was interested in applying. I asked Belinda "Isn't that strange?" Then I said, "They want to put spies in the camp." The other possibility was they wanted to be able to say Mr. Smith, who is Black, was discriminating against Hispanics. Even though Belinda's last name was Williams she was Hispanic.

Then the secretary from the legal firm out of Houston, which was hired by Corpus Christi ISD, called and first made the statement; they had not seen "The Motion to Compel" dated June 5, 2006 until now. She wanted to know why Belinda hadn't sent it certified. Belinda stated she told them she had E-Filed it which is a requirement now in the state of Texas. The secretary told her she had gone on vacation and when she arrived back all this stuff for Corpus Christi ISD was on her desk. She then wanted to know what format the judge required for the witness list. Belinda said she told her, "In the order the court tells you how they want it done."

All this happened in three days. Mr. Smith told me this was nothing. Next week would probably be even worst. I told him I think the district is now getting desperate because they know this is definitely going to court.

Well the bottom fell out of our case. Six days before I was to go to trial, Judge Owsley sent his decision not to allow my case to move forward to Mr. Smith's office. He had decided I would not be allowed to go to trial because it would be a waste of time. When I heard this you can only imagine what I felt. It was as if I had been kicked in the stomach and had all the air knocked out of me. I collapsed in a chair and just sat staring out into space. I couldn't believe I was being denied my day in court. Belinda sat solemnly as I sat stunned after hearing the news. She tried to console me. She knew I had been discriminated against but I had not been allowed to try and prove it. Mr. Smith came in to talk with me. He explained that I had another opportunity to try and overturn the judge's decision. I could appeal his decision. There was an appeals lawyer he knew that was very reasonable. His name was Mr. Christopher McJunkin.

I couldn't see giving up now and a meeting was scheduled. Once I met with Mr. McJunkin and he agreed to take my case, I felt I still had a chance. Even though I didn't have the money to pay his fee, I was able to get a loan from the bank.

After reviewing the judge's decision Mr. McJunkin felt the judge had made up his mind long before he officially rendered judgment. He just needed to make sure he covered all his bases, especially since I had file three separate charges involving different federal laws. He also told me something that nearly broke my heart. Immediately after the judge rendered his decision and it became a part of public domain my case was cited in another school district where someone had filed a discrimination lawsuit against that district. I had fought this so hard in an effort to not only help myself but to also help those that had been discriminated against and now it was being used to hurt them.

On August 17, 2007 I received a letter from Mr. McJunkin informing me that the appellate court had rejected my appeal and upheld the decision of the lower court in Corpus. He did say I could appeal that decision as well but I could see no purpose in that. I had sacrificed so much to get the money to fight to this point already. I felt I was throwing good money after bad.

One last thing I ask of Mr. McJunkin before I walked away from this was would it be possible to find out just how much money was spent by Corpus Christi ISD to fight me. I knew they could have shut me down for $25,000; I was just curious to see how much they eventually spent. He told me this information was a matter of public record and he would request that information for me. They spent over a $100,000 to fight me.

CORPUS CHRISTI INDEPENDENT SCHOOL DISTRICT
P.O. BOX 110 Corpus Christi, Texas 78403-0110 • 801 Leopard Street
(361) 886-9067 Fax: (361) 844-0283
www.ccisd.us

August 31, 2007

Mr. Christopher E. McJunkin
Attorney at Law
2842 Lawnview
Corpus Christi, Texas 78404

RE: Public Information Request
        Frankie J. Monroe vs. Corpus Christi Independent School District
        EEOC Charge No. 360-2005-00072
        Federal District Court Civil Action No. C-05-234
        Fifth Circuit Court of Appeals No. 06-41337

Dear Mr. McJunkin:

This will acknowledge receipt of your public information request dated August 20, 2007, and received in our office on August 24, 2007. Pursuant to your request, please find below the following responses:

1.   A record of all attorneys hired by Corpus Christi Independent School District (CCISD) related to services regarding the above-referenced EEOC (Equal Employment Opportunity Commission) Charge of Discrimination, federal lawsuit and appeal.

     RESPONSE:

          a.   The EEOC complaint was handled internally.
          b.   The federal lawsuit and appeal were handled by the law firm of Henslee, Fowler, Hepworth & Schwartz, LLP.

2.   A record of all funds paid by Corpus Christi Independent School District (CCISD) to each attorney listed in the previous request.

     RESPONSE:

     Please see attached spreadsheet reflecting invoice amounts and dates paid to Henslee, Fowler, Hepworth & Schwartz, LLP.

Should you have any questions, please do not hesitate to contact the undersigned.

Sincerely,

Imelda Martinez

Imelda Martinez, In-House Counsel
Office of Legal Services

mas

Enclosure

Frankie J. Monroe
Henslee, Fowler, Hepworth & Schwartz, LLP.

	Amount	Date Paid
	$6,855.50	8/17/2007
	$17.00	4/13/2007
	$124.00	3/23/2007
	$127.49	2/9/2007
	$20.02	1/12/2007
	$17,067.77	12/15/2006
	$1,927.50	12/8/2006
	$234.11	10/20/2006
	$85.00	9/29/2006
	$10,174.53	9/29/2006
	$19,141.50	9/15/2006
	$11,353.52	8/4/2006
	$16,616.29	8/4/2006
	$7,209.19	5/26/2006
	$1,853.00	3/10/2006
	$1,819.00	3/10/2006
	$2,669.00	2/3/2006
	$4,836.44	12/16/2005
TOTAL	$102,130.86	

Chapter XI

And the Band Played On

After what I felt was a complete failure of the justice system to defend me I continued to apply for different positions and continued to be rejected. Because of the intake person that held this position the entire time I was on my quest to advance into administration I questioned the school districts hiring practices. I constantly questioned whether my applications were being submitted by Mrs. Maria Villarreal. Personally I believe if you have someone that has a hidden agenda to systematically block others, whether they are Black, White, Hispanic or whatever; from even getting into the school district simply by failing to submit their applications this is a problem. Once this suspected problem is presented to those in higher authority I felt it should have been addressed. This wasn't the case, and as late as July 2009 which was the last time I submitted an application with Corpus Christi ISD this same person, whom I continuously complained about, was still holding the position of Human Resource Specialist. When I inquired about the application I had submitted for **Special Education Behavior Intervention Specialist** she blatantly admitted to me, after she told me a week earlier that all my necessary material had been received, she didn't submit my application because I was lacking two more references in time to be considered.

Even though I complained to all of those in authority, Dr. Jesus Chavez, Superintendent, Mrs. Mary Kelly, acting Superintendent, Mr. Scott Elliff, the present Superintendent of Corpus Christi ISD, Mr. Jacob Perez III the Director of Certified Personnel, Mrs. Jackie Turner, the Director of Special Education, and Dr. Connolly, the Superintendent of Special Education about this situation nothing was done. Mr. Jacob Perez III did respond, but only to inform me he was no longer the Director of Certified Personnel. He had been moved to assistant principal at Kaffie Middle School. This gentleman had been allowed to hold a temporary position as Director of Certified Personnel for nearly three years until he had enough work experience behind him to be hired permanently after Mr. Briones was elevated to Director of Human Resource. In this position Mr. Briones was over both certified and none certified personnel. How about that he was rewarded for committing perjury and getting away with it?

That's just like Corpus Christi ISD; they have employees that have been caught committing adultery, stealing district funds, falsifying test scores, and host of other illegal activity and those very same people are advanced into other high paying positions.

I was notified by e-mail that the position of **Special Education Behavior Intervention Specialist** had been offered to someone else. When asked for the person's qualification during the last EEOC mediation meeting in August 2010; we were told no one was hired. A week later I was contacted by Mr. McJunkin and told that the district contacted him and admitted they had made a mistake; someone was hired but they still failed to supply the qualifications of that applicant. This is just one more way to manipulate the situation to their advantage.

I even requested in an e-mail to the Superintendent and Personnel Director to be transferred to another campus as a special education teacher given I hadn't been allowed to advance in my career. That was rejected. This has been year after, year after, year of rejections with no recourse.

July 16, 2009

Corpus Christi Independent School District
Human Resource Dept
801 Leopard St.
Corpus Christi, TX

Attention: Mr. Jacob Perez,

My name is Dr. Frankie J. Monroe. I currently work on the Ray High School Campus. I would like to submit my letter of interest for the position of Special Education Behavior Intervention Specialist.

I have updated my application. Please inform me if there is any additional information currently needed to complete my files. I will submit all necessary documents as soon as possible. Once received, I request that these documents be uploaded into my application.

Any consideration in reference to this position will be greatly appreciated.

Respectfully submitted,

Dr. Frankie J. Monroe
fjmonroe2000@yahoo.com

Thank you for applying with Corpus Christi Independent School District Friday, July 10, 2009 5:40 P

From: "Corpus Christi Independent School District Human Resources" <ccisdjob@ccisd.us>

To: "Frankie Monroe" <fjmonroe2000@yahoo.com>

From: ccisdjob@ccisd.us

Dear Frankie,

We have received your application and are in the process of reviewing it.
Complete applications are reviewed and selected applicants are contacted by administrators/principals to schedule interviews. Please do not call administrators, principals, schools or sites for an interview.

If you are recommended for hire by a school or site administrator, the Human Resources Department will contact you to officially offer you employment.

If you need to make any changes to your application, visit www.ccisd.us

and log in using your User ID and password.

Your User/Applicant ID: fjmonroe
Password Hint: Grandmother

Your application will remain on file for 2 years. If you wish to reactivate your application, be sure to UPDATE your application.

Thank you for your interest in the Corpus Christi ISD!

The Department for Human Resources
Corpus Christi ISD
361-886-9061
E-mail link: ccisdjob@ccisd.us

280

Re: Updated Resume   Monday, July 20, 2009 12:47 PM

From: "Maria Villarreal" <MGVillarreal@ccisd.us>
  To: "Frankie Monroe" <fjmonroe2000@yahoo.com>
       1 File (218b)

Maria Vill...

Thank you Ms Monroe....I will add to your file...

****
Maria G. Villarreal
Human Resource Specialist
Phone: 361-886-9075
Fax :   361-886-9057

CONFIDENTIALITY NOTICE: This email and attached documents, if any, may contain confidential information. All
information is intended only for the use of the named recipient(s). If you are not the named recipient, you are not
authorized to read, disclose, copy, distribute or take any action in reliance on the information and any action other than
immediate delivery to the named recipient is strictly prohibited. If you have received this email in error, please immediately
notify sender by telephone (886-9075) or priority email to arrange for a return of the original documents. If you are the
named recipient, you are not authorized to reveal any of this information to any other unauthorized person.
E-Mail: mgvillarreal@ccisd.us

>>> Frankie Monroe <fjmonroe2000@yahoo.com> 7/20/2009 12:20 PM >>>
Ms. Villarreal,

Here is an updated resumed that list all of my qualifications for the latest position that I have applied for.

281

DEPARTMENT FOR HUMAN RESOURCES
Office of Certified Personnel

CORPUS CHRISTI INDEPENDENT SCHOOL DISTRICT
P.O. BOX 110 Corpus Christi, Texas 78403-0110 • 801 Leopard Street
Office: (361) 844-0314 • Fax (361) 886-9057
Website: www.ccisd.us

July 23, 2009

Frankie J. Monroe

Dear Ms. Monroe:

Thank you for your interest in the Special Education Behavior Intervention Specialist position. In order to consider your application, the documents checked below must be received on or before the advertised deadline. Advertised Deadline: Open until filled.

On-Line Application

Transcript(s) (Copy)

Resume must include related work experience in the position named above

Certification (Copy)

Professional Development and Appraisal System Certificate (Copy)

Highlighted topics need to be addressed (see attached)

x   References – send copies of the enclosed forms to three (3) references, which must be returned to the Department for Human Resources at the address on the form before the deadline date

If you have any questions, please contact the Department for Human Resources at 361/886-9075.

Sincerely

Jacob Perez, III
Director for Certified Personnel

282

Fwd: Special Education Behavior Intervention Specialist position   Thursday, February 4, 2010 9:14 AM

From: "Frankie Monroe" <fjmonroe@ccisd.us>

  To: fjmonroe2000@yahoo.com

    1 File (248KB)

Special E...

Forwarded Message: Special Education Behavior Intervention Specialist position

                                               Friday, August 14, 2009 3:32 PM

Special Education Behavior Intervention Specialist position

From: "Frankie Monroe" <fjmonroe@ccisd.us>

  To: "Scott Elliff" <DSElliff@ccisd.us>, "Frankie Monroe" <FJMonroe@ccisd.us>, "Jacob Perez III" <JAPerez@ccisd.us>, "Jacqulyn Turner" <JJTURNER@ccisd.us>, "Katherine Conoly" <KAConoly@ccisd.us>

  Cc: fjmonroe2000@yahoo.com

    1 File (185KB)

Letter to ...

Please read attachment.

August 14, 2009

Corpus Christi ISD
801 Leopard St
Corpus Christi, TX 78401

To Whom It May Concern:

My name is Dr. Frankie J. Monroe. I am currently assigned to the Ray high school campus. I am writing this letter in reference to the position Special Education Behavior Intervention Specialist. After conducting a job search on the district website I went online and updated my application. On July 16, 2009 I took a letter of interest in to the human resource office. I spoke to Ms. Maria Villarreal. She told me that she had received my online application and everything was in order. I specifically asked her if my references were in order because this had seemed to be a problem in the past when I applied for positions. She stated that she had checked my references and they were still good.

On July 23, 2009 I received a letter from Mrs. Villarreal stating that I needed to update my references. I called and questioned her because on July 16, 2009 she told me everything was in order. She said she was sorry but that was not the case. I then asked if she could mail the reference forms so that I could try to contact people.

I went to the main office today (August 14, 2009) to take care of some other matters and decided to check to see if all the paperwork was in order for the above mentioned position. Ms. Villarreal informed me that my application had not been submitted because my references were not received in time and the position had closed. I asked when did this occur and she told me that the position closed on August 3, 2009. She further stated that she had only received one reference on time and the other two references were received after the closing date. According to the letter I received from Ms. Villarreal on July 23, 2009 there was no closing date (Open until Filled).

I was told in the past that my references were good for at least two years. I have applied every year since 2000 for different positions. For some reason it seems that I am being required to get references each time I apply for a position.

I have dedicated 15 of my 25 years of service in education to Corpus Christi ISD. In those years I have received glowing annual evaluations and was even nominated as Teacher of the Year runner up, on the campus I worked on, twice.

I have continuously sought to improve my academic skills in order to be worthy of moving into administrative positions. Not only do I have a Superintendent and Principal certifications I also have a Doctorate in Educational leadership. In spite of all of my accomplishments I have been repeatedly denied the opportunity to advance past special education teacher. In many instances Mrs. Villarreal has been the application intake

284

person. She is the one that has contacted me over the years to inform me on the status of my applications and provided reasons why my application was not submitted for consideration in the interviewing process. I have constantly tried to make sure all of my information is updated and submitted but something is always missing according to Ms. Villarreal. In this instance there was no deadline posted but according to Ms. Villarreal I missed it anyway

I would like to be provided the opportunity to interview for this position. Any consideration would be greatly appreciated.

Sincerely,

Dr. Frankie J. Monroe

Fwd: Re: Special Education Behavior Intervention Specialist position

Monday, September 28, 2009 5:14 PM

From: "Frankie Monroe" <fjmonroe@ccisd.us>

To: fjmonroe2000@yahoo.com

1 File (4KB)

Re: Speci...

Forwarded Message: Re: Special Education Behavior Intervention Specialist position

Re: Special Education Behavior Intervention Specialist position

Friday, August 14, 2009 3:35 PM

From: "Jacob Perez III" <JAPerez@ccisd.us>

To: "Frankie Monroe" <FJMonroe@ccisd.us>

Ms. Monroe,

I am no longer in the HR department.

Thanks,

Jacob Perez III
Assistant Principal
Kaffie Middle School
Corpus Christi ISD
Phone: 361-994-3600

JAPerez@ccisd.us

CONFIDENTIALITY NOTICE: This email and attached documents, if any, may contain confidential information. All information is intended only for the use of the named recipient(s). If you are not the named recipient, you are not authorized to read, disclose, copy, distribute or take any action in reliance on the information and any action other than immediate delivery to the named recipient is strictly prohibited. If you have received this email in error, please immediately notify sender by telephone or priority email to arrange for a return of the original documents. If you are the named recipient, you are not authorized to reveal any of this information to any other unauthorized person.

>>> Frankie Monroe 08/14/09 3:32 PM >>>
Please read attachment.

CCISD Application for Employment

Friday, September 25, 2009 2:11 PM

From: "Maria G Villarreal" <mgvillarreal@ccisd.us>
To: "fjmonroe2000@yahoo.com" <fjmonroe2000@yahoo.com>

Dear Frankie,

Thank you for expressing interest in employment with the Corpus Christi Independent School District (CCISD). Your application was considered along with others for the following position:

Special Education Behavior Intervention Specialist (Lozano)

Although another applicant was offered the position, we encourage you to monitor our website for future openings.

Should another vacancy be advertised for which you wish to be considered, you are welcome to reactivate your file by submitting an online application and a new letter of interest to the Office of Certified Personnel.

Best wishes in your future endeavors.

Sincerely,

Donna R. Adams
Director for Certified Personnel

DRA:mv

Fwd: Re: Transfer   Thursday, February 4, 2010 9:07 AM

From: "Frankie Monroe" <fjmonroe@ccisd.us>
To: fjmonroe2000@yahoo.com
1 File (4KB)

Re: Trans...

Forwarded Message: Re: Transfer

Re: Transfer   Tuesday, June 17, 2008 9:36 PM

From: "Frankie Monroe" <fjmonroe@ccisd.us>
To: "Scott Elliff" <DSElliff@ccisd.us>
Cc: "Jacob Perez III" <JAPerez@ccisd.us>

Thank you Mr. Elliff for your prompt response. I veiwed the job
postings and saw that there are special education teacher positions
being sought by the district at the secondary level. I hope that I will
be considered before new people are hired and I hope my credentials will
be provided to the principals that are seeking special education
teachers.

Again thank you for responding.

Have a good day.

>>> Scott Elliff 06/17/08 1:38 PM >>>
Good afternoon Ms. Monroe:

Thank you for your email. The Department for Human Resources has your
transfer request, as submitted. Transfers are approved based on the
recommendation of the principal at the receiving campus. If there is an
opening in your area of certification, and a recommendation forthcoming
from a principal for you to fill that opening, then your transfer will
be accomplished.

Sincerely,

D. Scott Elliff
Superintendent of Schools
361-886-9003
Every student a learner...every learner a graduate...every graduate a
success!

CONFIDENTIALITY NOTICE: This email and attached documents, if any, may
contain confidential information. All information is intended only for
the use of the named recipient(s). If you are not the named recipient,
you are not authorized to read, disclose, copy, distribute or take any
action in reliance on the information and any action other than
immediate delivery to the named recipient is strictly prohibited. If

http://us.mc336.mail.yahoo.com/mc/showMessage?sMid=10&fid=Old%2520E%252dmails&filterBy=&.rand=...   8/24/2010 you have received this email in error, please immediately notify sender by telephone (361-886-9020) or priority email to arrange for a return of the original documents. If you are the named recipient, you are not authorized to reveal any of this information to any other unauthorized person.

>>> Frankie Monroe 6/14/2008 10:23 AM >>>
Good Morning Mr. Elliff,

My name is Frankie J. Monroe. I met you several years ago when I participated on one of the community action committees for your "Even One dropout is to much" campaign.

I know you are very busy and I don't want to impose, but I have a concern that perhaps you can help me with. I realize that no matter how much education I receive and how many certifications I get, I probably will never be allowed to advance into an administrative position with CCISD because I had the audacity to question their hiring practices.

Every year for the past 8 years I have applied for entry level positions in administration, basically assistant principal positions, but have been repeatedly over looked. Do you think a person should be penalized for doing there job well? I have been told that because I have worked in special education, in every subject and grade level with varying handicapping conditions for 25 years, met with a great deal of success with this student population, and considered an expert in behavior management, they cannot afford for me to leave the classroom. My response to this statement is "If I wanted to remain in the classroom I would not have pursued any additional certifications into administrations."

Having said all that this is what I would like for you to assist me with if you can. I have worked on the Ray High School Campus for 6 years. For three of those years I have requested to be transferred to a middle school campus. This school year I submitted two transfer request, one in November and one in February. I have contacted Mr. Perez the Certified Personnel Director as well. I don't want to be on the Ray campus when school starts this year. I have 11 years of middle school experience and would like to return to that student population. I requested Haas Middle School as my first choice for consideration if positions were available and then Martin and Cunningham prospectively. I also informed Mr. Perez if those positions were not available I would be open to other middle school campuses.

Any assistance in this matter will be greatly appreciated.

Have a Great Day!

From: "Maria G Villarreal" <mgvillarreal@ccisd.us>
  To: "fjmonroe2000@yahoo.com" <fjmonroe2000@yahoo.com>

Dear Frankie,

Thank you for expressing interest in employment with the Corpus Christi Independent School District (CCISD). Your application was considered along with others for the following position:

  Assistant Principal - All Levels - District Wide

Although another applicant was offered the position, we encourage you to monitor our website for future openings.

Should another vacancy be advertised for which you wish to be considered, you are welcome to reactivate your file by submitting an online application and a new letter of interest to the Office of Certified Personnel.

Best wishes in your future endeavors.

Sincerely,

Jacob Perez, III
Director for Certified Personnel

JP:mv

Chapter XII

No Peace Within

I thought I had released everything after the final decision was rendered in my 2004 discrimination lawsuit but something happened. It started with the fall at school on November 12, 2008. I have already given you some information concerning the fall and I don't feel I need to go any further as far as the initial incident but I will provided you with an exchange of letters between Mr. Clark Adkins, Director, Office of Employee Benefits and Risk Management, Mr. Scott Elliff, current superintendent of Corpus Christi ISD and I because of the fall at work.. As you already are aware I was not allowed to return to work with restrictions and was sent a letter which provided alternative options. I chose to take a leave of absence without pay for one year because some additional medical issues developed stemming from my initial fall and I didn't want to loose my job.

I thought I would receive a letter confirming my request for leave of absence without pay for one year but instead I received a letter from the superintendent, Mr. Scott Elliff stating I had resigned, which wasn't the case. This letter was the tipping point. Every hurt I had ever experienced, due to the treatment I received from Corpus Christi ISD, bubbled up inside me. I actually couldn't function for a time and sank into a deep depression. I was given an opportunity to voice some of what I felt in a Corpus Christi ISD Employee Separation Questionnaire as well and I will share that with you along with my response to the Superintendents letter.

OFFICE OF EMPLOYEE BENEFITS
and RISK MANAGEMENT

CORPUS CHRISTI INDEPENDENT SCHOOL DISTRICT
P.O. BOX 110 Corpus Christi, Texas 78403-0110 · 801 Leopard Street
Office: (361) 886-9851 · Fax (361) 886-9857
www.ccisd.us

Wednesday, September 09, 2009

Frankie J Monroe

Dear Ms. Monroe,

This is to acknowledge receipt and approval of your request for a leave of absence without pay for Temporary Disability for the period August 21, 2009 through February 16, 2010.

If you wish to keep your group health insurance and other benefits in force while you are on leave, you may pay the premiums directly to CCISD. Please contact Payroll at 886-9175 for information regarding these arrangements.

Prior to your return, our office must receive your written request to active status, along with a physician's statement indicating your ability to resume regular duties. A Return to Work/Work Status form are enclosed for your convenience.

If you are unable to return to work you must (1) submit a written request for a leave of absence without pay to the appropriate Director of Human Resources for at least one semester or no more than one calendar year; or (2) resign from your position. Failure to comply shall be deemed an election not to report and employment shall be terminated according to appropriate dismissal policies

If you have any questions, please contact our office at 886-9044.

Sincerely,

Clark Adkins, Director
Office of Employee Benefits and Risk Management

rb
cc: Principal/Supervisor
    Human Resources
    Becky Carter
    File

January 28, 2010

**OFFICE OF EMPLOYEE BENEFITS
and RISK MANAGEMENT**

P.O. BOX 110 Corpus Christi, Texas 78403-0110 • 801 Leopard Street
Office: (361) 886-9851 • Fax (361) 886-9857
www.ccisd.us

Tuesday, January 12, 2010

Frankie J Monroe

Dear Ms. Monroe,

This is to notify you that you have used at least 150 days of your temporary disability leave and that your scheduled return date is February 17, 2010. You have 30 calendar days from the date of this letter to notify the District of your intention for continuation of employment, along with a physician's statement indicating your ability to resume regular duties.

If you are unable to return to work at the end of your approved temporary disability leave period, you must (1) submit a written request for a leave of absence with out pay to the appropriate director in the Department of Human Resources; or (2) resign from your position. Failure to do so shall be deemed an election not to report, and your employment may be terminated according to appropriate dismissal policies.

If you have any questions, please contact our office at 886-9044.

Sincerely,

Clark Adkins, Director
Office of Employee Benefits and Risk Management

rb
cc: Principal/Supervisor
    Human Resources
    Leave File

January 28, 2010

Corpus Christi ISD
Clark Adkins, Director
Office of Employee Benefits
And Risk Management
801 Leopard Street
Corpus Christi, TX 78401

Attention: Mr. Clark Adkins:

My name is Dr. Frankie J. Monroe. I am currently assigned to the Ray High School Campus as an AE teacher. I am writing you this letter in response to the letter I received dated January 12, 2010 and postmark stamped January 21, 2010. This letter was issued to notify me that I had used at least 150 days of my temporary disability leave and my scheduled return date is February 17, 2010. It stated that I had 30 calendar days from the date of this letter to notify the school district of my intention for continuation of employment, along with a physician's statement indicating my ability to resume regular duties.

If I have not exhausted all of my temporary disability leave I would like to request continued temporary disability at this time. I am submitting another physician's statement indicating my inability to return to regular duty.

This letter went on to say if I was unable to return to work at the end of my approved temporary disability leave period I had to submit in a written request for a leave of absence without pay to the appropriate director in the Department of Human Resources.

If I have exhausted all of my temporary disability leave due to continued medical problems that restrict me from returning to full duty I want this letter to be considered my written request for leave of absence without pay to the Director of Human Resources.

Your attention to this matter will be greatly appreciated.

Respectfully submitted,

Dr. Frankie J. Monroe

Attachments

294

CCISD

This form must be completed in full and sent to the Office of Employee Benefits and Risk Management

I. EMPLOYEE INFORMATION

Monroe   Frankie   J.

Last Name   First Name   Middle Initial   Social Security Number

Home Address   City   State   Zip   Home Phone

Reg/Sp Ed   Cissy Perez   Teacher

Campus/Department   Supervisor Name   Job Position   Work Phone

Select status type from the following:

☐ **Return to Work** – I am requesting to return from a leave of absence. Per my Physician's Statement below, I can return to work effective _____ *(insert date).*

☒ **Work Status** – I am requesting a continuation of my current leave.

II. STATEMENT OF ATTENDING PHYSICIAN

To Be Completed By Employee's Physician:

Recommendations For Work:

☐ **Return to Full Work Duties/No Restrictions** – Effective Date: _____

☐ **Return to Work Duties With Restrictions** – Effective Date: _____

☒ **No Work** – Estimated Length of Time: _____

Physical Restrictions:

Limit Lifting/Carrying to:	Limit Pushing/Pulling to:	Other Physical Limitations:	
☒ 0-10 lbs	☐ 0-10 lbs	☐ No use of right/left hand	☐ Other: _____
☐ 11-20 lbs	☐ 11-20 lbs	☒ No reaching above shoulders	
☐ 21-35 lbs	☐ 21-35 lbs	☒ No reaching below waist	
☐ 36-50 lbs	☐ 36-50 lbs	☒ No exposure to vibrating tools	
☐ Over 50 lbs	☐ Over 50 lbs	☒ No operation of moving machinery	
☐ No lifting/carrying	☒ No pushing/pulling	☐ No driving of motor vehicle	
☐ Other: _____	☐ Other: _____	☐ Standard ☐ Automatic	
		☒ No climbing:	
		☐ Stairs ☐ Scaffold ☐ Ramp ☐ Ladder	

Time Restrictions/Other Restrictions:

☒ Work requiring repeated stooping, crawling, kneeling, or being in a cramped position limited to _____ minutes per hour

☒ Continuous walking limited to __2__ minutes per hour __4__ hours per day

☒ Continuous standing limited to __10__ minutes per hour __4__ hours per day

☒ Continuous sitting limited to __10__ minutes per hour __4__ hours per day

☒ Repetitive hand/wrist motion limited to __NA.__ minutes per hour _____ hours per day

☒ Workday limited to __0__ hours per day

☐ Environmental Restrictions (heat, cold). Please list: _____

☐ Special Instructions (dressings, eye patch, etc.): _____

☐ Orthotic Devices (braces, splints, etc.): _____

Duration of Restrictions: _____

Physician's Signature: _____ Office Phone: _____ Date: 1-27-100

Corpus Christi Independent School District
Office of Employee Benefits and Risk Management
P.O. Box 110 Corpus Christi, TX 78403-0110
Phone: 361-886-9044 Fax: 361-886-9857

CORPUS CHRISTI INDEPENDENT SCHOOL DISTRICT
P.O. Box 110 Corpus Christi, Texas 78403-0110
Office: (361) 886-9002   Fax: (361) 886-9109
Website: www.ccisd.us

January 29, 2010

Frankie Monroe

Dear Ms. Monroe:

The Corpus Christi Independent School District (CCISD) is in receipt of your letter dated January 28, 2010, regarding your decision to resign effective February 17, 2010. This letter is sent to notify you that your resignation is hereby accepted as per CCISD Board Policy DFE (Local) which states that: "Once submitted and accepted, the resignation of a contract employee may not be withdrawn without consent of the Board or the Superintendent."

On behalf of CCISD, please accept our thanks for your dedicated service to the children of this district. If you have questions, I may be reached at (361) 886-9003.

Please contact the Payroll Office at (361) 886-9175 regarding your final check.

I would also like to extend to you the opportunity to reclaim some to of the original documents from your personnel file after your last work day February 17, 2010. If you are interested in obtaining any of the documents, submit your request in writing to the Department for Human Resources.

Sincerely,

D. Scott Elliff
Superintendent of Schools

DSE/lg

cc: Cissy Perez

296

February 6, 2010

Office of the Superintendent
D. Scott Eliff, Superintendent of Schools
801 Leopard Street
Corpus Christi, TX. 78401

Attention Mr. D. Scott Eliff

I received your letter dated January 29, 2010 but postmarked February 5, 2010 accepting my letter of resignation. There seems to be a misunderstanding. According to the letters received from Mr. Clark Adkins on dated September 9, 2009 and the other dated January 12, 2010, I was given two choices (1) submit a written request for a leave of absence without pay to the appropriate Director of Human Resources for at least one semester or no more than one calendar year: or (2) resign from my position. Failure to comply would be deemed an election not to report and employment would be terminated according to appropriate dismissal policies. I am attaching a copy of those letters.

I submitted a request for a leave of absence without pay allowing me up to one calendar year to return to work. I do not wish to resign at this time. Immediate attention to this matter would be greatly appreciated.

Respectfully submitted,

Dr. Frankie J. Monroe

cc: Clark Adkins, Director
    Cissy Perez

CORPUS CHRISTI INDEPENDENT SCHOOL DISTRICT
Office of Certified Personnel

Employee Separation Questionnaire

Please check reasons for leaving (*Please include any comments you feel appropriate. You may add a separate piece of paper or use the back of this form*).

Other (Please explain):

I am being required to leave the school district due to medical problems that arose after a fall I had in my adaptive education class. Despite all efforts to improve my health and strength to return to the position that I held as an adaptive education teacher I was unsuccessful. My medical physician refused to release me to full duty without restrictions because he felt it would jeopardize my healing process. My duties required lifting students that weighed upwards of a 110lbs or more, excessive bending stooping, squatting and in some case chasing mentally and physically challenged students.

I was notified by a district representative that I had exhausted all of my temporary disability leave and since I was not able to return to full duty without restrictions I had a few choices (1) take a **Leave of Absence without pay,** (2) **Resign**, or (3) **be terminated.** I opted to take a **Leave of Absence without pay**. I had applied for other positions within the school district but was never selected for an interview.

What did you like about your experience as a District employee?

I have worked 27 years in education 18 years of which were dedicated to teaching special needs students with varying handicapping conditions in every subject from Math, English, Texas History, Science to Adaptive education within the Corpus Christi Independent School District. In that time I have worked with many administrators. Some were very effective as administrators and some were not. The one thing I enjoyed was the respect I was given from my immediate administrators and colleagues. Often times I would be called in by some administrators and asked my opinion on several issues the campus was facing. Many times I was called in and asked how I would handle certain volatile issues involving students and parents. I understood human behavior and knew how to deal with confrontational issues. I also enjoyed mentoring new teachers who knew pedagogy but could not teach due to their inability to control their classes. As you know if you can't control your students you can't teach. What I enjoyed most of all were my students. So many of them had never met with success but I made sure they left my class knowing that they were respected and cared for but I also had high expectations of them. I always provided them with choices. For years I had a banner in my room that I would refer to when I was challenged by one of my students that read "Let the Choices You Make Today be the Choices You Can Live with Tomorrow."

What did you dislike about your experience as a District employee?

The district has many excellent qualifications but it also has many flaws. As a minority in the school district I have been let down repeatedly. That old adage "It's not what you know but who you know", definitely applies within the Corpus Christi Independent School District. I have witnessed and experienced discrimination and favoritism first hand over the years. If you are not a relative or a close friend to certain administrators you are never given an opportunity to advance in your career; at least that has been my experience.

I never expected to be given any administrative position without preparing myself first. For years I worked hard to gain the knowledge necessary to advance in my career. I took all the courses, did all the work and passed all the test at Texas A & M University to obtain a Doctorate in Educational Leadership, Masters degree Educational administration, Superintendent Certification, Principal Certification and all the training the school district offered to hopefully one day be able to move into an administrative position.

Feeling confident I would be allowed to at least be hired in an entry level position as and (assistant principal) I applied over and over and received rejection letter after rejection letter. In those letters the explanation given for me not being selected, even to go on an interview, was that the positions had been filled by more qualified people than me. Initially I accepted that explanation because I had not been able to obtain the necessary experience the district required. As time went on I started observing people who were younger than me, with only 2 to 3 years of teaching experience, advance to administrative positions. When I questioned Dr. Jesus Chavez and Mr. Briones in 2003, why I was not being allowed to advance in my career after repeated times of applying for different administrative position, I was told by administration they had me where they wanted me, which was working with special needs students. I was even told by the in-house districts attorney that perhaps the reason I had not advanced was because I was doing the job of four people. She told me she had looked at my entire record which covered over twenty years and she had never come across a record quite like mine. There was not one bad note from any administrator I had ever worked for, every evaluation I had received was of exceptional quality, not one complaint from any parent, nothing that reflected negatively on my job performance. My question was "Do you mean to tell me that just because I do my job well I am penalized?"

Do you have any comments or suggestions to improve the District?

I think the district dropped the ball in my case but I am also aware of so many others that you have done this too. It is probably too late for me but I think you as a district need to reassess your hiring practices.

Would you recommend the District to others as a place to work?

Like I said in the beginning I feel that the district has many excellent qualities but it comes with flaws. If the district can reevaluate it's hiring practices, especially when it comes to hiring blacks that do qualify for certain positions, revisit the school boards duties and the role they should actually play in the hiring process, (**not to dictate who is hired in an academic capacity because many of them are not trained in that area but accept who the superintendent chooses after a fair selection process**), I would have no qualms about recommending others to work in the district.

A few months after I answered this questionnaire I discovered my teaching certification was being used without my knowledge. I had been denied the right to return to work with restrictions and was never offered any accommodations. Now they were going to reap benefits from me again through the use of my certification. I filed discrimination charges with EEOC. I have already provided information on that earlier.

Chapter XIII

Time Winding Down

It had been nearly a year since I had attempted to apply for a position with CCISD and decided to look at what they had available. I discovered they had posted assistant principal positions at all levels. The opening date was December 16, 2010 and the closing date was January 7, 2011 so I decided to apply. With such a short window to get information completed it didn't give me much time but I managed to get it done.

The very first contact I received was a confirmation letter indicating that they had received my application and it was in the process of being reviewed. This was automatically generated through the application system and then the games began once again. I received an e-mail from Mrs. Maria G. Villarreal, I'm not sure what her official title is because on one document she states she is a Human Resource Specialist and on another she states she is a Professional Applicant Specialist. She informed me once again off all the things I was missing in my application. I had to provide a letter of interest to Ms. Donna R. Adams, the Certified Personnel Director, update my resume, and provide one reference for the specific position I applied for which had to be an immediate supervisor.

Since I had not worked for over a year I didn't have an immediate supervisor. In the letter that I hand delivered to the certified personnel director I asked if I could just use prior supervisors as references. I don't know if she ever received the letter because I was only contacted by Mrs. Villarreal. I was now also required to take an online Principalinsight test. In the past only principals took test, assistant principals hadn't been required to.

I followed Mrs. Villarreal's instructions and then was notified by e-mail that not all of my references had been received. This was dated January 6, 2011. Ten years have passed and we are still doing this dance. Mind you she stated all I needed to get turned in was one reference. I checked my status on Winocular the districts application website and discovered that three of my references had been submitted dated 12/31/10, 01/03/11 and 01/04/11. Two of the three had been administrators that evaluated my job performance in prior years.

Once I received notice that EEOC was finished investigating my charges and were closing my case I received an e-mail from Mrs. Villarreal informing me that the district had decided not to hire anyone one for the Assistant Principal All Levels position. All of this maneuvering seemed very suspicious to me. I will submit documents so that you can follow this paper trail.

Once I contacted the superintendent concerning my supposed resignation in 2010, he did send me another letter which allowed me to take a year leave of absence without pay. On February 17, 2011 my year would be up and I had to let the district know if I would be returning. I still wasn't able to return to an AE classroom which required me to lift students 100+ pounds but the doctor did feel he could release me back to work with limited restrictions.

On February 15, 2011 I hand delivered a letter to Superintendent, Scott Elliff, Certified Personnel Director, Donna Adams, and Risk Management Director, Clark Adkins informing them that I had been released back to work with limited restrictions and asked to be put back on the employment list. I went to each one of their departments and submitted my letter and received a stamp and dated copy for myself. Today is February 24, 2011 and I still have not heard from them. I really don't expect to because in the letter I received from the Superintendent in 2010, it indicated that it was up to the school districts discretion whether they retained me or not.

Job Postings

POSITION AVAILABLE

JOB CATEGORIES >   ADMINISTRATOR POSITION TYPES >   Campus Based POSITIONS

JOB STATUS: Open

POSTING DATE: 12/16/2010

CLOSING DATE: 01/07/2011

POSTING NUMBER: 00003242

LOCATION: CAMPUS

POSITION TITLE: Assistant Principal - All Levels

REPORTS TO/SUPERVISES: School Principal

QUALIFICATIONS: **Education/Certification Required:**

- Master's Degree
- Texas mid-management/Principal Certificate or other appropriate Principal Certificate

Technology Proficiency: Level 2 Required:

- Use of technology for specific, but limited purposes

Special Knowledge/Skills Required:

- Thorough understanding of school administrative operations.
- Strong organizational, communication, and interpersonal skills

Experience Required:

- Three years experience as a classroom teacher

FUNCTION: Assist the campus principal in the administration of the instructional program and operations. Coordinate student activities and services as assigned.

MAJOR RESPONSIBILITIES & REQUIREMENTS: **INSTRUCTIONAL MANAGEMENT:**

- Participates in the development, implementation, coordination, and monitoring of the Campus Action Plan.
- Participates in the development, implementation, coordination, and monitoring of all aspects of the instructional program.

- Recognizes, evaluates, and analyzes elements of effective instruction and ensures that the instructional program is responsive to student needs.
- Provides instructional resources and materials to support teaching staff in accomplishing instructional goals.

SCHOOL/ORGANIZATIONAL CLIMATE:

- Communicates and promotes high expectations for special education/regular education staff and students performance, provides recognition of excellence and achievement which promotes a positive image to the community, and maintains positive staff morale.
- Coordinates supporting activities to accomplish the goals and objectives of the instructional program.

SCHOOL/ORGANIZATIONAL IMPROVEMENT:

- Fosters collegiality and collaboration among staff; mediates and facilitates resolution of conflicts; involves staff in planning/decision making.

PERSONNEL MANAGEMENT:

- Assists in defining expectations for staff regarding job performance.
- Evaluates personnel in accordance with state and District policies.
- Assists in identifying and providing opportunities for and encourages participation in staff development options to address school/district/employee goals identified through the goal-setting process.
- Works cooperatively with the Department for Human Resources in the selection of campus staff, and in closely monitoring the certification status of staff members when appropriate.

ADMINISTRATIVE AND FISCAL/FACILITIES MANAGEMENT:

- Complies with district policies, and state/federal laws and regulations.
- Manages all school facilities, requisitions, repairs as needed, and supervises custodial staff.
- Implements programs within budget limits, maintains fiscal control, and accurately reports fiscal information.

STUDENT MANAGEMENT:

- Implements and communicates to students, staff, and parents, a consistent, equitable discipline management plan with guidelines for student conduct that have been developed collaboratively with staff.
- Provides assistance in assessing the physical, mental, social, and emotional needs of students.
- Conducts conferences with parents, students, and teachers concerning school and student issues.

PROFESSIONAL GROWTH AND DEVELOPMENT:

- Assumes responsibility for acquiring knowledge, skills, and attitudes necessary for fulfilling job duties and improving leadership skills.
- Conducts himself/herself in a professional, ethical manner in accordance with generally accepted community standards; complies with Texas Education Agency code of ethics for educators.

SCHOOL/COMMUNITY RELATIONS:

- Involves parents and community in a positive, proactive manner by articulating the

school's mission through emphasizing and promoting two-way communication between the school and community.
- Articulates the school's mission to the community and solicits it's support in realizing the mission.

ADDITIONAL DUTIES:

- Performs other job-related duties as assigned by the principal.

SUPERVISORY RESPONSIBILITIES:

- Shares supervisory responsibility for professional staff with principal. Supervises teachers, custodians, paraprofessionals and clerical personnel and others when assigned by the principal.

WORKING CONDITIONS:

- Mental Demand: Ability to communicate effectively (verbal and written); interpret policy, procedures and data; coordinate District functions, maintains emotional control under stress.
- Physical Demands/Environmental Factors: Occasional District and statewide travel; frequent prolonged and irregular hours.

OTHER INFORMATION: The following MUST be submitted to HR for your file to be complete:

- Letter of Interest (MUST list level you are interested in: Elem, Middle, High School)
- Resume
- Three completed references (see below)
- Transcripts & Certifications
- Gallup Assessment

Interested applicants must complete the following:

- Online **Professional** Application (link at bottom of page), uploading a current resume, copies of transcripts and certifications, and letter of interest addressed to Ms. Donna Adams, Director of Certified Personnel.

- Our online application system will email "links" to the references listed in your application, if you provide email addresses. That person then uses the emailed link to complete the online reference form (accepted in place of a paper form). When you check your application status online, "returned" means that the reference has completed the online form. Any forms that were faxed and uploaded are available to us, but won't show as "returned."

- If you don't provide email address, or your references don't complete the online form, download the Professional Reference form, and provide to the 3 references listed in your online application. Copies of completed reference forms may be initially faxed to HR, but signed original reference forms must be provided to CCISD Human Resources by the job closing date.

Submit required documents to:

Office of Certified Personnel,
Attention: Ms. Donna Adams, Director of Certified Personnel.
PO Box 110,
Corpus Christi, Texas 78403-0110

or fax to 361-886-9057

or contact:
Maria G. Villarreal - (361) 886-9075
Professional Applicant Specialist
mgvillarreal@ccisd.us
CCISD Human Resources

801 Leopard
Corpus Christi, Texas

APPLY TO: Select the **Professional** Application in our online application system (link below).

SALARY: AP5 - $234.27 - $351.41 / daily rate
AP6 - $252.42 - $378.62 / daily rate
AP7 - $271.98 - $407.98 / daily rate

See the CCISD 2010-2011 Salary Schedule handbook for information regarding initial salary placement.

DAYS:

FROM -   TO -

GRADE / STEP: AP5-Elementary (200 days), AP6-Middle School (201 days), AP7-High School (203 days)

START DATE: Upon Hire

YAHOO! MAIL

Missing Documents

Monday, January 3, 2011 12:48 PM

"Maria G Villarreal" <mgvillarreal@ccisd.us>

"fjmonroe2000@yahoo.com" <fjmonroe2000@yahoo.com>

Frankie Monroe

Thank you for your interest in employment with the Corpus Christi Independent School District(District). The District is always looking for qualified applicants for Assistant Principal - All Levels with the deadline of January 7, 2011.

In reviewing your on-line application I noticed there were documents missing to complete the application process. Below is the list of items to submit.

1. A letter of interest to Donna R. Adams, Certified Personnel Director.
2. Resume
3. PrincipalInsight
4. References (1) for the specific position you are applying for. As per new directives: no letters, must be on District (CCISD) form, no part time assistant principals, no co teachers and 1 must be your immediate supervisor.

If you have any questions please do not hesitate to call me at (361) 695-7261.

Sincerely,

Maria G. Villarreal
Professional Applicant Specialist
Corpus Christi Independent School District
Phone - (361) 695-7261
Fax - (361) 886-9057
Email - Maria.Villarreal@ccisd.us

January 5, 2011

Donna Adams, Certified Personnel Director
CCISD Human Resource Dept
801 Leopard Street
Corpus Christi, TX 78401

Attention: Ms.Adams

My name is Dr. Frankie J. Monroe. I reside at 2962 Water Lily Dr. Corpus Christi, TX 78415. My phone number is (361) 851-1704. I am submitting my letter of interest for the position of Assistant Principal all- levels. I have enclosed a copy of my Resume.

I was instructed by Mrs. Maria Villarreal to have my immediate supervisor provide a reference for me. At this time I do not have an immediate supervisor so I have to rely on previous supervisors that were familiar with my work ethic.

It is also indicated that I only need one reference. Could you please have Mrs. Villarreal contact the references I provided by email through CCISD's application system on line. It will be greatly appreciated.

Any consideration in this matter will be greatly appreciated.

Sincerely,

Dr. Frankie J. Monroe

RE: CCISD PROFESSIONAL APPLICATION   Monday, January 3, 2011 12:48 PM
From: "Villarreal, Maria" <Maria.Villarreal@ccisd.us>
To: "fjmonroe2000@yahoo.com" <fjmonroe2000@yahoo.com>

Thank you for applying for a Assistant Principal position with the Corpus Christi Independent School District. We believe that Assistant principals are critical to student success, and we are committed to placing Assistant principals in positions where they will be most successful.

As an initial part of our process, we require that you take a Web-based assessment designed by Gallup, Inc. The assessment comes from research conducted with principals viewed as most successful.

• *PrincipalInsight* will require approximately 30 minutes of uninterrupted time.

• You can access *PrincipalInsight* using the URL below as a hot link or entering the URL from a Web browser.

• At the *PrincipalInsight* Log In page, you will be asked to create a username (use this e-mail address for your username) and a unique password. Please follow the directions carefully for creating the password. You should retain the username and password to re-enter the *PrincipalInsight* system.

• You will be asked to provide a district code as the means for identifying yourself in the system. The district code is provided below.

• *PrincipalInsight* consists of three question types: multiple choice, Likert scale (responses on a one-to-five scale), and open-ended items (in which you write your response). Specific instructions are contained within *PrincipalInsight* for each set of items.

• You should use Internet browsers with these versions or higher for best results: Microsoft Internet Explorer® 5.5+, Netscape® 6.1+, or AOL® 9.0+. A minimum of 56k modem is required.

• You must complete *PrincipalInsight* prior to the closing date for this position as advertised on our website (or within the next three days if there is no closing date), to be considered for this position.

• If you have completed *PrincipalInsight* within the last 12 months for CCISD, and the same version of *PrincipalInsight* is in use, *PrincipalInsight* will not admit you. If 12 months have elapsed, you will be admitted to the assessment for CCISD.

• If you have registered in more than one district using *PrincipalInsight* you may select to copy the results of the last assessment within 12 months or retake *PrincipalInsight*. If you wish to copy results from one school district to another school district within 12 months of the first assessment must use the same username and password for both districts.

• Following completion of the assessment, Gallup will forward the results to CCISD to be used in our selection process.

You may access *PrincipalInsight* with this URL: https://gx.gallup.com/principalinsight.gx

Use this district code:

If you need help, contact the Gallup client support team at srihelp@gallup.com or call 877-425-5872.

Maria G. Villarreal
Human Resource Specialist
Phone: 361-695-7261 (Internal 17261)

FW: RE: Reference form   Monday, January 10, 2011 9:12 AM

From: "Villarreal, Maria" <Maria.Villarreal@ccisd.us>
  To: "fjmonroe2000@yahoo.com" <fjmonroe2000@yahoo.com>
      1 File (20KB)

Referenc...

This reference must be a PRINCIPAL, even a previous Principal.....Please let me know if I can be of further assistance.   I will need this reference as soon as possible.

Maria G. Villarreal
Human Resource Specialist
Phone: 361-695-7261 (Internal 17261)
Fax: 361-886-9057
Email: Maria.Villarreal@ccisd.us

CONFIDENTIALITY NOTICE: This e-mail and attached documents, if any, may contain confidential information. All information is intended only for the use of the named recipient(s). If you are not the named recipient, you are not authorized to read, disclose, copy, distribute or take any action in reliance on the information and any action other than immediate delivery to the named recipient is strictly prohibited. If you have received this emial in in error, please immediately notify sender by telephone (886-9075) or priority email to arrange for a return of the original documents. If you are the named recipient, you are not authorized to reveal any of this information to any other unauthorized person.
E.Mail: Maria.Villarreal@ccisd.us

From: Villarreal, Maria
Sent: Thursday, January 06, 2011 3:00 PM
To: 'fjmonroe2000@yahoo.com'
Subject: RE: Reference form

Dr. Monroe

I have attached the reference form for you to use. I am aware as per your letter you do not have a supervisor to obtain a reference from....it can be a previous supervisor.......remember the deadline January 7, 2011... thanks

Maria G. Villarreal
Human Resource Specialist
Phone: 361-695-7261 (Internal 17261)
Fax: 361-886-9057
Email: Maria.Villarreal@ccisd.us

CONFIDENTIALITY NOTICE: This e-mail and attached documents, if any, may contain confidential information. All information is intended only for the use of the named recipient(s). If you are not the named recipient, you are not authorized to read, disclose, copy, distribute or take any action in reliance on the information and any action other than immediate delivery to the named recipient is strictly prohibited. If you

http://us.mc336.mail.yahoo.com/mc/showMessage?sMid=0&fid=School%2520E%252dM...   2/24/2011

have received this emial in in error, please immediately notify sender by telephone (886-9075) or priority email to arrange for a return of the original documents. If you are the named recipient, you are not authorized to reveal any of this information to any other unauthorized person.
E.Mail: Maria.Villarreal@ccisd.us

Documents on File / Reference Status

Listed below are documents that have been received as part of your application. We require original copies of transcripts and three letters of reference/recommendation from supervisors. The page count column indicates transcripts from multiple universities or multi-page transcripts.

Document Type	Date Added	Page Count
REFERENCES	01/04/2011	1
REFERENCES	12/31/2010	1
REFERENCES	01/03/2011	1

Please close out this window to continue your application.

Assistant Principal - All Levels   Wednesday, February 9, 2011 8:29 AM

"Maria G Villarreal" <mgvillarreal@ccisd.us>
"fjmonroe2000@yahoo.com" <fjmonroe2000@yahoo.com>

Frankie,

Thank you for expressing interest in employment with Corpus Christi Independent School Distict (CCISD). The District has elected not to fill the position of Assistant Principal - All Levels at this time.

Should another vacancy be advertised for which you wish to be considered, you may reactivate your file and submit a new letter of interest to the Department for Human Resource.

Donna R. Adams, Director
Office of Certified Personnel

CONFIDENTIALITY NOTICE: This email and attached documents, if any, may contain confidential information. All information is intended only for the use of the named recipient(s). If you are not the named recipient, you are not authorized to read, disclose, copy, distribute or take any action in reliance on the information and any action other than immediate delivery to the named recipient is strictly prohibited. If you have received this email in error, please immediately notify sender by telephone or priority email to arrange for a return of the original documents. If you are the named recipient, you are not authorized to reveal any of this information to any other unauthorized person.

http://us.mc336.mail.yahoo.com/mc/showMessage?sMid=21&filterBy=&.rand=14110373...   2/24/2011

CORPUS CHRISTI INDEPENDENT SCHOOL DISTRICT
P.O. Box 110 Corpus Christi, Texas 78403-0110
Office: (361) 886-9002 Fax: (361) 886-9109
Website: www.ccisd.us

February 8, 2010

Frankie Monroe
2962 Water Lily Dr
Corpus Christi, TX 78415

Dear Ms. Monroe:

Your request for leave of absence has been given staff approval effective February 17, 2010, with February 17, 2010 , being your last work day, for the 2009-2010 school year.

Your placement, when your leave of absence expires, will be in accordance with Board Policy DEC (Local) concerning leave of absence which states the following:

> "A full-time employee on leave of absence other than temporary disability covered under state law, shall notify the Executive Director for Human Resources of the desire to be restored to duty 30 days before the effective date for termination of the leave of absence. Unless otherwise required by applicable federal law, employees electing to return to duty from leave of absence shall be placed on a priority list for not more than one calendar year and not less than 90 school days, and shall be entitled to restoration to duty contingent upon there being a vacancy for which the person is qualified subject to selection and recommendation by the principal or supervisor."

If you desire to return to teaching at the termination of your leave of absence, please let the personnel office know, in writing, prior to February 17, 2011. If we do not hear from you, your name will be presented to the Board of Trustees as an automatic resignation from leave.

Please contact Payroll in the Office of Finance at 886-9179 for the appropriate paperwork to be completed. If we can be of further assistance, please do not hesitate to contact our office.

Please take a few minutes to complete and return the enclosed forms to the Office of Certified Personnel in the attached envelope or fax to (361) 886-9057.

Sincerely,

D. Scott Elliff
Superintendent of Schools

DSE/lg

cc: Cissy Perez

314

February 14, 2011

D. Scott Elliff, Superintendent
Corpus Christi ISD
801 Leopard St.
Corpus Christi, TX 78401

Attention: Mr. Elliff,

My name is Dr. Frankie J. Monroe. As you are aware I was taken off work by my physician due to continued medical issues stemming from a fall I sustained on the Ray High School campus as an AE Teacher on November 12, 2008. I was contacted by Mr. Clark Adkins, Director of Office of Employee Benefits and Risk Management in January 2010 and presented three choices I could take at that time, 1) take a leave of absence for one year without pay, 2) resign or 3) be terminated if I did not respond by a certain date. I opted to take a leave of absence without pay for one year which you approved.

On February 17, 2011 my one year leave of absence will be up. I have been under constant medical supervision since that time and my physician feels I can now return to work with limited restrictions. I will attach a copy of the Return to Work Notice/Work Status report.

I realize that the position I held as an Adaptive Education Teacher is no longer available but my special education certification covers all levels. I have taught on all grade levels in several subjects areas such as math, science, reading, Texas History, etc. The majority of my teaching experience has been on secondary levels in middle and high school. I did work as a highly qualified resource language arts teacher on the Ray High School campus for six years before returning to Adaptive Education.

I look forward to hearing from you, in the near future, on this matter and hope to be offered accommodations for the limited restrictions that my physician has placed on me.

I will forward copies of this letter and my physician's statement to Mr. Clark Adkins, Director of Risk Management and Mrs. Donna Adams, Certified Personnel Director.

Respectfully Submitted,

Dr. Frankie J. Monroe

Dr. Frankie J. Monroe

RECEIVED

FEB 1 5 2011

OFFICE OF SUPERINTENDENT
CORPUS CHRISTI ISD

315

This form must be completed in full and sent to the Office of Employee Benefits and Risk Management

I. EMPLOYEE INFORMATION

Monroe   Frankie   J

Last Name   First Name   Middle Initial   Social Security Number

Home Address   City   State   Zip   Home Phone

N/A   Sp. Ed Teacher

Campus/Department   Supervisor Name   Job Position   Work Phone

Select status type from the following:

☑ **Return to Work** – Per my physician's statement below, I can return effective _Feb 17 2011_ *(insert date).*
☐ **Work Status** – I providing a current update regarding my medical status.

Employee's Signature: _Dr. Freddie J. Monroe_   Date: _2-14-11_

II. STATEMENT OF ATTENDING PHYSICIAN

To Be Completed By Employee's Physician:

Recommendations For Work:

☒ **Return to Full Work Duties/No Restrictions** – Effective Date: _____
☒ **Return to Work Duties With Restrictions** – Effective Date: _2-17-11_
☐ **No Work** – Estimated Length of Time: _____

Physical Restrictions:

Limit Lifting/Carrying to:	Limit Pushing/Pulling to:	Other Physical Limitations:	
☐ 0-10 lbs	☒ 0-10 lbs	☐ No use of right/left hand	☐ Other: _____
☒ 11-20 lbs	☐ 11-20 lbs	☐ No reaching above shoulders	
☐ 21-35 lbs	☐ 21-35 lbs	☐ No reaching below waist	
☐ 36-50 lbs	☐ 36-50 lbs	☐ No exposure to vibrating tools	
☐ Over 50 lbs	☐ Over 50 lbs	☒ No operation of moving machinery	
☐ No lifting/carrying	☐ No pushing/pulling	☒ No climbing:	
☐ Other: _____	☐ Other: _____	☐ Stairs ☒ Scaffold ☐ Ramp ☒ Ladder	

Time Restrictions/Other Physical Restrictions:

☐ Work requiring repeated stooping, crawling, kneeling, or being in a cramped position limited to _____ minutes per hour
☐ Continuous walking limited to _____ minutes per hour _____ hours per day
☐ Continuous standing limited to _____ minutes per hour _____ hours per day
☐ Continuous sitting limited to _____ minutes per hour _____ hours per day
☐ Repetitive hand/wrist motion limited to _____ minutes per hour _____ hours per day
☐ Workday limited to _____ hours per day
☐ Environmental Restrictions (heat, cold). Please list: _____
☐ Special Instructions (dressings, eye patch, etc.): _____
☐ Orthotic Devices (braces, splints, etc.): _____

RECEIVED

FEB 1 5 2011

OFFICE OF SUPERINTENDENT
CORPUS CHRISTI ISD

Other Restrictions:

☐ Working unsupervised   ☐ Working in safety sensitive environment   ☐ Working in supervisory/decision making capacity

Duration of Restrictions: _____

Physician's Signature: _____ Office Phone: _____   Date: _2-14-10_

Corpus Christi Independent School District

Fertile Grown For Discrimination

My attorney stated Corpus Christi ISDs hiring process was a fertile area for discrimination. I will attach a few pages of the document he submitted to the courts on 6/05/2006 that explains why he came to that conclusion. You decide if he was right in drawing this conclusion.

ARGUMENT AND AUTHORITIES

36.   The record developed thus far in this civil action suggests that the District has used a selection scheme that has blocked the advancement and employment opportunities of Plaintiff. No logical explanation can explain the District's decision not to advance Plaintiff except for a discriminatory selection process.

37.   Based upon the structure and process used to evaluate and select various candidates, the District has demonstrated that discrimination can easily be made a part of the selection process because despite the experience and background of Plaintiff, she was not selected for various Assistant Principal positions. And, when compared against other candidates such as   ) (See   ) **Empl. App - Exh. I)** and (", it becomes even more obvious that no other explanation can explain why Plaintiff was not selected except for discrimination. **(Pl. Aff - Exh. A).**

38.   The record of this case also demonstrates that even after Plaintiff complained to various District officials, they were slow to respond, if at all, to address her concerns. Instead, she was retaliated against when her efforts to successfully get through the screening process was met with rejection.

39.   From a review of an inside perspective of the selection process, one need only examine the testimony of Michael Briones, who, among other things, testified that there were relatively few objective standards used by the District at the relevant period when Plaintiff applied for the positions in questions from 2001 through 2004. Specifically, with regard to the screening process, Mr. Briones talked about how the scoring for each criteria is used in screening the various applicants:

> **Q.   Can you tell us how the Screening Committee makes a determination of what score, if any, to give an applicant with regard to each of these separate nine criteria that make that up?**

Page -11-

318

A.   **Each of the nine criteria is taken individually. Someone can score from 0 points up to 4 points per criteria.**

(Briones Depo 18:14-20 - Exh. B).

40.   This is a fertile area for discrimination and an area Plaintiff contends was used to discriminate against her. The scoring for each criteria made by the screening committee is based upon each member's perception. **(Briones Depo 19:6-10 - Exh B).** As a result, the screening committee comes up with total score of their assessment of the narrative that is provided by the applicant. **(Briones Depo 19:17-19 - Exh B).**

41.   No committee member is required to explain how they arrived at the score they gave a particular applicant. **(Briones Depo 19:20-23 - Exh B).** The scores are then compiled at Human Resource office from high to low and the assistant superintendent determines how many to interview for the position. **(Briones Depo 20:11-17 - Exh B).** What's more, the number of people interviewed is left to the discretion of the Superintendent. **(Briones Depo 20:18-21 - Exh B).** Afterwards, the Superintendent makes the final recommendation for the assistant principal position to the Board of Trustees. **(Briones Depo 23:7-16).**

42.   This selection process, which includes a Paper Screening Committee, has been in place at Corpus Christi Independent School District for two years. **(Briones Depo 23:17-20 - Exh B).** Before 2004, the paper screening was done by the campus principal not a paper screening committee. **(Briones Depo 24:16-18 - Exh B).**

43.   Mr. Briones does not know if new or old forms were used for Plaintiff in June, 2004. **(Briones Depo 29:4-9 - Exh B)** How paper screening committee scores applicant criteria

Page -12-

319

Q.   Now, with regard to the paper screening form, can you explain how each Committee Member decides how to score a particular applicant as to his criteria?

A.   Each of the Committee Members that was doing the paper screening would look for evidence in the narrative that was provided by the applicants to determine their response, for instance "Number 1: Success in restructuring programs and/or schools, "they would look at the narrative and, as a Principal, assess the determination of that response, whether that would be a response where they would score a 1, a 2, all the way up to a 10. So we would leave it to the assessment of the Principal to determine by the narrative that was provided, did they feel that that response was a 5 or 8 or 10 or whatever. So it would be scored using the narrative.

(Briones Depo 29:10-25; 30:1 - Exh B).

44.   Eeach member makes his own determination. (Briones Depo 30:2-5 - Exh B).

Q.   What restraints, if any, does a Committee Member have as part of the Paper Screening Committee to decide what points, if any, to award a candidate regarding a particular line item on each of those criteria?

A.   The only one constraint that was they had to score no more than a maximum of 10 points.

(Briones Depo 30:6-12 - Exh B)

45.   Under this selection scheme used by the district, it is questionable whether or not there is an objective standard to screen each criteria used to evaluate each candidate

Q.   When a Screening Committee Member makes a decision on how to score an applicant on a particular criteria, is there an objective standard used by the District in guiding that Screening Committee Member in making that determination?

A.   Yes. When we went to this form, to the one that I was talking about where it has a possible score of zero to 4, each of those now have a description of what a score of zero to 4 should mean. In other words, we are trying to restrict the paper screeners and say: "Here is how a score of 2 should look like. Here is the descriptor of that response. "So, those scores sheets that we use now I think provide that descriptor for them to do that.

(Briones Depo 30:20-25; 31:1-8 - Exh B).

Page -13-

46.   The score sheets that are now used were made a part of the selection process sometime in 2004. **(Briones Depo 31:7-8, 11 - Exh B)**.

47.   Mr. Briones doesn't know if a screening criteria was used to score Plaintiff for those Plaintiff for those position subject of this litigation

> **Q.   But you don't know whether or not this was available or used in screening Ms. Monroe's application for an Assistant Principal position in June of 2004?**
>
> **A.   That is correct. I don't recall if it was used for that process or not.**
>
> **(Briones Depo 32:13-17 - Exh B)**.

48.   The relevant time period in this case includes a two year period preceding the date of this lawsuit, which is August 12, 2005. The limitations issue raised by the Defendant arguably could limit some of the claims as provided under Title VII jurisdiction. However, Plaintiff's 1981 claim provides the coverage necessary to support those claims made herein. Therefore, Plaintiff's claims are not barred by the statute of limitations.

CONCLUSION

This case represents an example where an individual, despite hard work, experience and dedication to the District was not afforded appropriate advancement or employment opportunities consistent with her experience and background. She was simply the victim of a discriminatory selection process that allowed the District to select lesser qualified individuals. What's more, this case represents a classic case wherein an individual is penalized for speaking out about a selection process that is used to perpetuate discrimination against certain groups. The summary judgment should be denied because it is largely based on a hearsay and unsubstantiated assertion that when viewed closely do not warrant a summary disposition of this case. Instead, Plaintiff should be allowed to present her claim so that she can show the history of her struggle to achieve those things to which others are easily provided.

WHEREFORE, PREMISES CONSIDERED, Plaintiff respectfully, requests that Defendant Corpus Christi Independent School District's Motion for Summary Judgment be denied, and be awarded her costs and attorney's fees and any other relief to which she may be entitled.

Respectfully submitted,

/s/Charles C. Smith
Charles C. Smith
Attorney for Plaintiff
615 N. Upper Broadway
Wells Fargo Tower, Suite 510
Corpus Christi, Texas 78477
Telephone Number: (361) 883-1055
Facsimile Number: (361) 883-4041
State Bar Number: 18550210
Admission Number: 4312

CERTIFICATE OF SERVICE

I, Charles C. Smith, certify that a true and correct copy of the foregoing Plaintiff's Response in Opposition to Defendant Corpus Christi Independent School District's Motion for Summary Judgment was forwarded to J. Erik Nichols, **Henslee Fowler Hepworth & Schwartz, LLP**, 3200 S.W. Freeway, Suite 1200, Houston, Texas 77027 on this the 5th day of June, 2006 by U.S. Regular Mail.

/s/Charles C. Smith
Charles C. Smith

Chapter XIV

Peace Be Still

I finally reached closure one beautiful Sunday morning as I prepared to get ready for church. The Bobby Jones Gospel Hour was coming on as I stood staring in the closet trying to decide what I was going to wear. I had lost a little weight and had given quite a few of my things away. My wardrobe had dwindled down to just a few choice pieces of clothing. I should have replaced some of the things I gave away but I really disliked going shopping. I know this is some sort of phobia but I can't remember what it's called right now. I get this icky feeling in the pit of my stomach when people crowd around me or block my way. If I do shop I generally do it early in the morning when people haven't gotten up yet. Usually I already know what I want before I go shopping and only spend about thirty to forty minutes in the store. Of course my husband loves it because I don't spend a lot of money on clothes. Here's the strange thing about my condition; it doesn't bother me to be in a high school with 2300 hundred students, pushing, shoving and talking loudly as they brush past me in the halls. I can't explain it, it just is.

I don't know why I was fretting so about what I was going to wear, because I don't go to church to impress anyone, I go because I need spiritual food for my soul. By the time we got dressed and made it to the eleven o'clock service I was literally feeling beat up by life. Our head pastor, Pastor Harvey Houston wasn't going to preach this Sunday, his wife, Co-Pastor, Teena Houston was going to be the speaker of the hour. I always enjoyed listening to her because she presented subjects that made you think. This particular Sunday she posed a question to the congregation that set something off in me that shook the very core of my being. She asked in this questioning voice, "If I were to ask how many of you could tell the story behind a scar on your body, I'm sure the majority of you could tell me exactly where and when you got it. Every scar has a story to tell"

As I listened, I thought about the many scars on my own body. I focused in on a barely visible crescent moon scar in the middle of my forehead. I remembered exactly what happened when I acquired it. It happened in McComb, Mississippi when I was in the fourth grade. I walked up to these two, huge heavy doors that could be pushed out or pulled open. As I approached the doors, not realizing someone was on the other side, one door flung open hitting me in the forehead. There was a split from the beginning of my widow's peak down to the bridge of my nose. I remember bursting into tears as the blood poured down my face. I was rushed to the school nurse to get it patched up.

Pastor Teena continued speaking. "It's a curious thing about the human body. Every time there's a cut, burn or puncture to the skin, when it heals there is generally a scar left. Sometimes we can barely make out what happened because it fades, but if you look closely enough you can see it and remember what happened. Some of our scars may not be just external (physical) they may be internal (emotional). These scars remind us of the hurt, pain, disappointment, and rejections we have experienced in life."

I really paid close attention as she started to list the characteristics of scars.

- Scars can be visible or invisible
- Scars can be mistakes that were inflicted by you or someone else.
- Scars can come from a sore that's constantly being picked at and reopened. Just when a scab is formed to help in the healing process you pull on it reinjuring it.
- Scars can be found deep within us, beneath the covering of the skin and clothes, buried as far as we can bury them.
- Some people are better at hiding their wounds because they don't want anyone to know they have them.
- Some have emotional scars that can haunt them and hurt much longer than physical wounds.
- Emotional wounds can be caused by hateful words spoken into someone's life causing that wounded person to look for comfort and validation in someone or something else. They may look for something to help hide the pain of depression, confusion, sadness, and hopelessness through the use of drugs, alcohol or toxic relationships, hoping it helps them just enough, to get through the day. (These are merely band-aids without remedy)
- Scars can come from being deeply hurt by people we loved and trusted (Family friends, spouses, children)
- Scars can come from a broken marriage, stressful relationships, painful childhood memories of abuse (sexual, mental or physical), neglect and rejection, betrayal, past failures and costly mistakes.
- Scars can fill a person with such bitterness, resentment, regrets, and anger; it can cause them to become critical and judgmental.
- Scars can be so deep that a person feels they have nothing to live for (Hopeless). They feel there is no way out and think of ending it all.

As I reflected on the words that flowed from Co-Pastors lips, the tears fell. She continued speaking in this soft, melodious voice, "But scars aren't meant to be dwelt on; or used to keep us stuck in the past. They are marks of healing and freedom known only in Jesus who took all of our pain, grief and sinfulness to the cross and left it there.

Hebrews 4:15 (Amplified) "For we do not have a High Priest who is unable to understand and sympathize and have a shared feeling with our weaknesses and infirmities and assaults of temptation, but one who has been tempted in every respect as we are, yet without sinning."

No one knows pain more than our Lord and Savoir Jesus Christ. Not only was he betrayed by his own disciple Judas; he was rejected, laughed at, accused, put down, criticized, gossiped about, ignored, hated, spit upon, scourged with a whip that was embedded with bone and metal causing his flesh to be ripped from his body. A twisted crown of thorns was thrust upon his head and nails were driven through his hands and feet. He was disfigured so badly you couldn't recognize Him. Jesus understands what you are going through because he has experienced every emotion and suffered every feeling you or I have ever had to go through. In addition to all that, He stooped down and shouldered all of our sins, sickness and sorrows. He literally took up our infirmities and carried our sorrows so he definitely has the power to deliver us from any bondage, oppression, or problem we may have.

Isaiah 9:6 "the government shall be upon His shoulder: and His name shall be called Wonderful, Counselor, Mighty God, the Everlasting Father, the Peace."

Isaiah 63:9, "Fear not; for I am with you: don't be dismayed; for I am your God: I will strengthen you; yes, I will help you; yes, I will uphold you with the right hand of my righteousness."

Her words pierced my very soul, and I was convicted in the spirit. How many times had I found myself in many of the situation she described in her sermon? How many times had I wanted to strike out against those that I felt wronged me? I knew what it said in the bible about revenge.

Romans 12:19, "Do not take revenge, my friends, but leave room for God's wrath, for it is written: "It is mine to avenge; I will repay," says the Lord."

Deuteronomy 32:35, "Vengeance is Mine, and retribution, in due time their foot will slip; for the day of their calamity is near, and the impending things are hastening upon them."'

These had been hard lessons for me. I wanted to pay them back for what they had done to me not later but immediately. I was going to get them back if it was the last thing I ever did, but God had to show me it wasn't up to me, it was up to Him and in due time He would give me permission.

Co-Pastor reviewed the beginning symptoms of hurt once again because she wanted us to recognize them.

- People with hidden hurts will try to escape the pain
- They will try anything to find relief
- They may bury themselves in their work
- Some turn to drinking or drugs to alter their state of mind
- Others try to find relief with false loves such as lust and infatuation
- Some try to inflict the pain they are suffering from onto others (blame)
- They blame others for all of their unhappiness
- They tend to take the role of a victim

She asked, "Do any of these responses work very well? They may provide some temporary relief but they are not remedies. They don't remove the pain permanently." The great thing about this sermon was; not only were problems presented, solutions to healing our hidden wounds was provided.

Step One: The first thing you have to do is reveal the hurt. Healing begins when you reveal or acknowledge your hurt to God. (Just like a child that shows his/her parent where it hurts.)

Psalm 3, (Amplified) David said, "When I kept silent, things to myself, my bones grew old through my groaning. I felt weak deep inside me. I moaned all day."

Psalm 39:2-3 David said, "I kept very quiet...but I became even more upset. I became very angry inside, and as I thought about it my anger burned."

Eventually David learned to open his heart, and reveal his hurt. He learned to be honest with himself. We need to be honest with ourselves and with God. We can do what David did by telling God exactly how we feel. God can handle our feelings because He was there when we were hurt and He will be there when we receive healing.

Step Two: The second thing we have to do to begin the healing process is release those who hurt us. We all have to make one very difficult decision: *Do we want to get well...or do we want to get even?* We can't do both! There is only one way to get rid of the hurt in our hearts. We have to forgive. Forgiveness works even if you are not a Christian. *Do you think they don't deserve to be forgiven?* None of us do, but God has forgiven each of us. If you want relief from the hurt you must release those who hurt you. Jesus taught us that we must forgive those who trespass (cross boundaries) against us. Forgiveness is the path to healing. We are not "victims" but victorious!!!

Step Three: The third thing we need to do is "Refocus" from the past to the future. We have to reprogram our thinking. We have to rehearse over and over in our mind what God said about us in His word!

Philippians 3:13 "Forget the past and look forward to what lies ahead."

How do we "Forget the past? By realizing our past doesn't have to be our future! You can't forget the past by focusing on the past. You forget by **Refocusing** on what God determined for you. Turn your attention from your hurt to your healer…Turn your attention from your pain to God's plan…

Step Four: The fourth thing we have to do to heal the hidden hurts is, "Reach out to help others." *How do we know when we've been healed?* When we reach out to help others… and share the cure with them. He wants those of us who have been healed to help heal those who are still hurting.

2 Corinthians 1:4, "God comforts us every time we have trouble, so when others have trouble, we can comfort them with the same comfort God gives us.

When Co-Pastor said, "God uses some of our most painful experiences to make us usable and shape us for service. The wounds we may want to hide, the pain that we may regret or resent are the experiences God will use to help heal us as well as others." The memories of my past hurts were so severe I wept. I had finally found the release I'd been seeking nearly my entire life and now I knew what I had to do to be healed.

I already knew I possessed many of the traits Co- Pastor preached about as far as wanting to help others that were hurting. This sermon just gave me confirmation that I was on the right path to being healed of my own past hurts. I know this because the more I wanted to strike out against those that hurt me the guiltier I felt about those that would be impacted negatively by my decision to strike, and then *I WEPT* uncontrollably.

Chapter XV

A New Beginning

Reliving these chapters in my life has been draining for me. It's like one of those sores that fester just underneath the scab. It looks healed but you keep getting pain when you shouldn't. It's not until you reopen the wound and allow it to drain that it starts healing from the inside out. That's what this process has felt like. All of that heaviness and helplessness inside of me seems to have dissipated. I have finally released the hurt and un-forgiveness I've harbored in my heart for so long; which in turn has set me free to move forward in my life. It's truly liberating.

I don't know what will happen once this information is published but just going through the process has all been worth it. Some one asked me, "What is the biggest thing you hope will happen after you tell your story?" I shared some of that with you earlier but I told them this……

"I did this for my children and grandchildren. They are all Summa's (Some of this some of that). They are of African, Indian, Mexican, White, Cuban, Spanish, and Asian decent. They come in all flavors, (dark chocolate, milk chocolate, caramel, vanilla, and white chocolate) I know that due to a trick of the genes, some of them will be judged very harshly. Their heritage is displayed on the outer layers of their skin and before people even get to know them personally they will be stereo-typed and then judged. My babies will have to be twice as good in anything they choose to do, academically, athletically, etc." Through everything that they will go through I don't want them to give up. I want them to know that Mahmaw already laid the ground work for them and all they have to do is build on that.

A Message from Mahmaw

I want to leave this message to my husband, children, grandchildren, nieces, nephews, grand nieces and nephews, cousins and greats to come and anyone else that reads my story.

God saw fit to snatch me from the grips of death three times in 2009. I don't know how much time He will allow me to live, on this side of life, but I want to leave this with you.

Life is short and death is sure. God blessed you with a gift of life that you personally don't have the right to contemplate ending. No matter how hard things get I promise, in time, it will get better, just stay the course. Make every moment of your life count.

Do something awesome to help mankind. We as humans need a human touch. When you greet people don't do it half heartedly tell them to "Hug me like you LOVE me!" and mean it. I want you to love hard and forgive easily no matter what the race, color, or religion, but don't be a fool.

Patience truly is a virtue. It took me fifty-eight years to get to this point. With God on your side it only takes one to stand up. When you truly do for others out of the goodness of your heart, it really does feel, *oh* so *wonderful*!

The very best advice I can give you is, "Watch what you **DO**! Watch who you do it **TO**! They might tell the world on **YOU**!

As my grandkids would say ; hit me up on my blog @ **www.fjmonroe.wordpress.com** or **www.psalm51ch7vs.blogspot.com**

I think I hear that theme song "Pretty Woman" resonating in my head.

Be Blessed!

To My Loving Cousin

Odell Williams Rest In Peace

February 9, 2011

Chapter XVI

The Four "Fs" of my Life

I have four "Fs" in my life that give me comfort. It is important to have these things to be complete.

Faith

Father, Son, Holy Spirit

Great Grandmother, Lannie Kitchum, her sister Aunt Harriette, Grandmother, Mary, Grandfather, Henry, Mother, Addie, Father, Frank, Godparents, Lucille and Pen Aunt Rose, Uncle Clarence, Aunt Willie Bee, Stepfather, Johnny Bee, Uncle Stance, Aunt Bernice, Ruth, Sylvester, Ethel Lee, Mr. Hill, Mamma Lou Brother, Melvin, Sister, Debra, Brother, Leonard, Brother, Pen, Brother, Martin, Sister-In-Laws-Rosie, Jean, Devita, Maria Husband, Eddie Sr., daughter, Tamika, Vicky, Earl, daughter, Catina, Jesse, Son, Demetrius, Son, Eddie Jr., Son-In-Laws-Dennis, Paris Sr. (aka Peter), Daughter-in-Laws-Selina, Michelle, Bridget, Sealy, Juan, Petra, Brenda,

Grandchildren

Gabriella, Aaliyah, Demetrius Jr. Jerry, Jackie, Dionna, Dahvon, Paris Jr., Jada, Kiara, Aja, Azelea, Jordan, Tamia, Kevin,

Nieces & Nephews

Family   Leota, Wayne, Charles, Nichole, Chandra, Aaron   **Friends**
James III., Levita, Angel

Cousins, grand nieces & nephews, friends

Robert, Thomas, Bradley, Vera, Rosemary, Jackie, Ledora Loretta, Odell, Elvertice, Henry, Von, Gloria, Frank, Willie Bee Jr., Lewis Yvonne, Sheryl, Roland, Mary Anne, Estella, Deborah, Bernadine, Jacqueline, Horace, Kevin, Mary Lou, Manuel, Mark, Monica Rhonda, Brandon, Stephen, Alexis, Mary Russell, Lydia, Maria, Diana, Harvey, Ruby, Diane, Sheryle, Dr. Walter, Anita, Dr. Kouzekanani, Dr. Moody, Dr. Prezas, Dr. Martin, Dr. Ryder, Dr. Sherritt, Anne Lee, Cindy, Dr. Breeling, Julia, Gloria,

Favor

For My Grandbabies

Here is why I wrote this. One day your Aunt Tamika came home crying because she had been picked on for being a friend to someone that wasn't Black. I wrote this song just for her almost 30 years ago and now it's just for you. The title is….. So What!

So What!

One sunny afternoon
Me and Debbie Lee
Were outside playing
Hide-n-go-seek
When Brenda Faye and her brother
Ran up to me

They ran up to me and called me a **Honky lover**
Brenda Faye and her brother
They called me a **Honky lover**

I jumped up and ran in the house
With tears streaming down my face
My mother asked me what was wrong
And I told her what they'd done

Brenda Faye and her brother
They called me a **Honky lover**
Mother Brenda Faye and her brother
They called me a **Honky lover**

My mother she sat me down
And wiped the tears from my eyes
And said baby, baby please don't cry

We can't blame Brenda Faye
It's her narrow-minded parents
Teaching her that way
We can't blame Brenda Faye
It's her narrow-minded parents
Teaching her that way
Baby mama wants you to remember this
And if you do there won't be no place you won't fit
You'll be welcomed by all nationalities
If you remember this reality

It doesn't matter what the color of your skin
Red, Black, Brown, White or Yellow
It doesn't matter whether you are kinth or kin
What does matter is that we are all human beings
And that's the only important thing

Now you listen to this

So what if they called you a **Honky Lover**
So what if they called you a **Nigger Lover**
So what if they called you a **Spic Lover**
So what if they called you a **Chink Lover**

It takes a lot of guts
To say so what

But

SO WHAT!

In time you will see
It's alright to be
A lover of all mankind
In time my child in time
Sure we are all unique in our own way
With different cultures in which we live
In which we live, work and play
But we all share one thing
And that is that we are human beings
And that's the only import thing

It takes a lot of guts
To say so what

But

SO WHAT!!!